Mastering Oracle Scheduler in Oracle 11g Databases

Schedule, manage, and execute jobs that automate your business processes

Ronald Rood

BIRMINGHAM - MUMBAI

Mastering Oracle Scheduler in Oracle 11g Databases

First published: June 2009

Production Reference: 1100609

Published by Packt Publishing Ltd.
32 Lincoln Road
Olton
Birmingham, B27 6PA, UK.

ISBN 978-1-847195-98-2

www.packtpub.com

Cover Image by Ninoslav Babić (nbabic@net.amis.hr)

Credits

Author
Ronald Rood

Reviewers
Hans Forbrich
Mennan Tekbir
Robin Buitenhuis
Syed Jaffar Hussain

Acquisition Editor
James Lumsden

Development Editor
Ved Prakash Jha

Technical Editors
Ishita Dhabalia
John Antony

Copy Editor
Sneha Kulkarni

Editorial Team Leader
Gagandeep Singh

Project Team Leader
Lata Basantani

Project Coordinator
Leena Purkait

Proofreader
Camille Guy

Indexer
Hemangini Bari

Production Coordinator
Shantanu Zagade

Cover Work
Shantanu Zagade

About the Author

Ronald Rood is an IT professional for over 20 years. His private domain is named after the first account that was created on a computer for him. That account was *ronr* on a DPS9 system, and so his private domain is called `ronr.nl` where you can contact him using `ronr@ronr.nl`. He eagerly joined the Oracle community and became a skilled, innovating DBA and troubleshooter. He is a master of C, PRO*C, lots of scripting languages, and—of course—PL/SQL. Ronald's real power is in the combination of the rich Unix world and Oracle. According to him, there is no such thing as a problem that cannot be solved; it just might take a little time.

Ronald speaks several languages such as Dutch, English, German, and some French. In the private time that he shares with his wife and two children, he likes to take an occasional dive (from the sky), fly with radio-controlled models, ride recumbents, and work as a volunteer for a local water scouts group.

Currently, Ronald is one of the Ciber Oracle consultants in The Netherlands and cooperates in many projects for many large companies. Before writing this book, Ronald wrote Oracle-related articles for the Dutch Oracle user group magazine. On his blog, you can find some short articles about various items, but most are related to Oracle.

I would like to thank everyone who helped me writing this book. Not in the least, Sandra for having lots of patience for me while writing, Silvana and Alex for being great children I can be proud of, Robin and the other reviewers for challenging me to write better, and Harold for showing me that there is a way that might or might not be seen. I also would like to thank my colleagues of Ciber for being my colleagues, and Mark for giving me the challenges that I like so much. Without my parents, I would never have existed at all, but they gave me the opportunity to study without ever asking anything in return. Bedankt ma, bedankt pa zonder jullie was het nooit wat geworden.

About the Reviewers

Hans Forbrich has been around computers for 40 years. While studying for his B.Sc. EE in the 70s, he worked as a contract programmer to help pay for school. Hans has been working with the Oracle products since 1984. While at Nortel in the field service group, he met Oracle Database version 4. He joined Oracle Canada to work in the Communications vertical from 1996 to 2002. In 2003, Hans started Forbrich Computer Consulting Ltd., which has become a successful international Oracle consultancy and Oracle training partner based in St. Albert, near Edmonton, Alberta, Canada.

As an Oracle ACE Director and OCP, Hans frequently responds in various Oracle Forums, teaches for Oracle University, consults with Oracle customers on maximizing value from Oracle licenses, and speaks at Oracle User Group conferences around the world. He holds a strong belief that Oracle products provide significant value, and the key to extracting that value—and reducing the effective cost of the product—is in understanding the product and using the right tool for the job.

I thank my wife of 27 years for her patience, especially while I experiment in the lab. I also thank my two sons for their patience, their assistance at computer setups, and their help in those same experiments. (And I am proud to note that Son #1, aka Employee #2, aka Chief Network and Systems Administrator, has achieved his M.Sc. EE this past year!) Finally, I thank Edmonton Opera and my colleagues there for allowing me to break away from computers and unwind on stage with the Edmonton Opera Chorus.

Mennan Tekbir has a master's degree in Computer Sciences, and has worked for several telecommunications companies around the world. He is mainly focused on performance analysis, designing and implementing frameworks, automated PL/SQL code generation, and fraud detection with data mining.

Robin Buitenhuis is an experienced Oracle DBA. During his study at the Universiteit Twente, he came in contact with Oracle RDBMS 6.0 en Forms 2.3. From that moment on, he has always worked with Oracle products. He is also a member of the board of the Dutch Oracle Usergroup (`www.ogh.nl`).

Syed Jaffar Hussain has more than 16 years of Information Technology (IT) experience, which includes over eight years as a Production Oracle DBA. He is an Oracle ACE, Oracle 10g Certified Master (OCM), OCP DBA (v8i, 9i, and10g), and Oracle 10g RAC Certified Expert. He is currently involved in 8 node production and 6 node development RAC setup with more than 60 databases running across the nodes. He has a broad experience in Oracle advanced technologies such as RAC, DataGuard, RMAN, and Performance Tuning. He occasionally presents Oracle University five-day courses and one-day seminars on behalf of Oracle EMEA. He has also worked for a couple of multinational banks in Saudi Arabia. He is currently involved with the Oracle 11g RAC book.

He is a frequent contributor at Oracle OTN forums and regularly writes to his blog, (`http://jaffardba.blogspot.com`). He is reachable at `sjaffarhussain@gmail.com`

I would like to thank my wife Ayesha and my three kids Ashfaq, Arfan, and Aahil for allowing me to concentrate on this task.

Table of Contents

Preface 1

Chapter 1: Simple Jobs 7

Creating a user 8

Running your Jobs 8

PL/SQL block 9

Stored procedure 15

Executable 19

Program 20

Defining arguments for your jobs 22

Metadata arguments 22

Normal application arguments 25

Summary 27

Chapter 2: Simple Chain 29

Jobs 30

Chains 30

Statuses 30

Chains and steps 31

Rules 31

Evaluation interval 32

Privileges 34

Steps to create a chain 35

Hands-on with chains 35

Programs 36

SHUTDOWN 36

COPYFILES 36

STARTUP 37

Program state 37

DB Console 38

Chain definition 41

Running the chain 48
Tricks with chains 49
Manipulating the running chains 51
Analyzing the chain 52
Summary 55
Chapter 3: Control the Scheduler 57
Job creation 57
Job execution 63
Scheduler management 66
Logging 68
Log detail level 68
Log purging 70
Summary 73
Chapter 4: Managing Resources 75
Resource consumer group 75
Creating resource consumer groups 77
Class 80
Plan 82
Window 91
Window groups 92
Monitoring 92
Problems with Resource Manager 97
Problems that Resource Manager solves 99
Summary 101
Chapter 5: Getting Out of the Database 103
Security 103
Installation on Windows 105
Installation on Linux 110
Upgrading the remote job agent 111
Silent install of the remote job agent 112
Base release 112
Patch to the latest available level 112
Preparing the database for remote agent usage 113
Verifying the XDB installation 114
Setting the HTTP port 114
Creating remote Scheduler objects 115
Setting registration password 115
Configuring a remote agent 116
Troubleshooting 117

Multiple agents on the same host 118
Credentials 120
Creating job—targeting Unix 121
Creating job—targeting Windows 125
Runtime observations of the remote Scheduler 126
Resource Manager 127
Summary 127

Chapter 6: Events 129

Monitoring job events 129
Events in chains 130
Event-based scheduling 133
Summary 140

Chapter 7: Debugging the Scheduler 141

Unix—all releases 141
Windows usage 144
Bugs 145
Job environment 148
Checks to do in the database 149
Summary 152

Chapter 8: The Scheduler in Real Life 153

Statistics collection 153
The schedule_run procedure 154
The run procedure 154
The statob procedure 155
The drop_jobs procedure 155
Generating the jobs 155
Performing the analysis 158
Generating the scheduled run 158
Backups 160
Things that can scare you 160
Diving into the code 164
Reading the event queue 164
Scheduling for the HOT backups 167
Scheduling the DARC process 169
Scheduling the final BARC process 171
How to use the calendar 172
Tools 173
Summary 180

Chapter 9: Other Configurations **181**
RAC **181**
Job creation/modification 184
The job_class definition 190
Standby databases **191**
Creating jobs in a logical standby database 191
Running jobs in a logical standby database 193
Summary **194**
Chapter 10: Scheduler GUI Tools **195**
DB Console **195**
Grid Control **216**
DbVisualizer **216**
Summary **221**
Index **223**

Preface

Welcome to the world of Oracle Scheduler! Oracle Scheduler is a free utility included in the Oracle database that makes the Oracle RDBMS the most powerful scheduling tool on our planet (and in the known parts of the galaxy).

An overview of Oracle Scheduler

The Oracle Scheduler can be used to automate not only the simple maintenance tasks, but also the complex business logic. Traditionally, only PL/SQL could be executed in the Scheduler. Later, operating system scripts were added to it, and now we can run jobs on remote systems and cross platform as well. This can turn the Oracle Scheduler into the spider in your Web, controlling all the jobs running in the organization and giving you a single point for control.

Database background

Relational database management systems (RDBMS) can be very powerful. With a little code, we can use the RDBMS as a filesystem, mail server, HTTP server, and now also as a full-blown job Scheduler that can compete very well with other commercial job Schedulers. The advantage that Oracle gives us is in terms of price, flexibility, and phenomenal power. The scheduling capabilities are all a part of the normal Oracle license for the RDBMS, whereas others have a serious price tag and often require a database for the repository to store the metadata of the jobs.

Scheduling events in the database

Since Oracle added the procedural option to the database, they also included some scheduling power provided by `dbms_jobs`. Although a bit restricted, it was used extensively. However, no one would even think about using this as an Enterprise-level Scheduler tool. This changed when Oracle introduced 10gR2. In this release, Oracle could not only start jobs that ran outside the database, but they also added the job chain.

In 11g, Oracle also added the option to run jobs on remote systems where no database is running. Now it's time to rethink what the database actually is. In the early days, a database was just a bunch of code that could hold data in tables. Today, the Oracle RDBMS can do that—and that too well—along with many more things. In fact, the Oracle RDBMS can perform so many tasks so amazingly, that it's surprising that we still call it just a database. We could easily turn it into a personal assistant.

Oracle Scheduler 11g can:

- Run jobs where no database ever was before
- Use different operating system credentials per job
- React on events
- Schedule jobs on multiple platforms simultaneously
- Give a tight security

What this book covers

Chapter 1 will get you going with the Scheduler as quickly as possible. In the end, you will automate simple tasks that are now maintained in cron, task manager, or the good old **DBMS_JOB** package, for example.

Chapter 2 will show you a lot of possibilities of chains with many examples and explanations. In short, it will tell you all you ever wanted to know about chains, but were afraid to ask.

Chapter 3 is for all you people living in an organization that requires strict job separation. This chapter will show how to make good use of the Scheduler and apply job separation.

Chapter 4 is a very important chapter that explains how to crank up the power of a system to the limits by combining the Scheduler and the Resource Manager. Here you will find how to get the best out of your system.

Chapter 5 will be of a great help in setting up remote external jobs introduced in Oracle 11g. How is this related to the old-fashioned local external jobs that we know since Oracle 10g and why we should get rid of the old external jobs? Get your answers here.

Chapter 6 helps the reader to get a firm grip on events and explains how to make good use of events. Events sound like voodoo, but in the end are an extra tool found in the Scheduler.

Chapter 7 considers the fact that when the jobs get more complicated, it gets harder to understand why something works differently than planned. This chapter gives the reader a fresh look at how to follow and debug Scheduler jobs.

Chapter 8 will give you some creative implementations of more or less common tasks—this time implemented using the Scheduler. This chapter gives a working code with clear explanations. This broadens the horizon and will take down the barriers that might exist between other environments and Oracle.

Chapter 9 shows how the Scheduler can be used in other configurations such as standby databases and RAC.

Chapter 10 shows how the Scheduler can be managed and monitored remotely through a web interface.

What you need for this book

Most examples will run fine with just a database. When the Oracle Scheduler Agent is discussed, you will also need a remote Scheduler Agent installed and running. In this case, the version of the database has to be at least 11.1.0.6 because this is the first release that includes the remote Scheduler Agent support. The installation, upgrade, and configuration of the Oracle Scheduler Agent are explained in the book. The agent can be installed either local to the database or remote to the database, that is, on a different computer than where the database is running. The location of the agent does not make a real difference for working with the book. This book is about a very valuable tool in the database, the Oracle Scheduler. So it is quite understandable that you will need access to a database. It can run on any platform. At the time of writing this book, I used Enterprise Linux, Red Hat Linux, Solaris, and MAC OS X, and even Windows. The Oracle Scheduler Agent can be on a different platform than that of the database. It is helpful if you have access to DB Console or Grid control, but it is not required. All the examples are with the PL/SQL code, which can be used from any tool that we normally use to work with the database.

Who this book is for

This book is intended for administrators and developers who currently use tools such as cron, `DBMS_JOB`, and the task manager, but who now want more control or have a need to scale up to tools that can handle the network. Complex tasks can be built that can easily control business process and enable the completion of important tasks in a limited time.

The reader is expected to have some experience of Oracle Database Management, and a working knowledge of SQL and PL/SQL.

Conventions

In this book, you will find a number of styles of text that distinguish between different kinds of information. Here are some examples of these styles, and an explanation of their meaning.

Code words in text are shown as follows: "The `DBMS_SCHEDULER` package is available to the public."

A block of code will be set as follows:

```
CREATE OR REPLACE PROCEDURE SNAP as
begin
null;
insert into session_log select * from v$session where sid = (select
                                  sid from v$mystat where rownum = 1);
insert into session_stat_log select * from v$mystat;
end SNAP;
```

When we wish to draw your attention to a particular part of a code block, the relevant lines or items will be shown in bold:

```
!/bin/sh

# set this if you change your Agent home
EXECUTION_AGENT_HOME="/data/app/oracle/product/schagent/11.1.0.6"

# set this to use a different data directory for the Agent
# EXECUTION_AGENT_DATA=""
```

Any command-line input or output is written as follows:

```
ps -ef|grep ora_cjq0_${ORACLE_SID}
```

New terms and **important words** are shown in bold. Words that you see on the screen, in menus or dialog boxes for example, appear in our text like this: "For 10g, Resource Manager is on the **Administration** tab.".

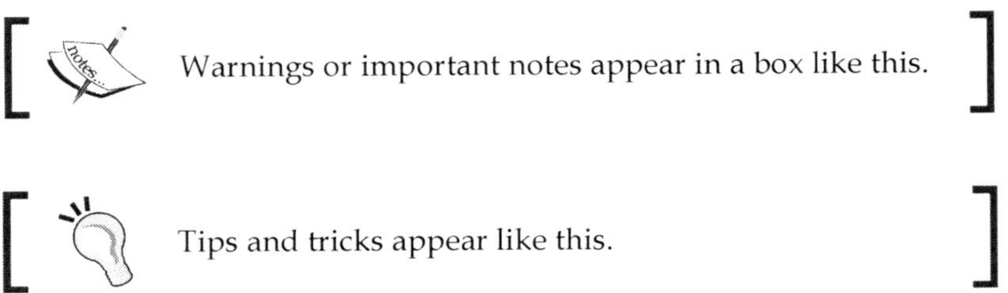

Warnings or important notes appear in a box like this.
Tips and tricks appear like this.

Reader feedback

Feedback from our readers is always welcome. Let us know what you think about this book—what you liked or may have disliked. Reader feedback is important for us to develop titles that you really get the most out of.

To send us general feedback, simply drop an email to `feedback@packtpub.com`, and mention the book title in the subject of your message.

If there is a book that you need and would like to see us publish, please send us a note in the **SUGGEST A TITLE** form on `www.packtpub.com` or email `suggest@packtpub.com`.

If there is a topic that you have expertise in and you are interested in either writing or contributing to a book, see our author guide on `www.packtpub.com/authors`.

Customer support

Now that you are the proud owner of a Packt book, we have a number of things to help you to get the most from your purchase.

Downloading the example code for the book

Visit `http://www.packtpub.com/files/code/5982_Code.zip` to directly download the example code.

The downloadable files contain instructions on how to use them.

Errata

Although we have taken every care to ensure the accuracy of our contents, mistakes do happen. If you find a mistake in one of our books—maybe a mistake in text or code—we would be grateful if you would report this to us. By doing so, you can save other readers from frustration, and help us to improve subsequent versions of this book. If you find any errata, please report them by visiting `http://www.packtpub.com/support`, selecting your book, clicking on the **let us know** link, and entering the details of your errata. Once your errata are verified, your submission will be accepted and the errata added to any list of existing errata. Any existing errata can be viewed by selecting your title from `http://www.packtpub.com/support`.

Piracy

Piracy of copyright material on the Internet is an ongoing problem across all media. At Packt, we take the protection of our copyright and licenses very seriously. If you come across any illegal copies of our works in any form on the Internet, please provide us with the location address or website name immediately so that we can pursue a remedy.

Please contact us at `copyright@packtpub.com` with a link to the suspected pirated material.

We appreciate your help in protecting our authors, and our ability to bring you valuable content.

Questions

You can contact us at `questions@packtpub.com` if you are having a problem with any aspect of the book, and we will do our best to address it.

1
Simple Jobs

For this book, I carried out an out of the box installation on Enterprise Linux with the Oracle-validated package applied to it. I made a simple database using DBCA, complete with sample schemas and DB Console. For storage, I made use of an NAS and openfiler on a separate installation presented as iSCSI targets.

Let's get started with simple jobs.

Simple jobs are the jobs that can easily be created using DB Console with little or no extra object creations required. The quickest way to get you started is by making the database perform actions for you. A simple job is not the same as a useless job. Far from that, many tasks can be performed using simple jobs. Sometimes we can go back and use easy, single-step jobs rather than using advanced jobs based on complicated rules.

The DB Console does provide some support for the Scheduler, which can be used for simple tasks. However, for more elaborate things we need to use a PL/SQL editor. Any PL/SQL-capable tool will do. If you like, use SQL*Plus, SQL Developer, DbVisualizer, or TOAD for a Windows-centric client. Let's start using DB Console and see what this gives us.

This chapter covers:

- Creation of a user who can handle the tasks
- A job that runs PL/SQL code
- A job that can start a stored procedure
- A job that runs an executable

Creating a user

When working with simple jobs, our basic need is to create a user. In DB Console, there is a default user `sysman`. We can use this or the user `system`. However, it is better to create a dedicated user for different tasks. This prevents us from giving too many privileges to jobs and maintains auditability. So, let's first create a normal user who does the work for us:

```
create user marvin identified by panic;
grant create session, create job to marvin;
grant select any dictionary to marvin;
create user stats identified by nopanic;
alter user stats quota unlimited on users;
create table stats.session_log as select *
                from v$session where 1 = 2;
create table stats.session_stat_log as select *
                      from v$mystat where 1 = 2;
grant select,insert,update,delete on stats.session_log to marvin;
grant select,insert,update,delete on stats.session_stat_log
                                                 to marvin;
create public synonym session_log for stats.session_log;
create public synonym session_stat_log for stats.session_stat_log;
```

The `select any dictionary` privilege is mainly because we want to use DB Console. For this, it must view a lot from the dictionary. Now start a web browser and connect to the freshly created user `marvin`. The Oracle Scheduler support is provided in the **Server** tab of the DB Console.

Running your Jobs

There are several kinds of jobs that we can run. The kind of job is defined by the `job_type`. What a job does is defined by the `job_action`. In this chapter, we will see an example of a job that calls:

- A PL/SQL block
- A stored procedure
- An external script
- A program

Now let's see each one in detail.

PL/SQL block

The simplest type of job is the one that runs a PL/SQL block as shown here. A PL/SQL block as a job action is just that—a normal anonymous block of PL/SQL code. The advantage of this type is that it is very simple to set up as it does not need anything else in the database to be defined. As we cannot give any arguments to a PL/SQL block, we cannot use arguments for this type of job—something to remember when you try to create a library of reusable code.

Once we are successfully connected as **MARVIN**, the DB Console shows us the database **Home** page. From here, we select the **Server** tab to reach the page presented in the following screenshot. We are interested in the **Oracle Scheduler** column. All the implementations towards using the jobs are done here. We can do a lot of things in DB Console. However, for now we will restrict ourselves to making a Job. Click on the **Jobs** entry in the **Oracle Scheduler** column as shown here:

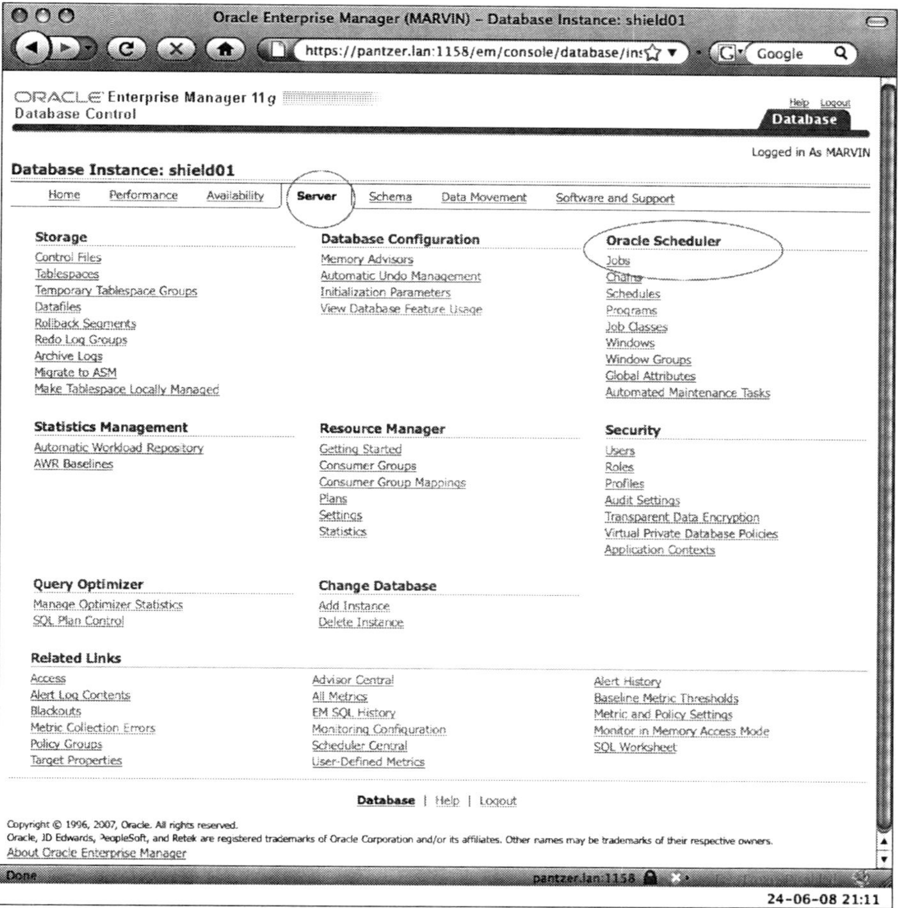

Click on the **Jobs** entry in the **Oracle Scheduler** column. In the screen that follows, we can see which jobs are already defined—or better, jobs that are yours or the jobs on which you have privileges:

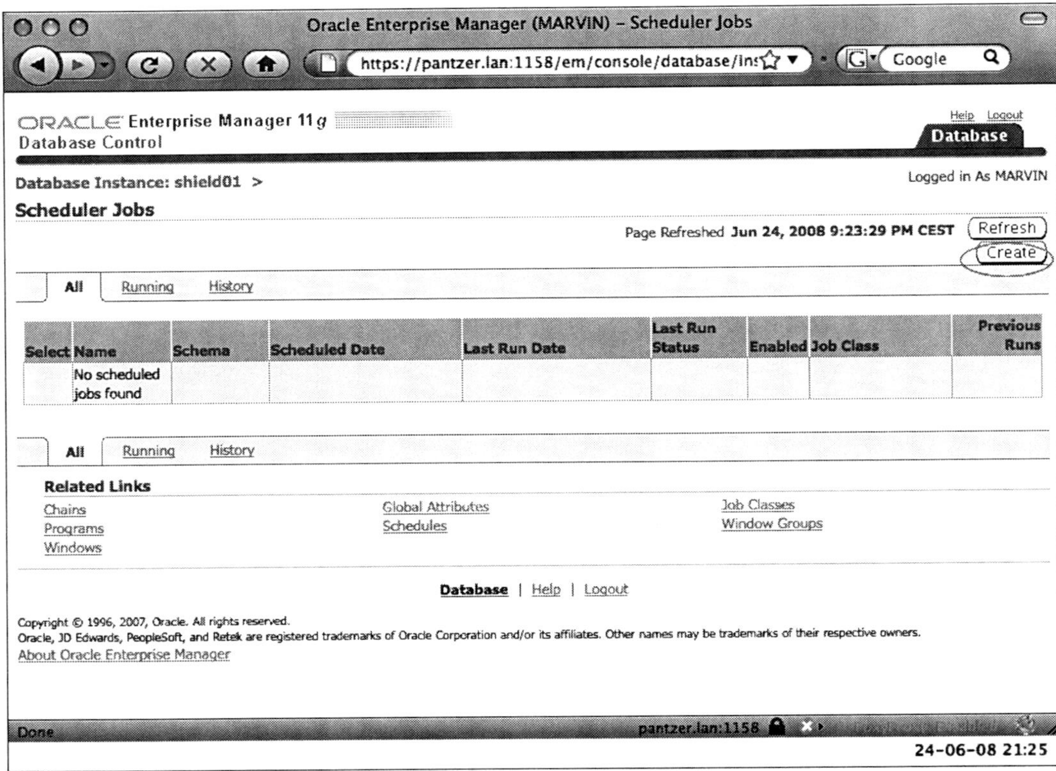

Apparently, `marvin` doesn't own jobs and has no privileges at all to run any job. We are going to change this quickly. To do so, click on the **Create** button to bring us to the **Create Job** screen where most of the job definition is handled.

It shows us a few of the job properties that can be entered, selected, or switched as follows:

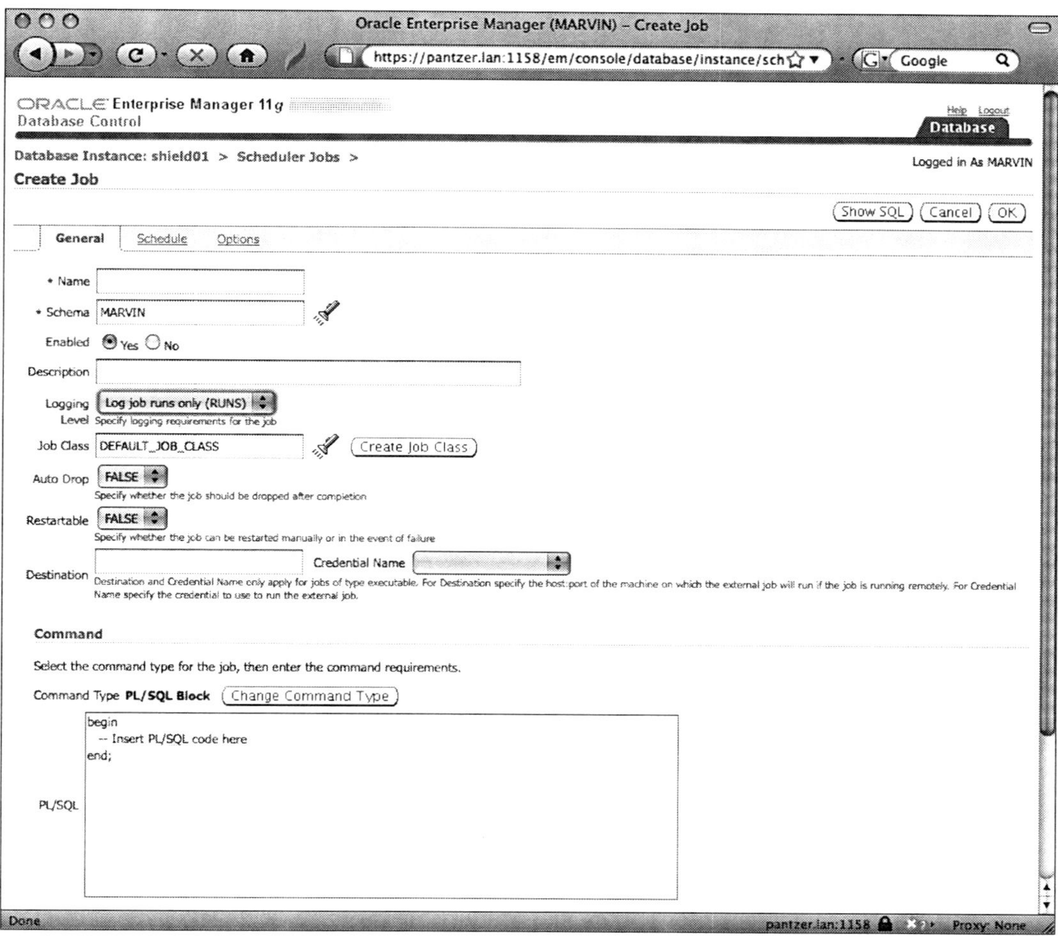

Here we can enter the properties of the job such as **Name**, **Command Type** of the job, and the action of the job. We can see what is entered. Because the default job type is of type **PL/SQL block**, we did not have to change anything for job type to get this going. Other attributes to note are the **Enabled** state and **Logging Level**.

If we create a job that has no other thing defined on it that regulates the execution of the job, such as a schedule or a window, the job will start running as soon as it is successfully created.

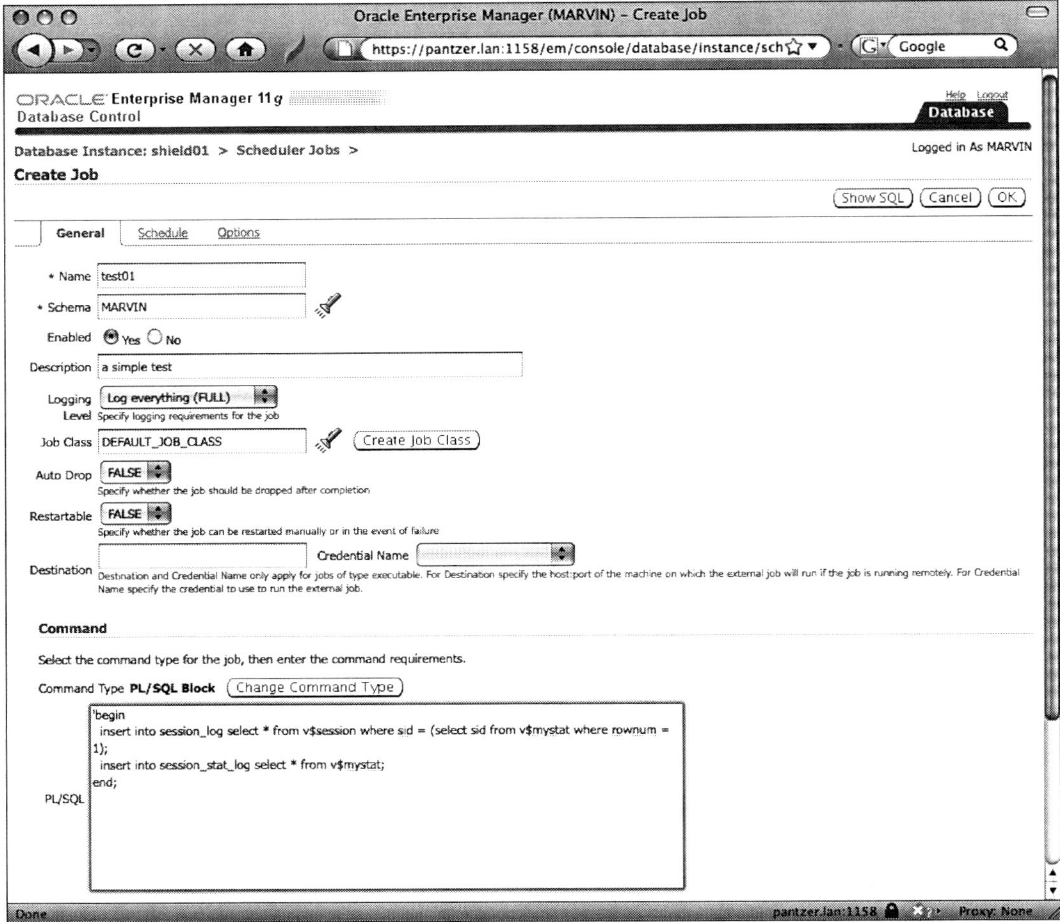

In the PL/SQL block, we can enter whatever code we want, as long as it is valid PL/SQL. In this case, there are a few simple inserts in a table.

Click on the **Show SQL** button. It will show the following code:

```
BEGIN
  sys.dbms_scheduler.create_job
    (
       job_name         => '"MARVIN"."TEST01"',
       job_type         => 'PLSQL_BLOCK',
       job_action       => 'begin
                            insert into session_log select * from
                            v$session where sid = (select sid from
                                       v$mystat where rownum = 1);
                            insert into session_stat_log select * from
                                                             v$mystat;
                            end;',
       start_date      => systimestamp at time zone 'Europe/Amsterdam',
       job_class        => '"DEFAULT_JOB_CLASS"',
       comments         => 'a simple test',
       auto_drop        => FALSE,
       enabled          => TRUE
    );
  sys.dbms_scheduler.set_attribute
   (
       name                 => '"MARVIN"."TEST01"',
       attribute            => 'logging_level',
       value                => DBMS_SCHEDULER.LOGGING_FULL
    );
  sys.dbms_scheduler.enable( '"MARVIN"."TEST01"' );
END;
```

Now, if we go back to the **Create Job** screen and click on the **OK** button, the job will be created and we will again come to the **Scheduler Jobs** screen. This time the list is no longer empty. It not only shows us our precious little job, but it also shows us that the job is in the **RUNNING** state as shown in the following screenshot:

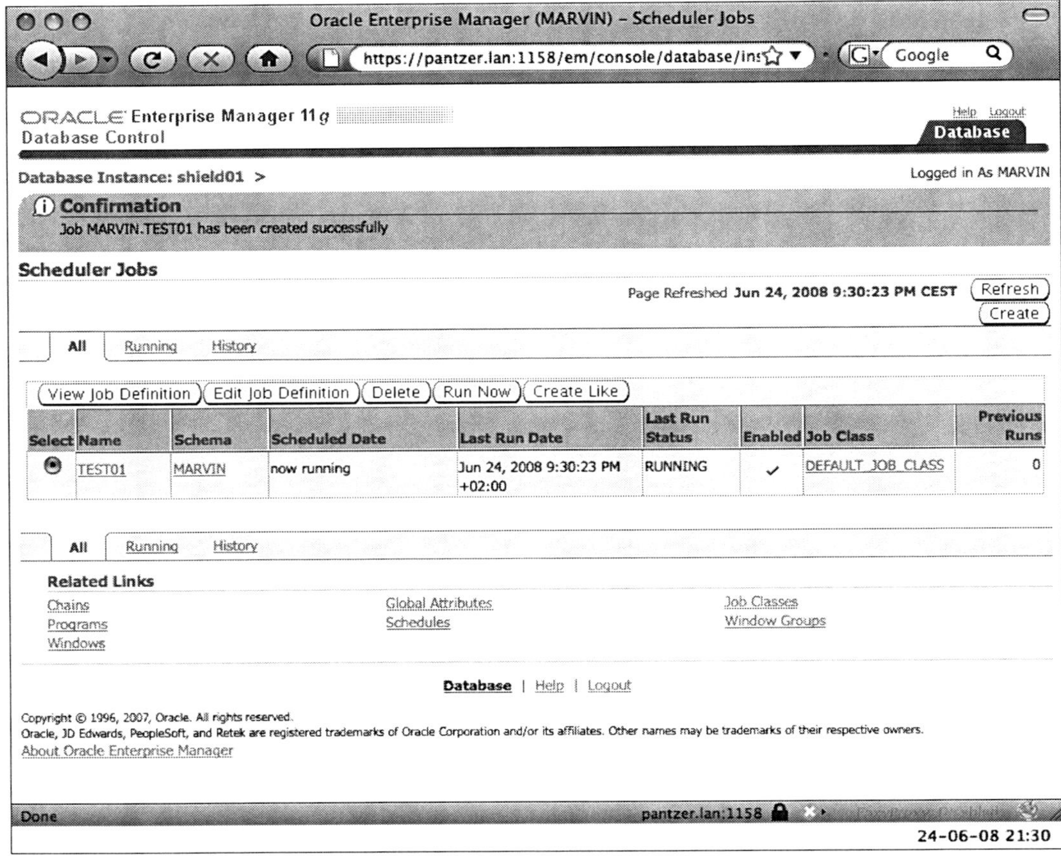

In case you do not want a job to start running directly upon creation, create it in the disabled state. In this case, we created the job in the **Enabled** state and so the job starts running automatically. To run it once more, just click on the **Run Now** button and off it goes. All this is done without having to use a command-line tool. In the rest of the book, all examples will be using good old SQL*Plus, SQL Developer, or DbVisualizer. The choice among them is mostly influenced by the contents of my glass!

Stored procedure

The next simplest type of job is the one that executes a stored procedure. A **stored procedure** is a piece of PL/SQL code that is stored in the database. It's not that this is more difficult; it's merely a question of creating the procedure and selecting it as `job_action`. In order to be able to select the procedure, we have to get the privileges to create the procedure. We can also select a procedure from another schema to use that in a job. In that case, we need the `execute` privilege on that procedure. However, we will create our own procedure. To be able to do that, grant `marvin` the correct privilege:

```
Grant create procedure to marvin;
```

And create a procedure called `SNAP`. It does not do much; it has the same contents as the PL/SQL block in the previous `TEST01` job:

```
CREATE OR REPLACE PROCEDURE SNAP as
begin
insert into session_log select * from v$session where sid = (select
                                sid from v$mystat where rownum = 1);
insert into session_stat_log select * from v$mystat;
end SNAP;
```

In DB Console, we need to change the **Command Type** by clicking on the **Change Command Type** button as shown in the following screenshot:

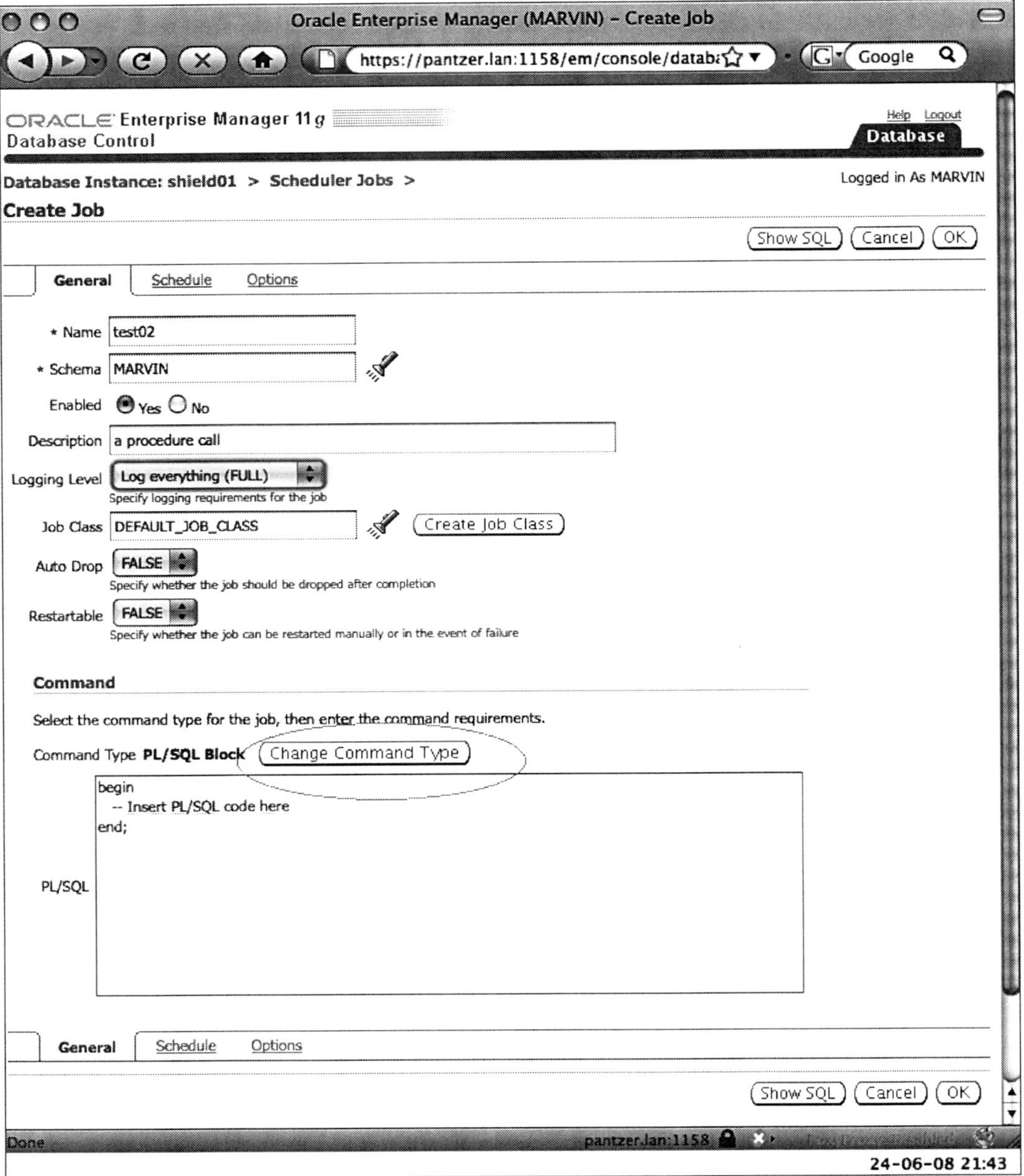

This brings us to the next screen where we can select the appropriate job type. In this case, it is **Stored Procedure** as shown in the following screenshot:

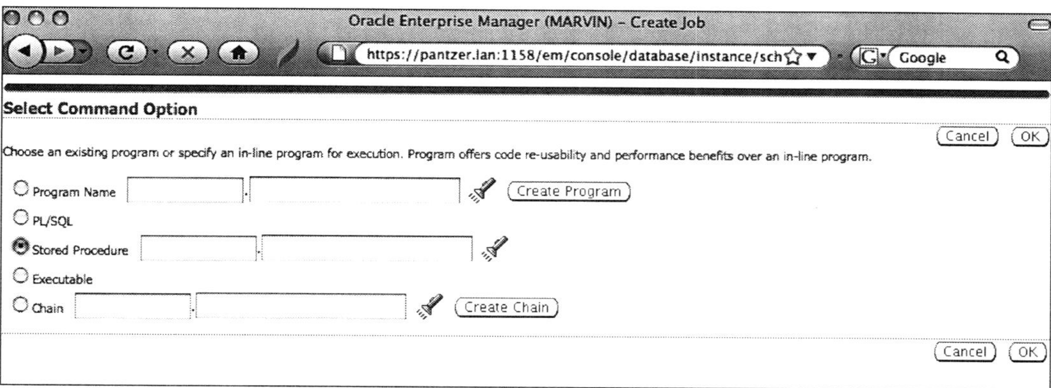

We can use the torch icon to select the procedure we want to run by the job as shown in the following screenshot:

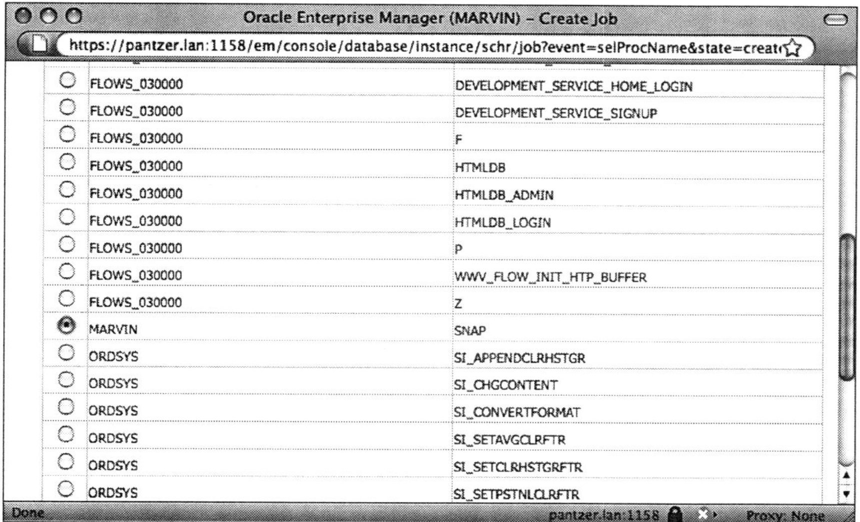

Here, we select the **SNAP** procedure from **MARVIN**.

After clicking on the **Select** button from near the bottom of the screen, we get back to where we started from—that is, our selection—but this time with the procedure name entered as shown in the following screenshot:

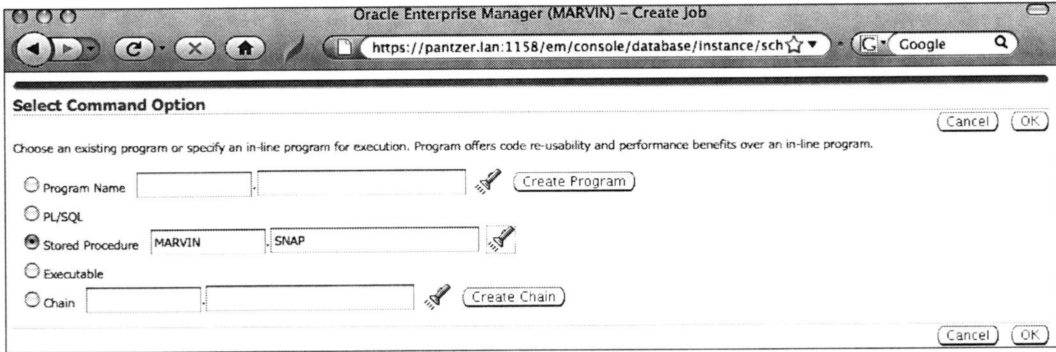

Clicking on the **OK** button brings us back to the main job creation screen as shown in the following screenshot:

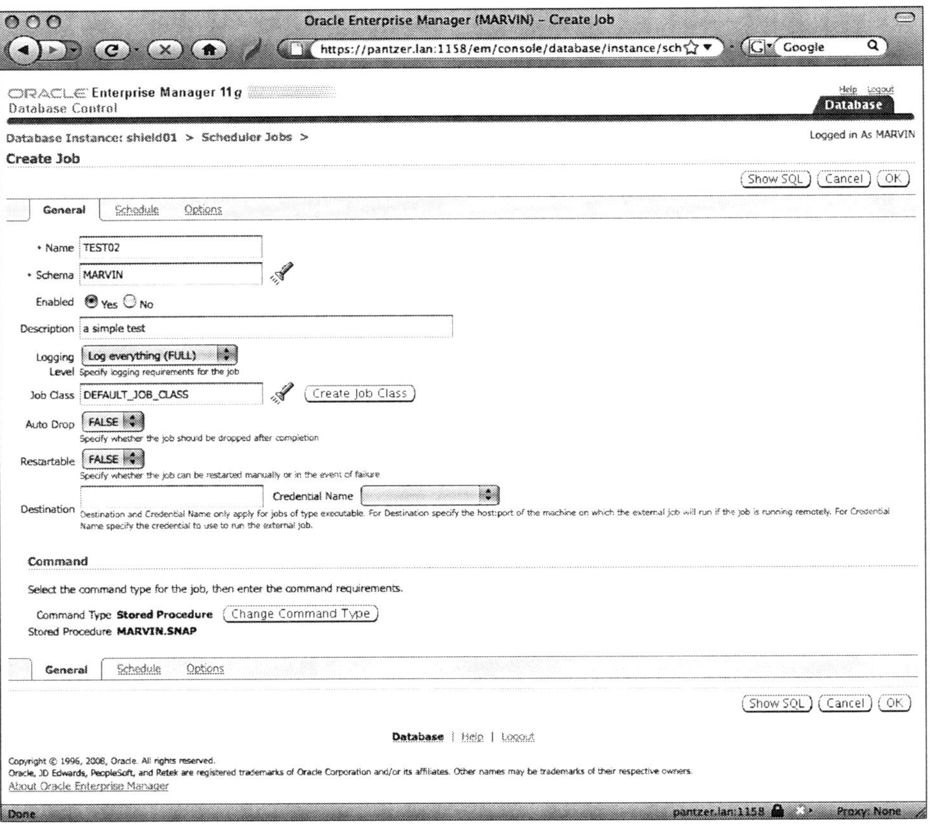

Using the **Show SQL** button will reveal the code that is generated for us:

```
BEGIN
  sys.dbms_scheduler9.create_job
    (
      job_name     => '"MARVIN"."TEST02"',
      job_type     => 'STORED_PROCEDURE',
      job_action   => '"MARVIN"."SNAP"',
      start_date   => systimestamp at time zone 'Europe/Amsterdam',
      job_class    => '"DEFAULT_JOB_CLASS"',
      auto_drop    => FALSE,
      enabled      => TRUE
     );
END;
```

The job performs the same function as the previous example, but this time by calling a stored procedure that has to do the work. Sometimes, a job type PL/SQL is sufficient for the task. But if you are planning to use job arguments, you can't use a job type of PL/SQL. In that case, you will need a job type of stored procedure or program, which we will discuss later.

Executable

A job type that starts an executable is the last type that can be created in the DB Console without having to create another Scheduler object type first. As compared to the DB-only PL/SQL or stored procedure, an executable can be an operating system script or binary program which the user *nobody* has `execution` privileges on. As the user *nobody* is not exactly a very powerful user, this mostly means that the script or binary program has to be executable by everybody. As this kind of job performs code that is not in the database, we also call it an external job. Later in the book, we will discover the preferred alternative for external jobs, **remote external jobs**, which is introduced in Oracle 11g.

To be able to create external jobs, `marvin` needs the extra privilege.

```
Grant create external job to marvin;
```

The code could very well look like this:

```
BEGIN
  sys.dbms_scheduler.create_job
    (
      job_name     => '"MARVIN"."TEST03"',
      job_type     => 'EXECUTABLE',
      job_action   => '/tmp/testje.sh',
      start_date   => systimestamp at time zone 'Europe/Amsterdam',
      job_class    => '"DEFAULT_JOB_CLASS"',
      comments     => 'an external job test',
```

```
        auto_drop    => FALSE,
        enabled      => TRUE
      );
  END;
```

And the script `testje.sh` is here:

```
#!/bin/ksh
{
  id
  env
} >/tmp/testje.log 2>&1
```

This may not be the most complex script, but it does show some important things about how the job is run. Without this information, it's a bit hard to get a working script. As most of us know, jobs that are launched by cron have a simple environment. But jobs started by the Oracle Scheduler win the game when it comes to simplicity. The environment is almost empty:

```
uid=99(nobody) gid=99(nobody) groups=99(nobody)
context=user_u:system_r:unconfined_t
_=/bin/env
PWD=/
```

The user who ran the script is by default the user `nobody`. The script that is started has slash (`/`) as working directory. So don't look surprised when you get hit by errors such as "permission denied". Another surprise might be that there is no job output shown in the Scheduler views—that is, if the job succeeds. Strangely enough, Oracle decided to show only job outputs in the Scheduler views when the job fails. The job gets a **FAILED** status when the error returned is other than `0`. The error code is interpreted by Oracle using the regular `errno.h`, which we all know from the good old C language hacking days. So if you invent an exit code, Oracle will interpret it using the standard error codes. The good news is that the first few bytes of `stderr` are logged in the **ADDITIONAL_INFO** column of the `*_scheduler_job_run_details` view. The `stderr` is always logged, even when the error code is `0`.

Program

A program is a database object that can be used to build a library of building blocks to create jobs or job chains. Just like a job, a program can be chosen from a few types such as:

- A PL/SQL block
- A stored procedure
- An executable

A **program** is not a runnable job by itself. It contains what a job or chain step should execute. It references the code and can easily be reused. When including programs in job steps, there are some limitations. But as long as we can do without arguments, we are OK. Let's create a few programs for the actions created above. When picking names, we need to think about the namespace where the jobs and programs live. They live in the same namespace. This means that if the **TEST01** job exists, I cannot create a program called **TEST01** as shown in the following screenshot. So, I will prefix the programs with P_.

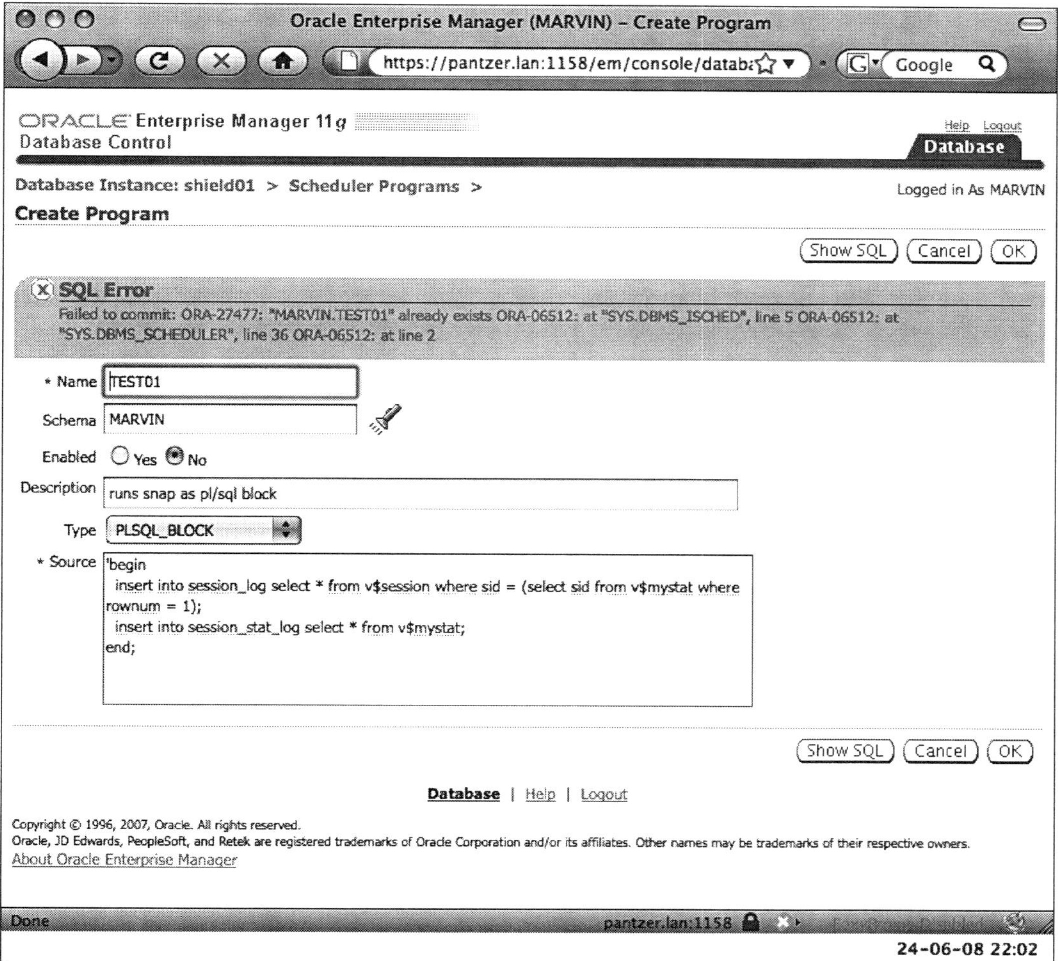

The TEST01 program is prefixed by P_, which gives P_TEST01. Now, don't forget to enable the program. Unlike jobs, the programs are not started at the enable time. In this case, it is just made useable for jobs or chains. Also, create the P_TEST02 program that selects the stored procedure `SNAP`, and P_TEST03 that calls the executable.

Defining arguments for your jobs

When using building blocks like stored procedures and programs, we might want to control what the code is going to do for us by giving it arguments. Arguments can also be given to external jobs such as command-line arguments. There are two types of arguments:

- Metadata arguments
- Normal application arguments

If you are using arguments for a job, you will start by specifying the number of arguments that the procedure, program, or external job is going to have. Next, you need to define the arguments and their values. Until all of the arguments are defined, it is not possible to enable the item for which you are defining the arguments.

Metadata arguments

A metadata argument is an argument that tells something about the currently running job.

There are several reasons for using metadata arguments in a program. One is that a program is executed by several different jobs and you want to know which job called the program. The `job_name` is one of the important metadata attributes for a metadata argument. The complete list of useable attributes is as shown in the following table:

Attribute name	Description
`job_name`	Name of the currently running job.
`job_subname`	Subname of the currently running job, if running in a chain. The combination of `job_name` and `job_subname` define the step that the chain is running.
`job_owner`	The owner of the currently running job.
`job_scheduled_start`	This tells when the job was scheduled to start.
`job_start`	This tells when the job really started.
`window_start`	If the job is connected to a window, this specifies the window open time.

Attribute name	Description
window_end	If the job is started by a window, this specifies the time at which the window is scheduled to close.
event_message	The contents of the event message that triggered an event-driven job.

This does look a bit mysterious, but a simple example will make things clearer. In this example, we make a small program that uses the job_name attribute to find out which job called the program.

First, give marvin the required privileges and quota to be able to create a log table:

```
Grant create table to marvin;

Alter user marvin quota unlimited on users;
```

Next, let marvin create the log table:

```
Create table log (job_name varchar2(30), dat_sys date);
```

Define a stored procedure that accepts one argument, the job_name:

```
--/
CREATE OR REPLACE PROCEDURE WHOCALLEDME (v_job varchar2) as
  begin
    insert into log (job_name, dat_sys) values (v_job, sysdate);
  end WHOCALLEDME;
/
```

Now, create a program that uses this stored procedure:

```
--/
BEGIN
  DBMS_SCHEDULER.CREATE_PROGRAM
    (
      program_name        => '"MARVIN"."P_CALLER"',
      program_action      => '"MARVIN"."WHOCALLEDME"',
      program_type        => 'STORED_PROCEDURE',
      number_of_arguments => 1,
      comments            => 'show which job called me',
      enabled             => FALSE
    );
end;
/
```

This program is created with `enabled` as `FALSE`. As not all of the arguments are defined, it cannot be enabled. Trying to run this code with `enabled=> TRUE` will result in an error message that will try to explain to us that not all arguments are defined. Now it is time to define the metadata argument to complete the job.

```
--/
begin
  DBMS_SCHEDULER.DEFINE_METADATA_ARGUMENT
    (
      program_name          => 'p_caller',
      metadata_attribute    => 'job_name',
      argument_position     => 1,
      argument_name         => 'v_job'
    );
end;
/
```

The program is now completely defined with all of the arguments, so we can enable the program. If this program is called by some job, the Scheduler automatically inserts the correct values in the first argument of this program.

```
--/
BEGIN
    dbms_scheduler.enable('P_CALLER');
END;
/
```

Now create the job that uses the enabled program, `P_CALLER`. The job name is `test_m_arg` and is defined as follows:

```
--/
BEGIN
  dbms_scheduler.create_job
    (
      job_name        => 'TEST_M_ARG',
      program_name    => 'P_CALLER',
      comments        => 'test using metadata argument',
      enabled         => TRUE
    );
END;
/
```

Because the job is enabled at the creation time and we have not tied the job to a schedule, an event, or a window, the job immediately starts running. So it makes sense to check the contents of the log table. Despite the fact that the job itself has no arguments, the job name is passed to the program that inserted it into the log table.

```
Select job_name from log;
```

This clearly reveals the name of the job that caused the program to be executed: TEST_M_ARG.

This example might look a bit silly, but this mechanism gives us countless possibilities. The other attributes have their own different uses. For example, the window_end attribute enables a job to find out how much time it has to complete its task before the window that started the job will close. This can help the code to decide whether or not to make an extra iteration to complete another batch of transactions.

Normal application arguments

Now that we have seen the mysterious metadata arguments, the normal application arguments, also known as regular arguments, are just a piece of cake. For this example, we use the same log table as for the metadata example. We create a separate procedure that also has one argument as follows:

```
--/
CREATE OR REPLACE PROCEDURE justaproc (v_arg varchar2) as
  begin
    insert into log (job_name, dat_sys) values (v_arg, sysdate);
  end justaproc;
/
```

The procedure used by a program is defined as follows:

```
--/
BEGIN
  DBMS_SCHEDULER.CREATE_PROGRAM
    (
      program_name            => 'P_ARG01',
      program_action          => 'JUSTAPROC',
      program_type            => 'STORED_PROCEDURE',
      number_of_arguments     => 1,
      comments                => 'pass an argument',
      enabled                 => FALSE
    );
END;
/
```

Now let's define the argument to complete the program description:

```
--/
BEGIN
  DBMS_SCHEDULER.DEFINE_program_ARGUMENT
    (
      program_name            => 'P_ARG01',
      argument_position       => 1,
```

```
        argument_name              => 'v_arg',
        argument_type              => 'varchar2'
    );
END;
/
```

The argument type is mandatory, but it is not the type checked by the Scheduler. So, if you are going to use it, you need to test the arguments definition before using it. Now that the program is complete, we can enable it.

```
--/
BEGIN
    dbms_scheduler.enable('P_ARG01');
END;
/
```

We are reaching the goal of creating a job that passes an argument to the code. Everything is in place, so create the job now:

```
--/
BEGIN
  sys.dbms_scheduler.create_job
    (
      job_name     => 'TEST_ARG',
      program_name => 'P_ARG01',
      comments     => 'test using a regular argument',
      enabled      => FALSE
    );
END;
/
```

You might have noticed that the job is created in the disabled state. This is the same as for the program arguments—all of the job arguments have to be defined and given a value before the job can be enabled. Failing to do so will result in **ORA-27457: argument 1 of job "MARVIN.TEST_ARG" has no value.** We don't want such errors, so we define the arguments before trying to enable—and run—the job:

```
--/
BEGIN
  dbms_scheduler.set_job_argument_value
    (
      job_name       => 'TEST_ARG',
      argument_name  => 'V_ARG',
      argument_value => 'manual'
    );
END;
/
```

And finally we are ready to enable the job. The job will start immediately, so we can check the log table right away. First enable the job like this:

```
--/
BEGIN
    dbms_scheduler.enable('TEST_ARG');
END;
/
```

If everything goes as expected, you will find another entry in the log table with "manual" in the `job_name` column. If you are experimenting with job arguments, you might notice that you don't need to disable a job to give its arguments a new value. As soon as you do, the job automatically becomes invalid. When you are ready, the job will not automatically get enabled again and you need to do so manually.

Summary

This was a quick glimpse of what the Scheduler can give us by using DB Console or Grid control. There is a lot more to say than this, as `dbms_scheduler` is full of surprises.

In this chapter we looked at:

- What are the minimal privileges a user needs to create and run scripts
- How to create a simple job that has only the PL/SQL code
- How to create a simple job that calls a stored procedure
- How to create a simple job that calls an executable
- How to create a simple job that uses a program
- How to assign metadata arguments to a program
- How to assign normal application arguments to a program
- How to use arguments in a job

In the next chapter, we will use the programs of this chapter to create a simple chain. Chains are really wonderful! You will love them. Here, you will see the real difference in `dbms_job`. Let's get us chained....

2
Simple Chain

At first sight, **chains** might look a little intimidating. Often, there is a lot of code which can be difficult to go through when you are trying to identify particular problems or issues. But fear not, things are not as bad as they seem. Chains are useful and can reduce a number of potential issues.

In many systems, problems are hidden in the form of scheduled tasks that rely on one task to be completed before the next task is started. A nice example of this is a cold backup, which is performed in three individual sections:

1. Shut down the database.
2. Copy the database files to a remote location.
3. Start up the database.

In the example above, when the cold backup was implemented, step 2 originally took four minutes. Therefore, the administrator decided that step 3 could be started five minutes after step 1 was completed. However, after a few weeks the database grew bigger and the copy phase of the backup took 20 minutes. This is what we might call a **time bomb**. Everything looks as though it is working fine. The database will run after the backup is completed and data files apparently get copied to a remote location. However, what will happen if the storage is hit by a power failure? In this case, a good backup is needed. But this backup does not exist because the original timings are no longer valid. Had the backup been implemented using a chain, this disaster could easily have been prevented. This chapter will show how this can be done.

Jobs

Before we start, we need to agree on what a job is. A **job** is a list of tasks that perform an action. This list can contain any number of tasks. The jobs we created in the previous chapter are valid jobs that all perform a single task. Next, we will see how the above-mentioned backup scenario can be fitted into a chained job. We will also see that a chained job doesn't mean that it will work correctly as there are opportunities for errors.

Chains

If we want to combine multiple logically-connected jobs or tasks, we should build a job chain. As the name implies, a chain is simply a group of concurrent or sequential jobs. Tasks that have no relation to the other tasks should be scheduled individually, and not as a part of a job chain.

[If we combine an individual task in a chain, we have to accept that it will depend on other links in that chain.]

In other words, an individual task can get skipped because another part in the chain has been skipped.

Clearly, skipping tasks in any chain is probably not something we want. In a job that consists of multiple steps, we want to see some kind of relationship between the steps. We describe this relationship with **rules**. The rules in a chain define the order in which the job steps are executed (or, maybe, not executed). Execution depends on the **status** of the previous job steps. Let's list the statuses and their meanings.

Statuses

The following is the list of statuses that we can use in rules to control what should be done next:

- `NOT_STARTED`: Set a chain step to this status to make it runnable again
- `SCHEDULED`: The normal status of a scheduled job when it is runnable
- `RUNNING`: The job or step is currently running
- `PAUSED`: The job or step is paused
- `STALLED`: The Scheduler does not know what step to perform next
- `SUCCEEDED`: The job or step is completed successfully
- `FAILED`: The job or step has ended in failure
- `STOPPED`: The job or step is completed with a Scheduler error

If a step is in the SUCCEEDED, FAILED, or STOPPED state, its completed attribute is set to TRUE; otherwise it is set to FALSE.

Chains and steps

As mentioned earlier, a chain consists of multiple steps that are logically connected together. We cannot say anything about the behavior of these steps in the job chain. In order to know when these steps are going to be executed, we have to know what rules are applied to them. All steps have a name. We are going to reference these names of steps in our rules, which we will define later. Now, let's return to the backup example and list the steps there:

1. SHUTDOWN: Take the database offline in a clean way.
2. COPYFILES: Copy the database files to a remote location.
3. STARTUP: Start up the database for a normal operation.

Without rules, nothing much will happen. The Scheduler will be looking for a step to start, but will be unable to find it. As soon as the Scheduler finds itself in a situation where it is given a chain and it cannot determine what to do next, the job gets a special job status—CHAIN_STALLED. This status means that the Scheduler does not know how to handle the chain. The chain will probably remain in this state indefinitely, unless we manually take over. If we ever find our job in such a state, it means that we have not taken into account all possible combinations of outcomes that the steps can have. Defining a good set of rules will mostly prevent us from getting in this state. Let's go to the rules now.

Rules

Rules in a chain describe the way the Scheduler should read the job description. A chain *must* have a proper starting point and end point. Steps in a chain are activated when the rules in the chain definition evaluate to true (as rules are Boolean) and mention the specific step names to be started.

Let's return to the backup example once more. We know there is only one location where it makes sense to start the job—the step that shuts down the database. How can we make the Scheduler know that? Let's start with an overview of what we know. The steps are:

1. Always start with SHUTDOWN.
2. If SHUTDOWN is successful, start COPYFILES.

3. If COPYFILES is successful, start STARTUP.
4. If STARTUP is successful, start END 0.

This lists the optimum order of executions, but does not take into account a situation with failures. What should we do if SHUTDOWN fails? What should we do if COPYFILES fails? What should we do if STARTUP fails? If it is important that we act on a status, we should tell this to the Scheduler. With the current list of rules, we would end up in CHAIN_STALLED as soon as one of the steps fails. To prevent this we should add at least one extra rule that tells the Scheduler what to do if any one of the defined steps fail.

5. If SHUTDOWN, or COPYFILES, or STARTUP fails, start END 1.

This last rule makes sure that our example backup always ends. It returns an error code 0 when everything succeeds and returns an error code 1 when any step in the chain fails. The error code 0 means "no error", and any other value means "failure". In this short example, it is easy to make one rule that handles all FAILED situations. When the list of steps grows, it is more likely that we forget to mention a step. In the long run, it might be smarter to give every step its own FAILED rule. In doing so, we end up with a larger list of rules but they are easier to check for completeness and should help us to prevent getting stuck in CHAIN_STALLED situations.

Evaluation interval

As Steven Jobs would often say:

> *There is one more thing ...*

There is one more thing to say about rules. The Scheduler normally checks *what to do* at the start and the end of each and every job step. In many situations this may be good enough, but there are situations where something more is required. One example is where one step of a job not only depends on the status of a former step, but also on the row count of a table or on the time of day. If this is the case, it would be best if the job step starts running as soon as the condition becomes true; and not after we had to manually intervene to make the Scheduler evaluate the chain again. We can give the chain an **evaluation interval** to make the Scheduler not only check the status of the job when it starts the job (or a job_step ends), but also to repeat the evaluations on a timed basis. To run these repeated evaluations, we have to specify evaluation_interval. The evaluation interval is the way to make the Scheduler check what to do next for moments other than job starts or at the job_step ends. We will need this as soon as a step can depend on something that is not a part of the chain.

An example could be that a step is allowed to execute only when the Nth step SUCCEEDED and there are less than 1000 sessions in the database. However, it might not be possible to predict the number of sessions in the database. The database may be regularly busy. We want this step to run as soon as enough people disconnect:

```
':stepn.state=''SUCCEEDED'' AND select count(*)
                               from v$session < 1000'
```

We can make the Scheduler re-evaluate the chain periodically by setting the evaluation_interval parameter at the time of creating the chain.

The evaluation_interval parameter cannot be less than a minute and more than a day.

The following is an example to define an evaluation interval at the chain creation time:

```
--/
BEGIN
  dbms_scheduler.create_chain
    (
      comments              => 'freezing cold backup',
      evaluation_interval   => numtodsinterval (5,'minute'),
      chain_name            => '"C_COLD_BACKUP"'
    );
END;
/
```

This creates a chain that has an evaluation interval (which makes the Scheduler check what to do) of five minutes. Forgetting things is human, and Oracle happens to know this. So it has given us the opportunity to add or modify the evaluation interval after the creation of the chain in the form of setting the following attribute:

```
--/
BEGIN
  dbms_scheduler.set_attribute
    (
      name         => 'c_cold_backup',
      attribute    => 'evaluation_interval',
      value        => numtodsinterval (6,'minute')
    );
END;
/
```

Finally, there is also a way to get rid of this by setting the `evaluation_interval` to `NULL. Use the set_attribute_null` procedure for this purpose as follows:

```
--/
BEGIN
  dbms_scheduler.set_attribute_null
    (
      name          => 'c_cold_backup',
      attribute     => 'evaluation_interval'
    );
END;
/
```

Privileges

Before we can go any further, we need some extra privileges. These privileges will come along with the `CREATE JOB` privilege that we saw in the previous chapter. We need to be able to create rule sets, rules, and evaluation contexts. We can do this by using the `DBMS_RULE_ADM` package to grant the user, `MARVIN`, the required privileges:

```
--/
BEGIN
  DBMS_RULE_ADM.GRANT_SYSTEM_PRIVILEGE
        (DBMS_RULE_ADM.CREATE_RULE_OBJ, 'MARVIN');
  DBMS_RULE_ADM.GRANT_SYSTEM_PRIVILEGE
        (DBMS_RULE_ADM.CREATE_RULE_SET_OBJ, 'MARVIN');
  DBMS_RULE_ADM.GRANT_SYSTEM_PRIVILEGE
        (DBMS_RULE_ADM.CREATE_EVALUATION_CONTEXT_OBJ, 'MARVIN');
END;
/
```

This tiny bit of code gives `MARVIN` the privileges to create rule sets, rules, and evaluation contexts.

We discussed earlier in the chapter what a rule is. A **rule set**, on the other hand, is a collection of the rules that control the chain. Mostly, we will not deal with rule sets as individual items and we will not even need to assign a name to them (but we could do so if we wanted). Normally, the names of rule sets and rules are generated by the system. We can even reuse a carefully defined rule set that relates to another chain. This chain would contain the exact set of steps, or rule set, as the original chain. Having said that, most of the time we will be happy with the system generated names. We will hardly ever refer to a rule set by name when using the Scheduler. Often, we will build new chains with custom rules for that chain. In rare cases, we can define the chain rules and the chain steps separately if needed.

Steps to create a chain

When creating a chain, there are certain steps that need to be followed:

1. List the actions that the chain should perform.
2. Create the programs that perform separate actions.
3. Enable the programs so that they can be used in the chain.
4. Design the rules that the Scheduler must follow to work through the chain.
5. Check if a chain step depends on events from outside the chain.
6. Create the chain.
    a. Use `evaluation_interval` when a step depends on something outside the chain.
    b. Leave `evaluation_interval` undefined when no external dependency exists.
7. Create the chain steps by calling the created and enabled programs.
8. Create the chain rules for every step with rules (at least) for success and failure.
9. Enable the chain.
10. Create a job that is going to run the chain.

Let's go through this list of actions in the upcoming sections.

Hands-on with chains

Let's get our hands dirty and play with chains for a while. The functionality of the programs we use in the chains is not important. What is important is that we can see what happens and why. We will use three programs that perform their own very important task: the first program for shutting down the database, the second program for copying the files, and the third program for starting the database after backing up.

All the three programs call `dbms_lock.sleep` to enable us to study job logging and see how the chains we have created are run. This is enough for us to simulate the backup scenario we have seen before. In other words, for this example, `dbms_lock.sleep` is used as a placeholder for the important tasks that the job may eventually run.

Programs

Programs are the building blocks of the chain (as well as a job, as mentioned in the previous chapter). We should start by creating programs that perform functions. For this part, we can work with the `SHUTDOWN`, `COPYFILES`, and `STARTUP` programs. They all perform the action of calling a block of PL/SQL, which in turn calls `dbms_lock.sleep` for a while.

`SHUTDOWN` runs for 30 seconds, `COPYFILES` runs for 130 seconds, and `STARTUP` will take only 10 seconds. Take the code provided in the next section and apply it in a database using SQL*Plus or any other tool that you feel comfortable with.

SHUTDOWN

Here is the code that simulates the `SHUTDOWN` as generated by DB Console. It can be applied using SQL*Plus or any other tool you prefer to use when working with Oracle. In real life, this program will differ from this code only in the `program_action` parameter. In our simple example, it calls `dbms_lock.sleep`. But in real life, this `program_action` action will call an operating system script that performs the `SHUTDOWN`.

```
BEGIN
  DBMS_SCHEDULER.CREATE_PROGRAM
    (
      program_name         => '"MARVIN"."SHUTDOWN"',
      program_action       => 'begin
                               dbms_lock.sleep(30);
                               end;',
      program_type         => 'PLSQL_BLOCK',
      number_of_arguments  => 0,
      comments             => 'simulate a database shutdown',
      enabled              => TRUE
    );
END;
```

COPYFILES

Here is the code we use to simulate the `COPYFILES` action in the chain. Again, this code consumes a lot of time. In this case, it is a fixed 130 seconds. Remember that in real life situations this time may vary according to the size of the database and the load on the system. When coding a real backup scenario, the `program_action` variable will likely point to an operating system script that performs the `COPYFILES` actions.

```
BEGIN
  DBMS_SCHEDULER.CREATE_PROGRAM
    (
      program_name          => '"MARVIN"."COPYFILES"',
      program_action        => 'begin
                                dbms_lock.sleep(130);
                                end;',
      program_type          => 'PLSQL_BLOCK',
      number_of_arguments   => 0,
      comments              =>'simulate a database backup',
      enabled               => TRUE
    );
END;
```

With regards to time, it is this part of the backup code that sees the most fluctuation.

STARTUP

We have three actions and here is the last piece of code used to simulate the backup scenario. As you can see, this is not really a startup of a database but just a sleep of 10 seconds. This gives us the chance to see that the step has run and has performed the given task. Again, in real life, the `program_action` would call an operating system script that performs the database `STARTUP`. In our case, we just want to simulate the database `STARTUP`.

```
BEGIN
  DBMS_SCHEDULER.CREATE_PROGRAM
    (
      program_name          => '"MARVIN"."STARTUP"',
      program_action        => 'begin
                                 dbms_lock.sleep(10);
                                 end;',
      program_type          => 'PLSQL_BLOCK',
      number_of_arguments   => 0,
      comments              => 'simulate a database startup',
      enabled=>TRUE
    );
END;
```

Program state

As we cannot use a program that is not enabled in a chain, it is very important to have all the programs enabled before trying to use them. This can save a lot of time and frustration.

DB Console

We can use DB Console's Job Scheduler admin pages to generate the code; the resulting code was given above. Here is how you can build the programs in DB Console. If you want to use DB Console, log in and navigate to the **Server** tab in DB Console as shown in the following screenshot:

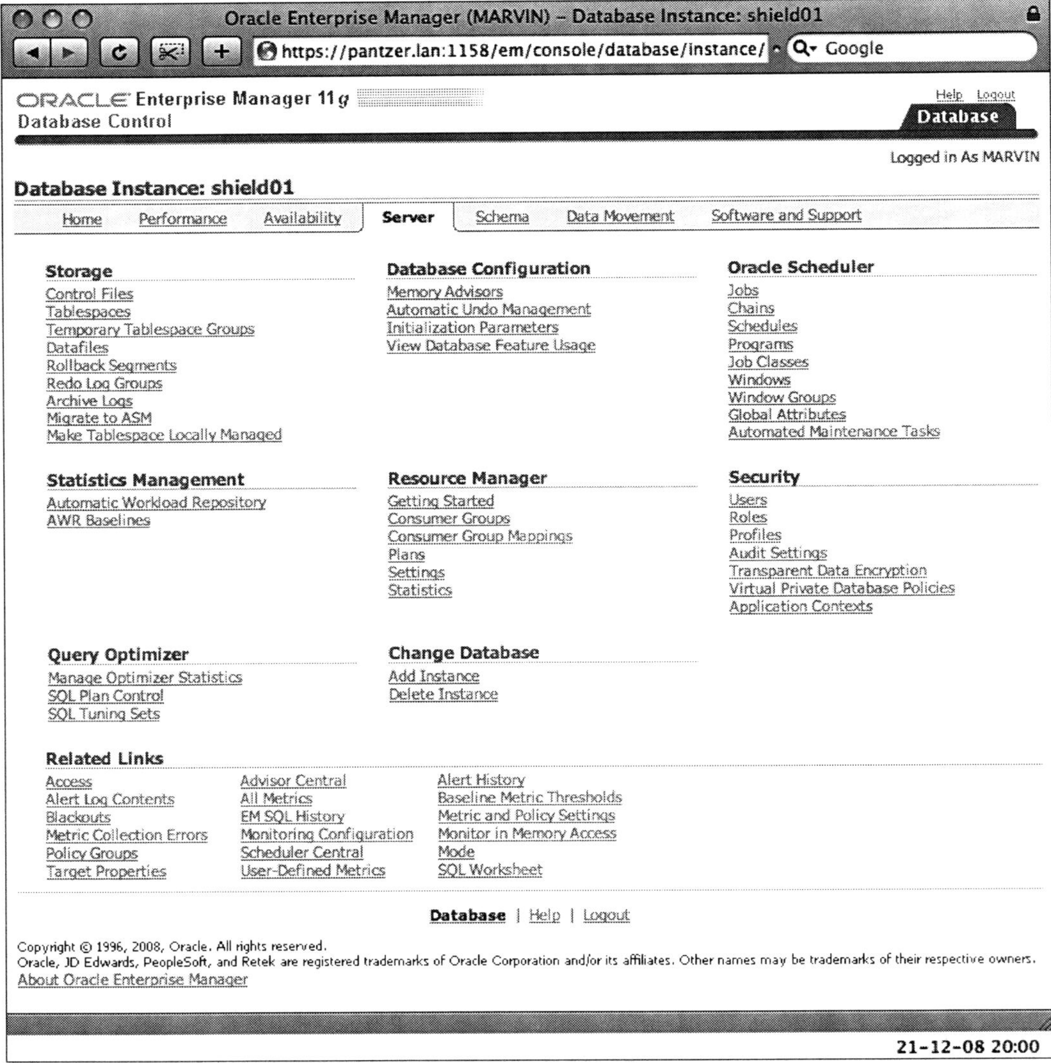

Select the **Programs** link under the **Oracle Scheduler** header, and then hit the **Create** button as shown in the following screenshot:

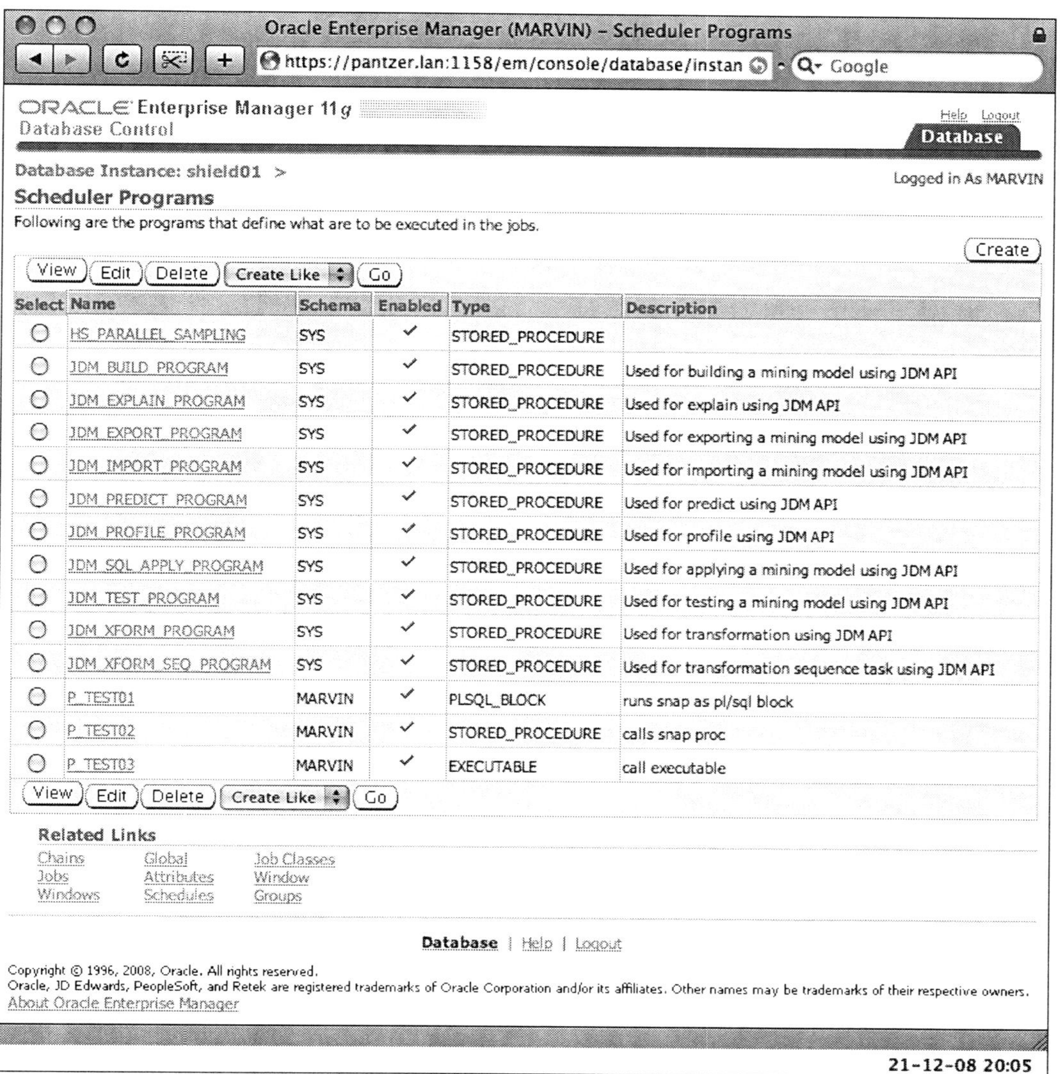

In the following dialog box that appears, enter the names and code as specified by using the values suggested earlier:

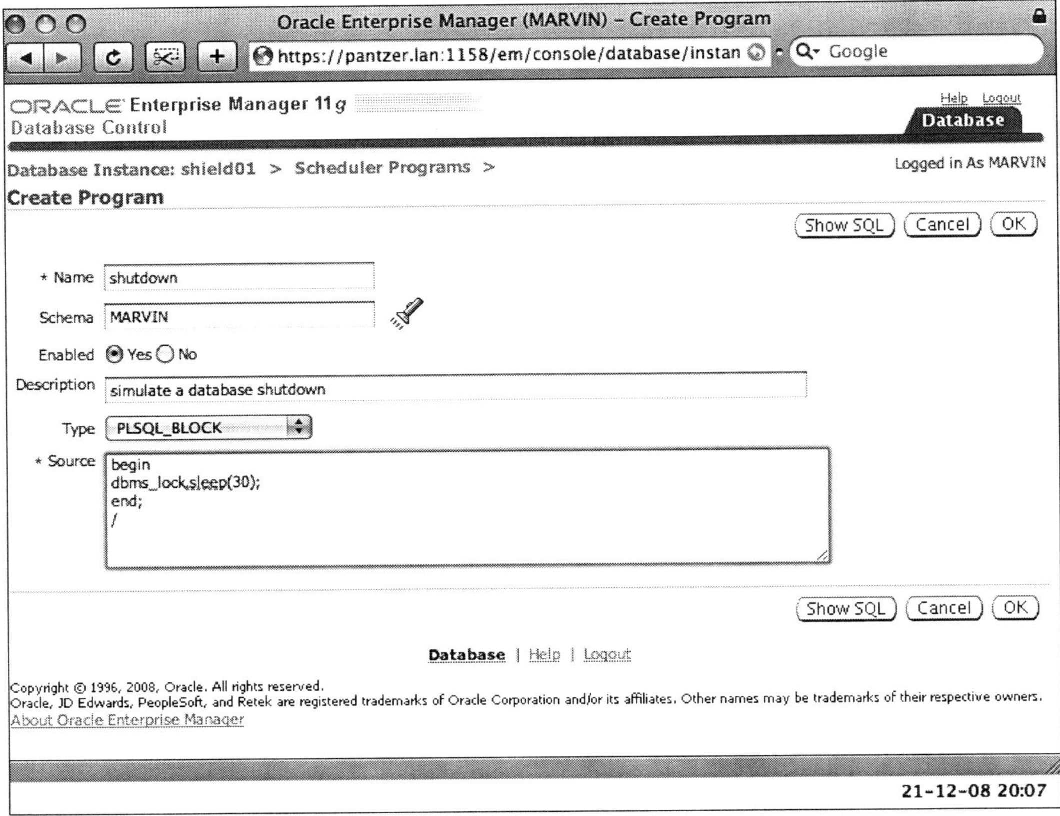

Repeat this for the other two programs. In the end, we should have the three programs—`SHUTDOWN`, `COPYFILES`, and `STARTUP`—in the programs overview as shown in the following screenshot. See to it that **MARVIN** has all the three programs as discussed.

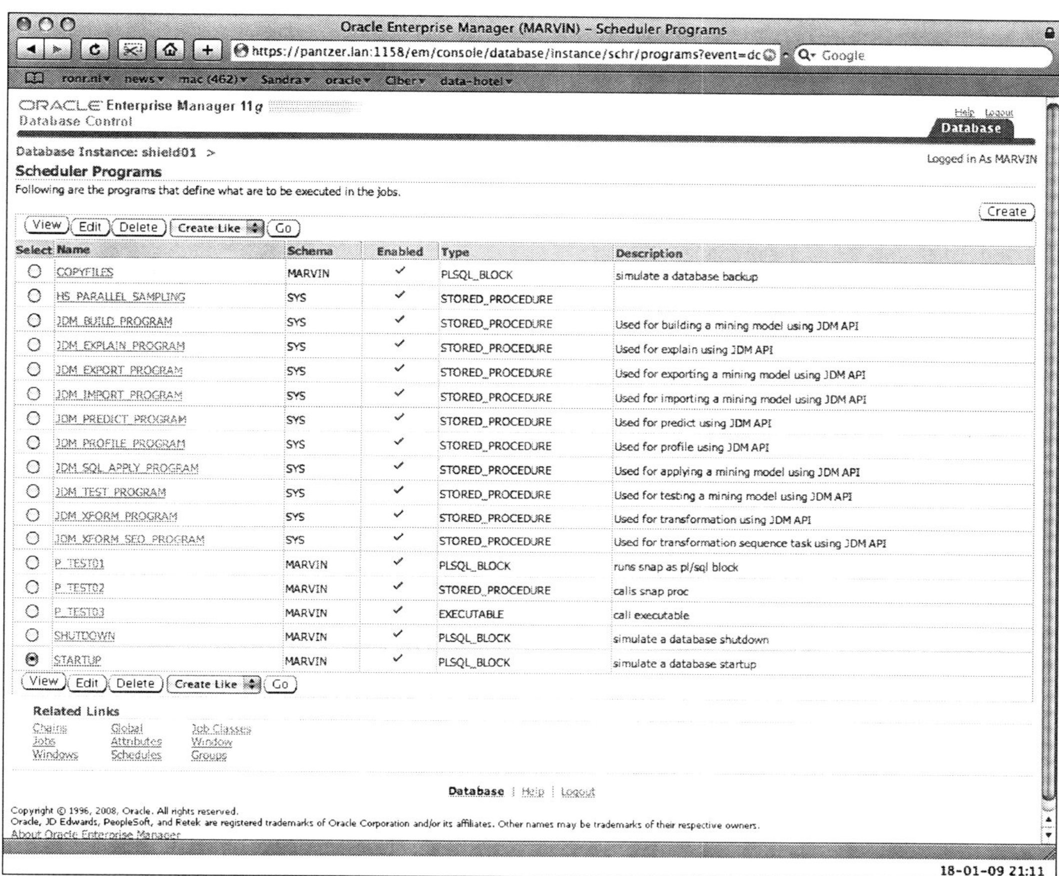

Chain definition

Did you see the status of the **Enabled** flag in the program creation part of this screenshot? They are all in the enabled state. We can use a chain only if all of its components are in an enabled state. In order to prevent a search for disabled components, we should enable them right at the definition time. The **Scheduler Programs** overview shown in this screenshot is able to find the enabled state of the program, but we can also check this using a good old SQL query such as:

```
select program_name, enabled from user_scheduler_programs;
PROGRAM_NAME ENABLED
COPYFILES TRUE
SHUTDOWN TRUE
STARTUP TRUE
```

For the chain definition, we can again use the DB Console. Do not use the **Programs** link in the **Oracle Scheduler** tab, rather select the **Chains** link. This brings us to the **Scheduler Chains** overview, as shown in the following screenshot:

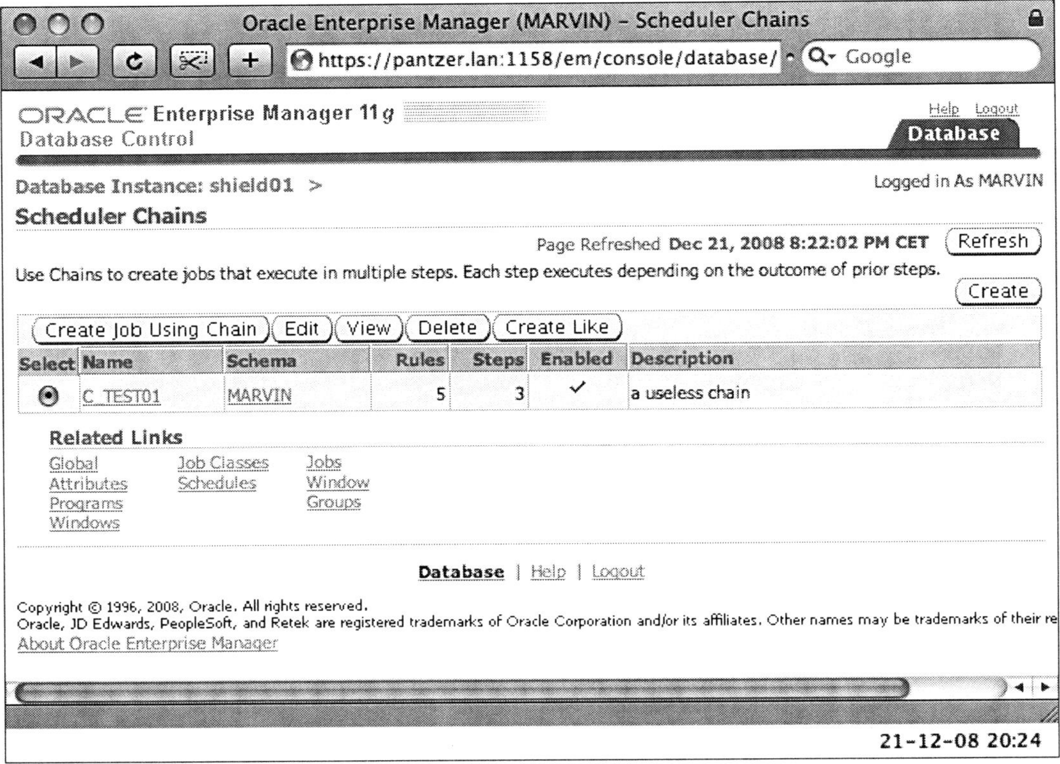

A quick glimpse at the screenshot reveals that the **Create** button is waiting for us to use it. Click on the **Create** button and enter the requested fields. Instead of entering the values manually, we can also use the torch symbol for a lookup list as follows:

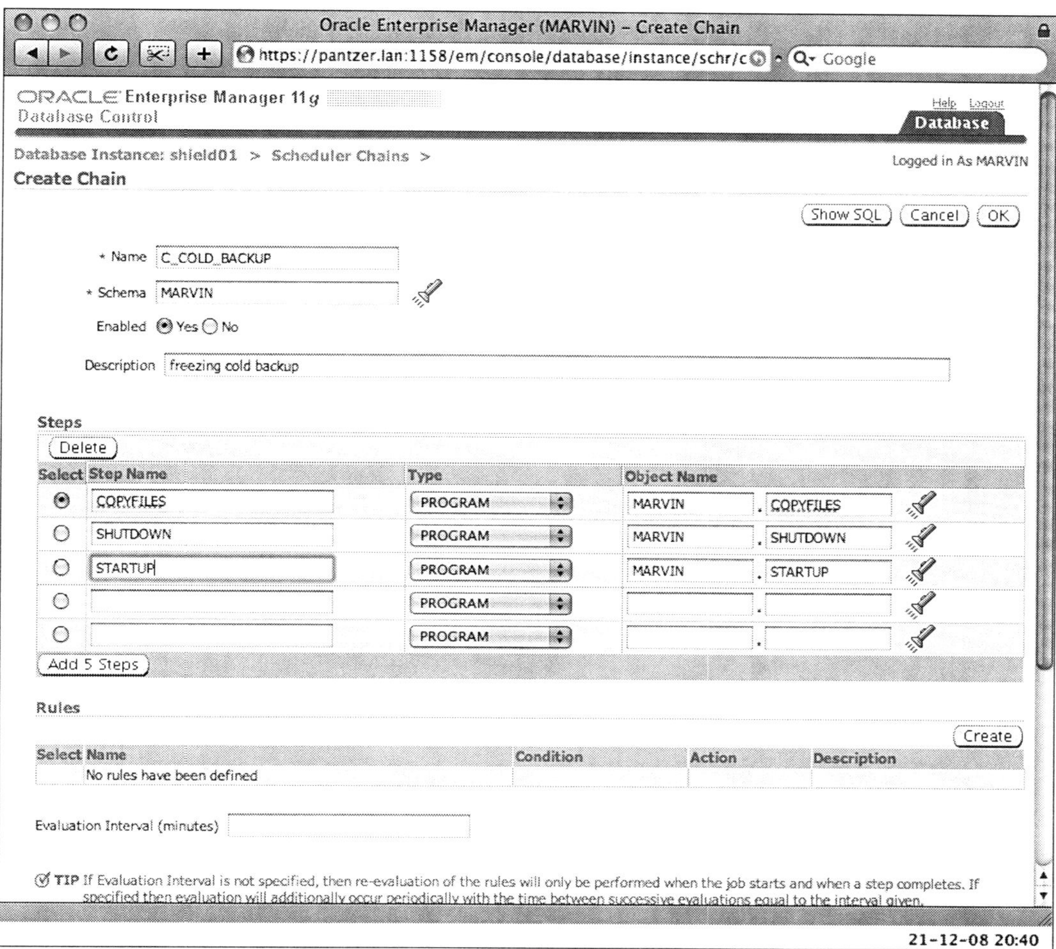

Note that the step names have been manually entered and the object names are in an arbitrary order. The step names have no meaning other than being the handles that the rules refer to. Step names will also be in the job logs. Giving them a useful name is a good idea. The DB Console has a very useful button called as **Show SQL** that gives the following code (shown after a little editing):

```
BEGIN
  sys.dbms_scheduler.create_chain
    (
      comments       => 'freezing cold backup',
      chain_name     => '"MARVIN"."C_COLD_BACKUP"'
    );
END;
```

This mere name and comment is a chain creation by itself. For every step that is added to the chain, there is `define_chain_step` as follows:

```
BEGIN
  sys.dbms_scheduler.define_chain_step
    (
      chain_name        => '"MARVIN"."C_COLD_BACKUP"',
      step_name         => '"COPYFILES"',
      program_name      => '"MARVIN"."COPYFILES"'
    );
END;
```

This might be welcome for those who have not configured DB Console for their database. This code references the `COPYFILES` code. Adjust it for the other two chain steps as shown next. The code generated by DB Console also sets the `SKIP` and `PAUSE` attributes to `false`.

```
BEGIN
  sys.dbms_scheduler.define_chain_step
    (
      chain_name           => '"MARVIN"."C_COLD_BACKUP"',
      step_name            => '"STARTUP"',
      program_name         => '"MARVIN"."STARTUP"'
    );
  sys.dbms_scheduler.define_chain_step
    (
      chain_name           => '"MARVIN"."C_COLD_BACKUP"',
      step_name            => '"SHUTDOWN"',
      program_name         => '"MARVIN"."SHUTDOWN"'
    );
END;
```

As we can see, there is no functionality in here; just references to the predefined programs. Normally, the programs contain the functionality. In this case, you can hardly call our programs "functional", but they do enable us to show the working. Now, let's concentrate on the Rules definition part of the DB Console screen for the chain definition. Click on the **Create** button and fill in the dialog box that appears next:

Oracle Enterprise Manager (MARVIN) - Edit Chain: MARVIN.C_COLD_BACKUP

https://pantzer.lan:1158/em/console/database/instance

Google

ORACLE Enterprise Manager 11g
Database Control

Help Logout

Database

Database Instance: shield01 > Scheduler Chains > Edit Chain: MARVIN.C_COLD_BACKUP >

Logged in As MARVIN

Create Rule

Cancel Continue

The rule will not actually be created until you click OK on the Create Chain page.

Name: Use System-Defined Name / Specify Name

Description: starting point of the chain

* Condition: true

Example: S1 SUCCEEDED

* Action: start shutdown

Example: START S4

TIP To specify rules, refer: Rule Language Specification

Cancel Continue

Database | Help | Logout

About Oracle Enterprise Manager

21-12-08 21:15

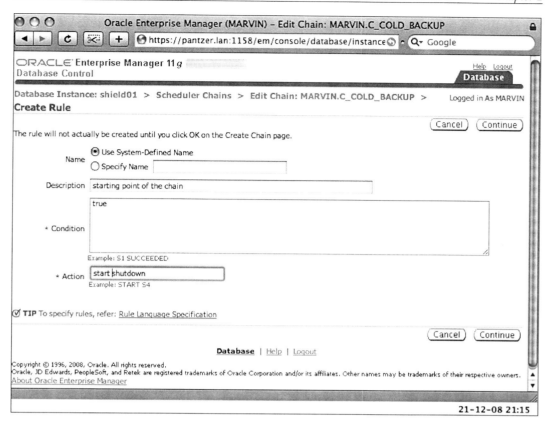

Enter all the rules we discussed earlier, which will give you the following screenshot:

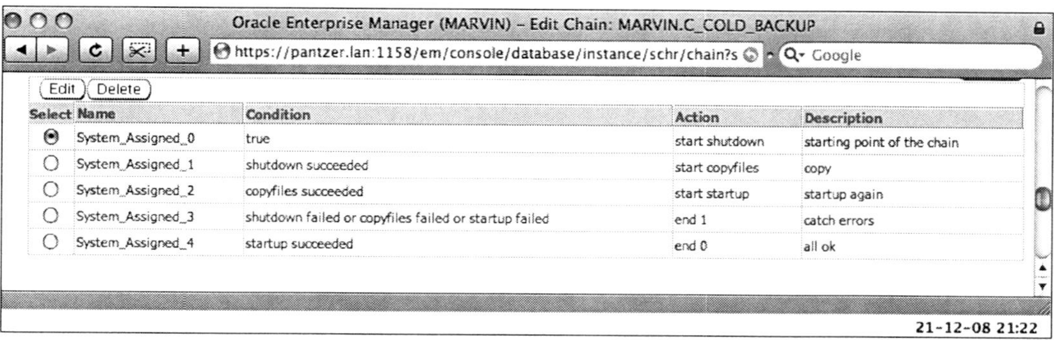

Oracle Enterprise Manager (MARVIN) - Edit Chain: MARVIN.C_COLD_BACKUP

https://pantzer.lan:1158/em/console/database/instance/schr/chain?s

Edit Delete

Select	Name	Condition	Action	Description
◉	System_Assigned_0	true	start shutdown	starting point of the chain
○	System_Assigned_1	shutdown succeeded	start copyfiles	copy
○	System_Assigned_2	copyfiles succeeded	start startup	startup again
○	System_Assigned_3	shutdown failed or copyfiles failed or startup failed	end 1	catch errors
○	System_Assigned_4	startup succeeded	end 0	all ok

21-12-08 21:22

As we did not give the rules any name, the rule names are system generated. This is fine for most situations.

The code for execution in SQL*Plus is as follows:

```
BEGIN
  sys.dbms_scheduler.define_chain_rule
    (
      chain_name          => '"MARVIN"."C_COLD_BACKUP"',
      condition           => 'true',
      comments            => 'allways start here',
      action              => 'start shutdown'
    );
END;
BEGIN
  sys.dbms_scheduler.define_chain_rule
    (
      chain_name          => '"MARVIN"."C_COLD_BACKUP"',
      condition           => 'shutdown succeeded',
      comments            => 'copy',
      action              => 'start copyfiles'
    );
  sys.dbms_scheduler.define_chain_rule
    (
      chain_name          => '"MARVIN"."C_COLD_BACKUP"',
      condition           => 'copyfiles succeeded',
      comments            => 'startup again',
      action              => 'start startup'
    );
  sys.dbms_scheduler.define_chain_rule
    (
      chain_name          => '"MARVIN"."C_COLD_BACKUP"',
      condition           => 'shutdown failed or
                              copyfiles failed or
                              startup failed',
      comments            => 'catch errors',
      action              => 'end 1'
    );
  sys.dbms_scheduler.define_chain_rule
    (
      chain_name          => '"MARVIN"."C_COLD_BACKUP"',
      condition           => 'startup succeeded',
      comments            => 'all ok',
      action              => 'end 0'
    );
END;
```

The chain is almost ready now. We must enable the chain either by setting the enabled property in DB Console, or by executing it:

```
begin
  dbms_scheduler.enable ('c_cold_backup');
end;
/
```

Now we can almost start the job. The job must first be created. There isn't any job available at this time because we have not yet created one. A chain needs a job that has the chain selected as an action. This is how the Scheduler was designed—without a job that runs the chain, there is no running of chain. A very convenient way to quickly create such a job is by using the DB Console button **Create Job Using Chain**, but the following PL/SQL works as well:

```
BEGIN
  sys.dbms_scheduler.create_job
    (
      job_name      => '"MARVIN"."J_COLD_BACKUP"',
      job_type      => 'CHAIN',
      job_action    => '"MARVIN"."C_COLD_BACKUP"',
      start_date    => systimestamp at time zone 'Europe/Amsterdam',
      job_class     => '"DEFAULT_JOB_CLASS"',
      auto_drop     => FALSE,
      enabled       => FALSE
    );
END;
```

Note that the job is not enabled at this moment. This is done to prevent it from running immediately, as when a job without a schedule is enabled, it will start running right away. We are now ready to get started. In the same way that we created other jobs (without chains) and still they could be started in several ways, similarly this job can also be started in several ways.

Several ways can be used, including the **Run Now** button in DB Console and the `dbms_scheduler.run_job` procedure in SQL*Plus. If you run `dbms_scheduler.run_job`, you must be prepared to cope with the error message **feature not prepared**. When you run a conventional job (a job that does not run a chain), you have a choice of running this job in the current session. With a chain, we can only use this procedure in the background. The default of `run_job` is `use_current_session = true`. Therefore, in order to start a job that runs a chain with SQL*Plus, we have to explicitly define the `current_session` parameter as `false`.

Running the chain

To run the job chain you can use the following:

```
begin
  dbms_scheduler.run_job
    (
      job_name              => 'j_cold_backup',
      use_current_session   => false
    );
end;
```

When the job is running, check the contents of the `user_scheduler_running_jobs` and `user_scheduler_running_chains` views. Officially, it is impossible for a chain to be listed in `*_scheduler_running_chains` without it being listed in `scheduler_running_jobs` as well. If you find this situation on your system, you need to apply the patch for `bug 5705385`. This bug is fixed in 11.1.0.7 and 10.2.0.5 with back ports available to 10.2.0.4 and 10.2.0.3.

In the `user_scheduler_running_chains` view, the complete execution of the chain is visible—as long as the chain is running, of course. This means that all the steps that are defined for the chain are visible, including `step_name`, `state`, `error_code`, `start_time`, and `duration`. We can use these steps to see how the chain progresses and what steps are still waiting to get started. `step_job_subname` is another column. For some reason, this column is `NULL` for the steps that are not active. The steps that are actively running are defined with `step_name`.

In the other view (`user_scheduler_running_jobs`), there are two entries listed—one for the chain itself and other for listing the details of the active step or `sub_jobname`. The entry that lists the chain also has the running total for `job_duration`.

To start a job, mostly `dbms_scheduler.run_job` will be used. But for chains, we also have another option—we can call `dbms_scheduler.run_chain`. Using this procedure, we can not only make a job run that runs the specified chain, but also specify at which step the chain should start. There is no need to specify that the job is to be started in the background. That makes sense because a chain can only be started in the background. If the `stepname` parameter is `NULL`, the chain starts right at the beginning as defined by the chain rules.

Tricks with chains

The fact that we use chains does not mean that we cannot build a disaster backup scenario! Using chains does not automatically mean that we can only use it in a predetermined way. In fact, we can make the job run exactly as the original scripts did and still have all the steps in one chain. Chain rules allow us to start a step, following a delay.

Let's assume that we want an action to happen after a delay of 1 minute and 5 seconds. In that case, we would code the rule with `after 00:01:05 start x`. This will start step x after a delay of 1 minute and 5 seconds. However, the system administrator who created the first backup scenario can accomplish exactly the same with the following rules:

```
true start shutdown
true after 00:05:00 start startup
true after 00:00:30 start copyfiles
startup succeeded end 0
```

The following screenshot shows how these rules will look in DB Console:

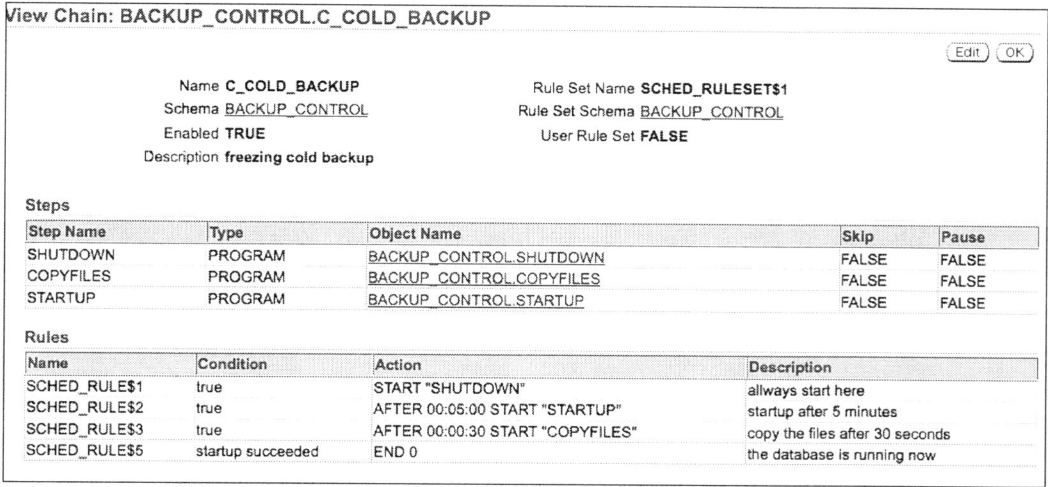

View Chain: BACKUP_CONTROL.C_COLD_BACKUP

(Edit) (OK)

Name **C_COLD_BACKUP**
Schema BACKUP_CONTROL
Enabled **TRUE**
Description **freezing cold backup**

Rule Set Name **SCHED_RULESET$1**
Rule Set Schema BACKUP_CONTROL
User Rule Set **FALSE**

Steps

Step Name	Type	Object Name	Skip	Pause
SHUTDOWN	PROGRAM	BACKUP_CONTROL.SHUTDOWN	FALSE	FALSE
COPYFILES	PROGRAM	BACKUP_CONTROL.COPYFILES	FALSE	FALSE
STARTUP	PROGRAM	BACKUP_CONTROL.STARTUP	FALSE	FALSE

Rules

Name	Condition	Action	Description
SCHED_RULE$1	true	START "SHUTDOWN"	allways start here
SCHED_RULE$2	true	AFTER 00:05:00 START "STARTUP"	startup after 5 minutes
SCHED_RULE$3	true	AFTER 00:00:30 START "COPYFILES"	copy the files after 30 seconds
SCHED_RULE$5	startup succeeded	END 0	the database is running now

Implementing these rules will shut down the database, copy the files, and then start up the database again. If the `startup` succeeds and ending the job returns `0`, it means that no errors occurred. It might work for a while. In this case, as soon as the database grows to such a size that `copyfiles` is still running when the `startup` triggers, `end 0` normally tells us that we are ready and have successfully completed a job. However, something extra might be happening when the Scheduler gets this status returned from a running chain. Then the Scheduler might actively stop other steps that are still running. Don't forget that the rules only say that after a given time the action has to be made active. So no matter how long the `copyfiles` step needs to be active, the startup step is started 5 minutes after the start of the chain. It appears that the `end 0` action not only returns a `0` to the system, it also terminates all the steps that are still running. This causes those steps to get the status of `STOPPED`. The `STOPPED` status means that the step did not end in a normal fashion. This indicates that there might or might not be a problem, depending on the application. In our case, it would likely mean that there is a problem because the copy of the database files would have been terminated.

All the steps that are evaluated to `true` are started when their triggering rule is evaluated to `true`. The rules listed earlier immediately start the shutdown, and then immediately start the countdown of 5 minutes—after which the `startup` will commence. This is because all the rules are `true` when the chain starts.

It is legal to start multiple steps concurrently using one rule. This enables us to run several steps in parallel. In our case, we could easily make the problems worse by specifying this:

```
true start shutdown, copyfiles, startup, end 0
```

Now all the steps will be run at once—something that we certainly don't want to do. Again, this is a valid syntax. But the correct use of this option depends a lot on your goal.

This rule would start all the mentioned steps at the same time. We can configure the system in such a way that they are started sequentially, but this would not be a very wise decision for our backup scenario.

We can even code loops in a chain, which can be useful. However, there is one little problem—we cannot code a clean exit. We can get lucky and get a clean exit if the looping step is not executing when the `END N` action is performed. However, this is sheer luck. Let's assume that we have a long-running piece of code, and for some reason we want a log switch every 5 minutes. In that case, we can implement rules like this:

```
true start longrunningstep
true after 00:05:00 start performlogswitch
performlogswitch succeeded after 00:05:00 start performlogswitch
longrunningstep succeeded end 0
longrunningstep failed end 1
```

This code starts a long-running step, and at the same time starts a countdown of 5 minutes, after which the `performlogswitch` program is called. If the `performlogswitch` program succeeds, a new countdown is started and this is our loop. It is hard to say how useful this is, but the rules do enable us to build this type of code.

The following chapter has an example with full code that shows another way of chaining jobs by using events instead of hardcoded chains. In many situations, a hard-coded chain will be preferable, because it is easier to understand. All the rules and the actions are available for making it easier to see what is happening.

Manipulating the running chains

Chains are very powerful, but they also provide opportunities for errors that we have never seen before. One of the errors is forgetting (as system administrator) how one or more rules might cause our chain to get stalled. Another error is forgetting the evaluation interval for a chain that depends on something that is not a part of the chain. Think about a chain step that is supposed to run only when the current number of sessions is below a specified value. This status could be `true` when the previous step ends. If not, the number of sessions should be evaluated repeatedly until the step is allowed to start.

In the situation where we can see that the chain step is ready to run (because all the prerequisites are met), but we forgot to implement the evaluation interval, we can manually force the job to evaluate its rules using this piece of code:

```
begin
dbms_scheduler.evaluate_running_chain (job_name => 'a_running_job' );
end;
/
```

This piece of code will evaluate the rules for the mentioned job, and there is a good chance that it will start running again. If this is not enough to get the chain running again, we still have another option—to manipulate the status of the chain steps manually using `dbms_scheduler.alter_running_chain`. This procedure allows us to set a step's state to a value that meets our goal. For example, if we have completely forgotten to implement the failure steps and have gotten into a situation where one of the steps of a chain failed, we are stuck in a `CHAIN_STALLED` status. In that case, we could manipulate the following step to start things:

```
begin
  dbms_scheduler.alter_running_chain
    (
      Job_name    => 'a_running_job',
      step_name   => 'step_to_manipulate',
```

```
        attribute  => 'state',
        value      => 'running'
      );
end;
/
```

This code just sets the state of a step to running, which actually makes it run. Whether this is enough to solve all the problems with this particular chain or not depends on the rest of the rules. The best thing is to prevent getting into this situation by making the chain rules as complete as possible. This is where our human origins will pop up; we tend to forget things.

Analyzing the chain

Chains can quickly become complex. Complexity makes it harder for us to have the rule definitions complete in a chain. Therefore, Oracle decided to build the `dbms_scheduler.analyze_chain` procedure. This procedure is of particular interest when we are lost. The exact definition is yet unknown, but it can be used to list all the dependencies of a chain. With a little luck, the results are presented in such a way that we can see what is missing or what is wrong. Here is an example based on our famous backup chain:

```
--/
declare
  rules sys.scheduler$_rule_list;
  steps sys.scheduler$_step_type_list;
  zout sys.scheduler$_chain_link_list;
begin
  dbms_scheduler.analyze_chain
    (
      chain_name     => 'c_cold_backup',
      rules          => rules,
      steps          => steps,
      step_pairs     => zout
    );
end;
/
```

The output is as shown as follows:

```
SHUTDOWN of type PROGRAM depends on "BEGIN" of type BEGIN . Based on
rule MARVIN SCHED_RULE$6 of type START
COPYFILES of type PROGRAM depends on SHUTDOWN of type PROGRAM . Based
on rule MARVIN SCHED_RULE$7 of type START
STARTUP of type PROGRAM depends on SHUTDOWN of type PROGRAM . Based on
rule MARVIN SCHED_RULE$7 of type START
STARTUP of type PROGRAM depends on COPYFILES of type PROGRAM . Based
on rule MARVIN SCHED_RULE$8 of type START
"END" of type END depends on COPYFILES of type PROGRAM . Based on rule
MARVIN SCHED_RULE$9 of type END_FAILURE
"END" of type END depends on STARTUP of type PROGRAM . Based on rule
MARVIN SCHED_RULE$9 of type END_FAILURE
"END" of type END depends on SHUTDOWN of type PROGRAM . Based on rule
MARVIN SCHED_RULE$9 of type END_FAILURE
"END" of type END depends on STARTUP of type PROGRAM . Based on rule
MARVIN SCHED_RULE$10 of type END_SUCCESS
```

The output is written using `dbms_output`. This output tries to tell us that the chain begins with `SHUTDOWN`, and `SHUTDOWN` depends on `BEGIN`.

If `SHUTDOWN` succeeds, it starts `COPYFILES` and `STARTUP`. (`COPYFILES` depends on `SHUTDOWN`, and `STARTUP` depends on `SHUTDOWN`). `STARTUP` also depends on the status of `COPYFILES`.

This clearly shows that there is something interesting in the chain definition. We expect that the order of execution will be `SHUTDOWN`, `COPYFILES`, and `STARTUP`. However, the output of `analyze_chain` suggests this:

- `COPYFILES` and `STARTUP` are started at the same time
- `STARTUP` can be started twice
- There are four ways to end the chain—three are controlled by `END_FAILURE` and only one exit has `END_SUCCESS`

The following screenshot shows what the chain definition looks like:

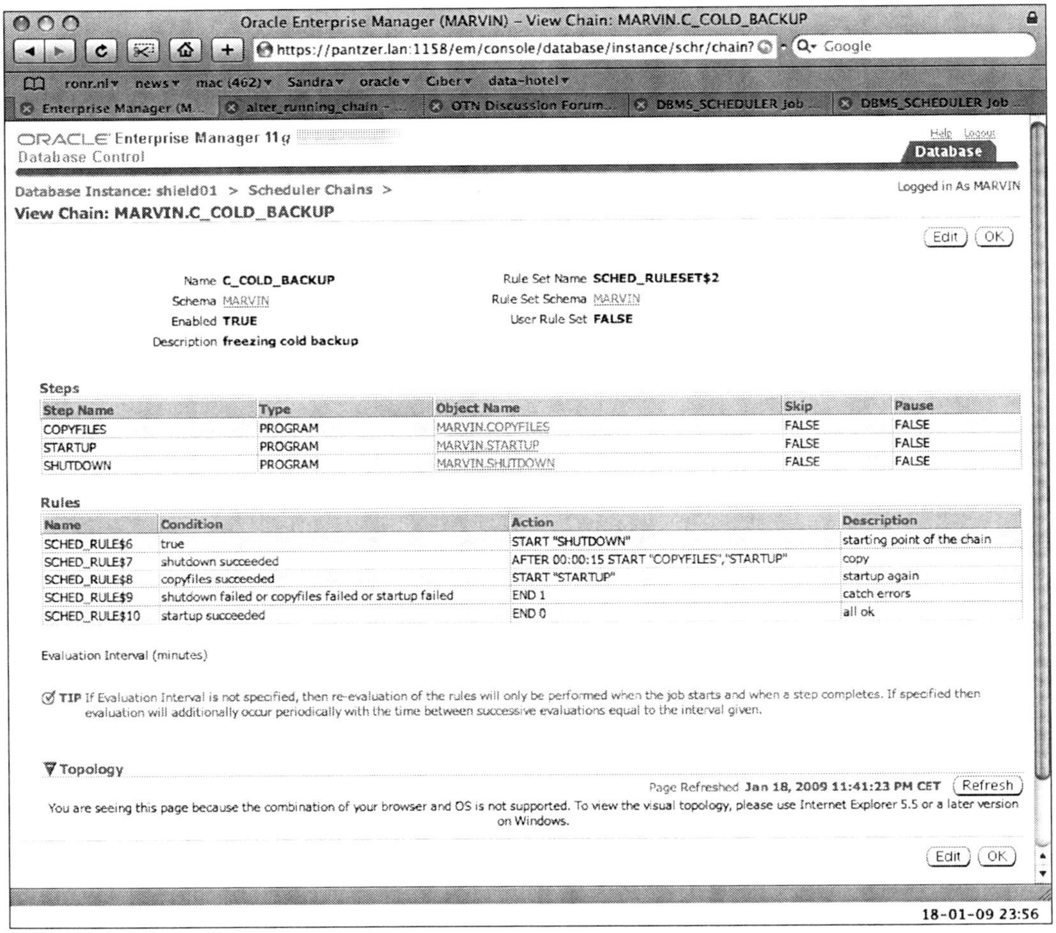

Oracle Enterprise Manager (MARVIN) - View Chain: MARVIN.C_COLD_BACKUP

https://pantzer.lan:1158/em/console/database/instance/schr/chain?

ORACLE Enterprise Manager 11g
Database Control

Help Logout
Database

Database Instance: shield01 > Scheduler Chains >
Logged in As MARVIN

View Chain: MARVIN.C_COLD_BACKUP

(Edit) (OK)

Name **C_COLD_BACKUP**
Schema MARVIN
Enabled **TRUE**
Description **freezing cold backup**

Rule Set Name **SCHED_RULESET$2**
Rule Set Schema MARVIN
User Rule Set **FALSE**

Steps

Step Name	Type	Object Name	Skip	Pause
COPYFILES	PROGRAM	MARVIN.COPYFILES	FALSE	FALSE
STARTUP	PROGRAM	MARVIN.STARTUP	FALSE	FALSE
SHUTDOWN	PROGRAM	MARVIN.SHUTDOWN	FALSE	FALSE

Rules

Name	Condition	Action	Description
SCHED_RULE$6	true	START "SHUTDOWN"	starting point of the chain
SCHED_RULE$7	shutdown succeeded	AFTER 00:00:15 START "COPYFILES","STARTUP"	copy
SCHED_RULE$8	copyfiles succeeded	START "STARTUP"	startup again
SCHED_RULE$9	shutdown failed or copyfiles failed or startup failed	END 1	catch errors
SCHED_RULE$10	startup succeeded	END 0	all ok

Evaluation Interval (minutes)

TIP If Evaluation Interval is not specified, then re-evaluation of the rules will only be performed when the job starts and when a step completes. If specified then evaluation will additionally occur periodically with the time between successive evaluations equal to the interval given.

Topology

Page Refreshed **Jan 18, 2009 11:41:23 PM CET** (Refresh)

You are seeing this page because the combination of your browser and OS is not supported. To view the visual topology, please use Internet Explorer 5.5 or a later version on Windows.

(Edit) (OK)

18-01-09 23:56

When looking at the table of rules in the screenshot above, the output of the `analyze_chain` procedure might become more recognizable. The chain definition is faulty because it starts `SHUTDOWN`. If `SHUTDOWN` succeeds, the `COPYFILES` and `STARTUP` steps are both started after a delay of 15 seconds. For a backup scenario, this is *not* what one wants. The database is normally not allowed to start at the same time as the starting of the `COPYFILES` action.

There really is no way to tell whether a chain definition is correct or not. All you need to know is what is supposed to happen and by what rules the different actions are allowed to happen.

The `analyze_chain` procedure can be of help in checking if all actions are executed when expected, and if the rules are complete enough to reach our goal. The database has no way to know what we want from a job if we do not tell it exactly what should be done and when.

Summary

In this chapter, we have seen:

- What are the steps involved in creating a chain
- How to define a chain
- How to define the steps of a chain
- How to use rules to make the steps run when we want them to run
- How to use programs in a chain
- What are the programs that need to be enabled before we can use them in a chain
- Why we shouldn't forget the error situations in rules
- How to manipulate a running chain
- How to force the Scheduler to evaluate the chain rules for a particular chain
- How to use the `analyze_chain` procedure
- How to use DB Console to create a chain
- How to grant privileges to be able to create a chain
- How using a chain does not guarantee a correctly functioning system

In the next chapter, we will see how to find out what happens in the Scheduler, and how we can keep the database happily running the Scheduler.

3
Control the Scheduler

Oracle Scheduler does a lot of out of the box things, and if the demands are not too high, Oracle Scheduler can cover most of the situations. When your application has to run many thousands of jobs in an hour and log them over a long period, a little more attention is needed. In cases where the demands are high, we need to take care of a few more things to keep the system happy. What we need to do depends on *how* the Scheduler is used and *what* kind of load it is supposed to handle.

In this chapter, we will take a closer look at how we can control this beast. We will take a look at the privileges for job creation, job execution, and Scheduler management. We will also examine how to control logging retention and find a way to prevent jobs from running when the database starts.

Job creation

Like most object types in the database, as seen at the beginning of Chapter 1, Oracle enables us to create Scheduler objects. The privileges `create job` and `create external job` are very important. They should normally be used when building an application system. Also, there is a `create any job` privilege, which can be useful when you need to create a job in a different schema. Normally, this privilege should not be granted to anyone. It will allow the grantee to run an arbitrary code on any schema, which is not particularly desirable. Instead, just log on to the correct schema and perform the tasks using the correct privileges. The following privileges can be used:

System Privilege	Description
`create jobs`	This privilege allows the grantee to create not only jobs but also chains, schedules, and programs. A schema can always alter and drop the scheduler objects in their own schemas even without the `create jobs` privilege. For chains, we need more privileges.
`create external jobs`	Using this privilege, we can create external jobs. Note that when the job references to a program that uses an executable, this privilege is also needed. In case another user created an external job in a schema, that schema still needs `create external jobs` to run that job.
`create any jobs`	This privilege is very powerful and should preferably not be granted to anyone. It allows a user to create a job in any schema, except `SYS`. The end effect is that the grantee is able to run arbitrary code in any schema, which should not be allowed.
`execute any class`	Using this privilege, we can have a job running in every job class that we want.
`execute any program`	Allows the grantee to use any program in a job.
`manage scheduler`	This privilege gives the possibility to manage job classes, windows, window groups, and logs. It also allows the grantee to set the Scheduler attributes.
`dbms_rule_adm.grant_system_privilege (dbms_rule_adm.create_rule_obj, '<schema_name>')`	Needed to be able to create chains.
`dbms_rule_adm.grant_system_privilege (dbms_rule_adm.create_rule_set_obj, '<schema_name>')`	Needed to be able to create chains.
`dbms_rule_adm.grant_system_privilege (dbms_rule_adm.create_evaluation_context_obj,'<schema_name>')`	Needed to be able to create chains.

Here, it is interesting to note that the `drop any job` privilege seems to be missing. For other object types, we have the `create any` privilege and also the `drop any` privilege. Making use of these *any* privileges looks smart at first glance. However, it makes a system less transparent and more difficult to maintain eventually. Preferably, objects are granted explicitly instead of falling back on *any* privileges when building an application. For example, select any table and you will observe that it is much harder to find how an application flows or what the impact of dropping an object is. If the privileges are explicitly granted, we can see that someone is using our object.

Mostly, it is smarter to create schemas using the least privileges principle. This means that one or more schemas contain tables that hold the data, and other schemas contain the procedures that act on the various tables. Users or roles should have privileges on the procedures.

The `DBMS_SCHEDULER` package is available to the public. The use of the package is controlled by the underlying privileges such as `create jobs`, `manage scheduler`, and the execution privileges on the products of the `DBMS_SCHEDULER` package such as jobs, programs, and job classes.

Privileges	Object type	Description
`execute`	`job_class`	To be able to use a job class, we need `execute any job` or `execute any class`, or `execute` privilege on the specified job class. Job classes are in the `SYS` schema. So when granting them, we need to prefix the job class with `sys`.
`execute`	`Program`	When we cannot use the `execute any program` privilege. We need an `execute` privilege on the specified program if it is in another schema.
`execute`	`Credential`	Needed to be able to use the credential if it is in a different schema.
`execute`	`Job`	Needed to be able to run a job from another schema.

Now we have enough information to create a job as far as the job system is concerned. The application-specific privileges that enable the job to perform its task should hopefully also be granted as a matter of course. Don't forget the synonyms. Having privileges is fine, but if the objects are not visible to you because you missed the public or private synonyms on the procedure, the job will fail. To avoid this failure, you can prefix the objects with the owner name or change the current schema using this:

```
alter session set current_schema;
```

Whether or not prefixing should be preferred over using synonyms is not the point of discussion of this book.

During job creation or alteration, we can assign a job to a job class. The default job class is `DEFAULT_JOB_CLASS`. The job class can be used to assign a job to a resource consumer group. It also specifies the logging level, the log history, and the service name that should be used for the class.

The `job_class` defines the resource consumer group that the job has to use. The logging level and the log retention are also defined by the job class. For the log settings, the job class gives more granularity than falling back to the Scheduler attributes without having to define the logging properties for each and every job. In addition to that, the job class is also the interface for service selection. Oracle is mainly aiming at having multiple applications in a database where each application can have a service name defined for itself. In doing so, we can choose the instance where the specific service is running. A service can run in multiple instances.

The logging level can be one of the following:

- `DBMS_SCHEDULER.LOGGING_OFF`: No logging at all.
- `DBMS_SCHEDULER.LOGGING_RUNS`: The starts and stops are recorded with timestamps and status information.
- `DBMS_SCHEDULER.FAILED_RUNS`: This logs only the failed runs.
- `DBMS_SCHEDULER.LOGGING_FULL`: This records not only the runs, but also the job creations and alterations. This enables us to see when a job was created, changed, enabled, disabled, or dropped. When you suffer from a lot of unexplained variations during the runtime, it can be useful to set the logging level to `FULL`. When the job is dropped, the fact that it was dropped as well as the definition of the job are logged.

Log history specifies the number of days the Scheduler should retain the log entries. Log entries for a chain are purged only when the chain has ended. This might be the cause of flooding in the log tables when you fix a problem that causes a chain to stall. However, you might have to forget to make the chain end. The log history is specified in days. It would be very useful to be able to specify the number of job runs to be retained in the logging. In order to be able to compare the last five runs of an end-of-year run, we are now forced to retain the logging of five years. The valid range of values is `NULL`, `0` (no logging at all) to `999`. When `NULL` is specified, the log history is inherited from the global Scheduler attribute.

As the logging of Scheduler jobs can grow quickly, it is good to know which tables are under the Scheduler log views. There are two tables that contain the job logs—the `SCHEDULER$_EVENT_LOG` table, (which also holds the Windows log) and the `SCHEDULER$_JOB_RUN_DETAILS` table. These tables are located in the `SYSAUX` tablespace. According to the `v$SYSAUX_OCCUPANTS` view, we cannot move them to another tablespace. This can be seen using the following query:

```
SELECT occupant_name, occupant_desc, move_procedure_desc,
space_usage_kbytes
FROM V_$SYSAUX_OCCUPANTS
WHERE occupant_name = 'JOB_SCHEDULER';
```

This gives us the following output:

```
OCCUPANT_NAME  OCCUPANT_DESC  MOVE_PROCEDURE_DESC  SPACE_USAGE_KBYTES
JOB_SCHEDULER  Unified Job    *** MOVE PROCEDURE   50368
               Scheduler      NOT APPLICABLE ***
```

So we need to monitor the `sysaux tablespace` usage closely when we use large volumes of jobs that use logging.

The service name that is specified in the `job_class` (which we connect the job to) is useful for tying a job to a specific service name in an RAC configuration. This can be used when there is a specially configured instance available in an RAC database that runs jobs, while other instances serve online users.

In the `ALL_SCHEDULER_JOB_CLASSES` view, we can see which classes exist and how they are defined. There are quite a few classes defined in an empty database. Oracle uses them for many of the automated background tasks such as statistics gathering, log purging, auto space, and advisory.

Other attributes of a job, which might be handy, are `job_priority`, `schedule_limit`, `restartable`, and `max_run_duration`. Each of these attributes can only be set using `DBMS_SCHEDULER SET_ATTRIBUTE`. Let's look at each of these attributes here:

- `job_priority`: This gives the Scheduler the power to select a higher priority job before a lower priority job. The priority count ranges from `1` to `5`, where the highest priority is `1`, the lowest is `5`, and the default is `3`. An example where using a job priority can be useful is the situation where we generate a statistics collection job for every object (table, table partition, or index) that has stale statistics or no statistics at all. All the jobs can be generated using the default priority and have the same job class. But due to the enormous impact of not having statistics at all, we should give highest priority to the jobs that generate statistics for an object that has no statistics to make sure that those statistics are generated the fastest. The use of `job_priority` only makes sense when the jobs that differ in priority are in the same job class and have the same `start_date`. Here is an example:

```
dbms_scheduler.set_attribute
  (
    name      => l_job_name,
    attribute => 'start_date',
    value     => NULL
  );
if i.last_analyzed is null
then
-- top prio for objects without stats !
dbms_scheduler.set_attribute
  (
    name      => l_job_name,
    attribute => 'job_priority',
    value     => 1
  );
end if;
```

- `schedule_limit`: This is meant to help with the decision to run a job later than the scheduled time (if the system is very busy) or to reschedule the job to a next scheduled time. If a specific task has to be completed before 09:00, it does not make sense to start it at 08:00 when normally, the task takes 4 hours to complete. The schedule limit is specified in minutes from the scheduled time. This parameter only makes sense for a repetitive job. Here is an example:

```
BEGIN
  sys.dbms_scheduler.create_job
   (
    job_name        => 'test',
    job_type        => 'PLSQL_BLOCK',
    job_action      => 'begin
 -- Insert PL/SQL code here
                          end;',
    repeat_interval => 'FREQ=DAILY;BYHOUR=4;BYMINUTE=10',
 -- should start at 04:10 (not guaranteed to start at this time)
    start_date       => systimestamp at time zone 'Europe/Amsterdam',
 -- available for scheduling immediatly
    job_class       => '"DEFAULT_JOB_CLASS"',
    comments        => 'testjob',
    auto_drop       => FALSE,
    enabled         => FALSE
   );
  sys.dbms_scheduler.set_attribute
   (
    name            => 'TEST',
    attribute       => 'schedule_limit',
    value           => numtodsinterval(240, 'minute')
   );
```

```
-- it does not make sense to start this job after 08:10
-- if the job is not started before 08:10, forget this run and
-- use the next schedule time (tomorrow at 04:10)
   sys.dbms_scheduler.enable( 'TEST' );
END;
```

- `max_run_duration`: This can help in making the decision about whether to stop or continue the job after it exceeds the maximum run duration. In such a case, the `job_over_max_dur` event is raised. (The job is not automatically stopped.) This is a more advanced parameter requiring a job event handler process that reads the event from the job event queue and notifies a user using mail, SMS, or whatever is appropriate. In a real-life example scenario, this is used to generate a notification when a back-up job takes more time than usually expected.
- `restartable`: This can be used to make the job restart if an error occurs during the running of the job. The `restartable` attribute is a Boolean and can be `TRUE` or `FALSE`. The Scheduler will retry a maximum of six runs, and will do so with a growing wait time interval. The first retry is for 1 second after the initial failure. For the second retry, the wait time is multiplied by 10, causing a wait of 10 seconds. For the other retries, the wait time is multiplied by 10 every time until all six retries are passed or failed, or the job finally succeeds. If the job fails for all the retries, the job is marked *broken* and will not be started again until we fix the problems and enable the job again. The Scheduler will stop retrying a job when:
    - The job succeeds
    - All the six retries fail
    - The next retry would make the job retry after the next scheduled normal run

  During the retries, the run count and the failure count are not incremented until the retry stops. At success, the run count is incremented by one and after the final failure, the failure count is incremented by one.

Job execution

It might look like kicking in an open door, but the job owner has automatic execution privileges on his or her own jobs. As `dbms_scheduler` works with `authid current_user`, the executing user also needs the privileges on the objects that are used in the job. Originally, Oracle had stored objects defined with definer's rights. This means that if you have an `execute` permission on a package, with definer's rights (the default), the package can use all the objects that it needs without having to call the user to have privileges on the objects that the package works on. With authid current_user, we run the package with the privileges of the user who calls the package. This means that if (for example) the package wants to insert a row into a table, the calling user needs to not only execute privilege on the package, but also insert privileges on the table. Scheduler objects that can be granted to others are—job_class and Program. In order to be able to associate a job with a job_class, the user must have the execute privileges on the job class.

For external jobs, all this is slightly more complicated because the script has its own rules on the machine where it runs. In the database, we can administer everything using Oracle privileges; whereas on the operating system, we have to take into account the way the operating system runs our external job. Normally, the jobs are run by a lower-privileged user on the machine where the database lives. This is administered in $ORACLE_HOME/rdbms/admin/externaljob.ora. On the Linux and Unix platforms, this is typically a user, nobody, within the nobody group. This is not what we want because on many systems, the Oracle software is shared by multiple databases. In that case, running all the jobs on all of the databases using the same operating system account is probably not desirable.

Starting with Oracle version 11g, we can also submit jobs to a remote agent and we can define the credentials to be used to run the job here. We will go into more detail about this in *Chapter 5, Getting Out of the Database*. This mechanism with the remote job agent is far smarter than the old external jobs we had to use in 10g. Even when a job runs locally, we should use a remote job agent to run the job because security is now handled in a much smarter way.

[When running external jobs, you cannot make any assumption about the environment that the script can use.]

Do you remember the results of TEST03 from Chapter 1? Even the working directory is unusable for us—no ORACLE_HOME and no ORACLE_SID. When working with Oracle, we need to define both of these to use the software. This is also the reason why many attempts to start Oracle tools directly from the Scheduler fail. Oracle does not support the direct calling of executables and strongly recommends using scripts to initialize the environment at runtime. As no ORACLE_SID is specified, I assume that many external job scripts will have ORACLE_SID as one of their parameters. One simple example is that of an export. Start with making an operating system script and decide how (and with what parameters) it should be called. Make sure that is also able to run using cron. If the job runs correctly using cron, it is very likely that it also runs correctly using the Scheduler. Cron also has a very limited environment, and so many users have problems getting their scripts running with cron. In the following code, you will see a generic setup that will work for most Unix installations where, by default, the oraenv, coraenv, and dbhome scripts are located in the /usr/local/bin directory. At the start of the script, we make sure that the normal Unix binaries are resolvable using PATH and the Oracle environment script oraenv that calls dbhome. Most Oracle-related scripts should be able to use this. When site or application specific code is used that is in a different directory, the directory should also be added to the PATH, or those scripts should be called fully qualified.

```
#!/bin/bash
# this script takes ORACLE_SID as argument 1
#              and the full qualified parameterfile as argument 2
PATH=$PATH:/usr/local/bin:/usr/bin
export PATH
ORAENV_ASK=NO
ORACLE_SID=$1
PARFILE=$2
. oraenv
$ORACLE_HOME/bin/exp parfile=$PARFILE
```

Save this script in a known location. There are many possible locations; one choice could be /usr/local/bin/run_exp.sh. The location has to be usable and referenced from the job that has to call the script, as shown next.

Now, make an Oracle Scheduler job that calls this script with the two required arguments, ORACLE_SID and the full qualified parameter file name. This can be done as follows:

```
BEGIN
  sys.dbms_scheduler.create_job
   (
    job_name            => 'RUN_EXP',
    job_type            => 'EXECUTABLE',
    job_action          => '/usr/local/bin/run_exp.sh',
    start_date          => systimestamp at time zone 'Europe/Amsterdam',
    number_of_arguments => 2,
    enabled             => FALSE
   );
  sys.dbms_scheduler.set_job_argument_value
   (
    job_name              => 'RUN_EXP',
    argument_position     => 1, argument_value => 'ORCL'
   );
  sys.dbms_scheduler.set_job_argument_value
   (
    job_name              => 'RUN_EXP',
    argument_position     => 2,
    argument_value        => '/tmp/exp_parameters.par'
    );
  sys.dbms_scheduler.enable( 'RUN_EXP' );
END;
```

The job is defined in two parts—one part defines the job, and the other part assigns the variables for the job. As this has to be done in two parts, the job has to be defined with `enabled => FALSE` to prevent it from starting before the variables are defined. The location for the parameter file is not where we would normally put these files—for this example, it is a convenient location that exists on most systems, but is a very bad choice for a production environment. Again, the file has to be usable from the Scheduler job and readable by the operating system user who runs the job.

Scheduler management

Managing the Scheduler in the database is a little vague. Most things are defined very clearly, but there is no such thing as the ability to stop or start the Scheduler in a supported way. In the Oracle RDBMS, there is the system privilege `MANAGE SCHEDULER` that enables you to define job classes, windows, and window groups. Setting and reading Scheduler attributes is controlled by this privilege, as is purging the Scheduler logs. The Scheduler attributes are listed in the `ALL_SCHEDULER_GLOBAL_ATTRIBUTE` view. Not all attributes listed here can be modified, and not all Scheduler attributes are listed. The `current_open_window`, for example, is a read-only and changes when the next window opens or the current window closes.

`max_job_slave_processes` can be used to limit the number of processes the Scheduler is allowed to use. The `max_job_slave_processes` parameter cannot be set to `0`. In the earlier versions of Oracle, we could prevent the `dbms_jobs` jobs from running by setting `JOB_QUEUE_PROCESSES` to `0`. In 11g, this parameter (`JOB_QUEUE_PROCESSES`) is deprecated and maintained only for backward compatibility. In fact, there is no parameter that controls the status of the Scheduler at instance startup.

So how can we prevent jobs from running during unplanned maintenance? The simple answer at this moment is: we cannot, not in a supported way. However, it is possible to make a database event trigger that disables the Scheduler during a normal database shutdown. Just set the `SCHEDULER_DISABLED` attribute to `true` as follows:

```
begin
DBMS_SCHEDULER.SET_SCHEDULER_ATTRIBUTE ('SCHEDULER_DISABLED','true');
end;
/
```

It is nice to have this setting. It only fails to help when "unplanned" events occur, which means that it is caused by a database crash. In such a scenario, it is sensible to have the database quiet until the DBA decides that it is safe to run jobs again. Imagine a schedule in which jobs are spawned every second. By the time we disable the Scheduler, several jobs will have started running. For this reason, it is smarter to define the `on startup` trigger in such a way that it disables the Scheduler on database startup. When everything is working the way it should be, a separate process should enable the Scheduler. The problem is that even in this case jobs can already be started before the disable scheduler could take place.

It makes sense to have a normal `init` parameter that defines the state of the Scheduler after the database startup. In the old-fashioned `dbms_job`, we could do this by setting `JOB_QUEUE_PROCESSES` to `0`, so why not have something similar with the Scheduler? The following code can be used to handle this:

```
CREATE OR REPLACE TRIGGER "SYSMAN"."DISABLE_SCHEDULER" AFTER
STARTUP ON DATABASE begin
dbms_lock.sleep(3); -- The docs say the trigger is executed after
--                  -- the database opens … in 11.1.0.7 it is before.
DBMS_SCHEDULER.SET_SCHEDULER_ATTRIBUTE ('SCHEDULER_DISABLED','true');
end;
```

When the database is open, check the `ALL_SCHEDULER_GLOBAL_ATTRIBUTE` view to see the status after startup:

```
SQL> col value form a10
SQL> select value from ALL_SCHEDULER_GLOBAL_ATTRIBUTE
  2  where attribute_name = 'SCHEDULER_DISABLED';

VALUE
----------
true
```

Don't forget to enable the Scheduler when the system is checked and found to be in a good working state. This can be done in SQL*Plus as follows:

```
SQL> exec DBMS_SCHEDULER.SET_SCHEDULER_ATTRIBUTE ('SCHEDULER_
DISABLED','false');

PL/SQL procedure successfully completed.
```

It is funny to see that this state can be set to `false` multiple times without any error. When the `SCHEDULER_DISABLED` status is `false`, the row no longer exists in the `ALL_SCHEDULER_GLOBAL_ATTRIBUTE` view, so don't be surprised when the query to check the `SCHEDULER_DISABLED` state does not return any row. It just means that the Scheduler is enabled.

As the Scheduler is tightly coupled to the resource manager, it would be fair to have the Scheduler administrator administer the resource manager plans. To arrange all this work neatly, the resource manager plan and the job classes have to be documented and defined very clearly. Developers should try to create jobs and link them to the desired job class.

Logging

One benefit of `dbm_scheduler` over `dbms_job` is the fact that it records job actions and (if needed) the actions on the jobs. This enables us to find out when jobs ran and compare the runtime behavior based on recorded execution times, instead of vague user estimations and assumptions. Not everything we would wish for is recorded. It is very useful to add some performance metrics to the detailed logging. This can help us spot where the longer job runtime came from. For example, when we see that a job that normally runs for 2 seconds and performs 4,000 buffer gets, now ran for 3 hours and performed 800,000,000 buffer gets, it's clear that some investigation is required.

The disadvantage of this logging is that it has to be configured and maintained. For this, we have the `log_detail_level` and the `log_history` parameters of the job, `job_class`, or the Scheduler.

Log detail level

The log detail level can be defined at several locations. It can be defined in the job creation and `job_class`, where the `NULL` value for the job means its `log_detail_level` is inherited from the `job_class` to which the job belongs. Logging can be found in the `ALL_SCHEDULER_JOB_RUN_DETAILS` and `ALL_SCHEDULER_JOB_LOG` views.

JOB_NAME, JOB_ID, and **JOB_CLASS** are recorded (among others) in **Scheduler job Logs**.

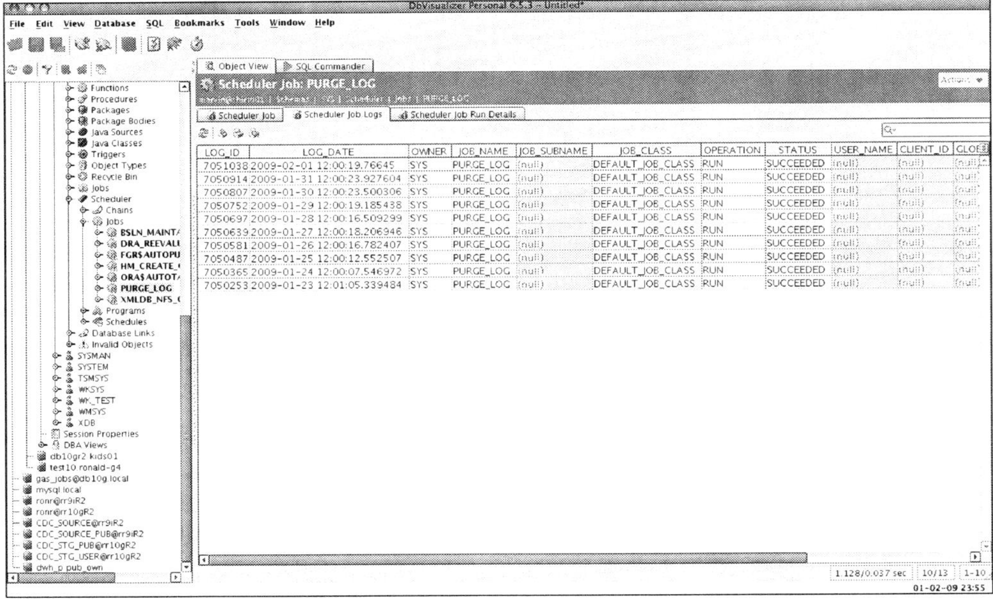

In this DbVisualizer screenshot, you can see that this particular job only logs the runs. When job logging is defined with `DBMS_SCHEDULER.LOGGING_FULL`, it logs runs and modifications of the job. The DROP is also in the log. This can be useful when there are jobs that are of the *run once* type and have `auto_drop` set to `true`. These jobs are dropped automatically when they are complete. In that case, we can still find the definition of the dropped job in the `ALL_SCHEDULER_JOB_LOG` view in the **ADDITIONAL_INFO** column. Look at the following screenshot:

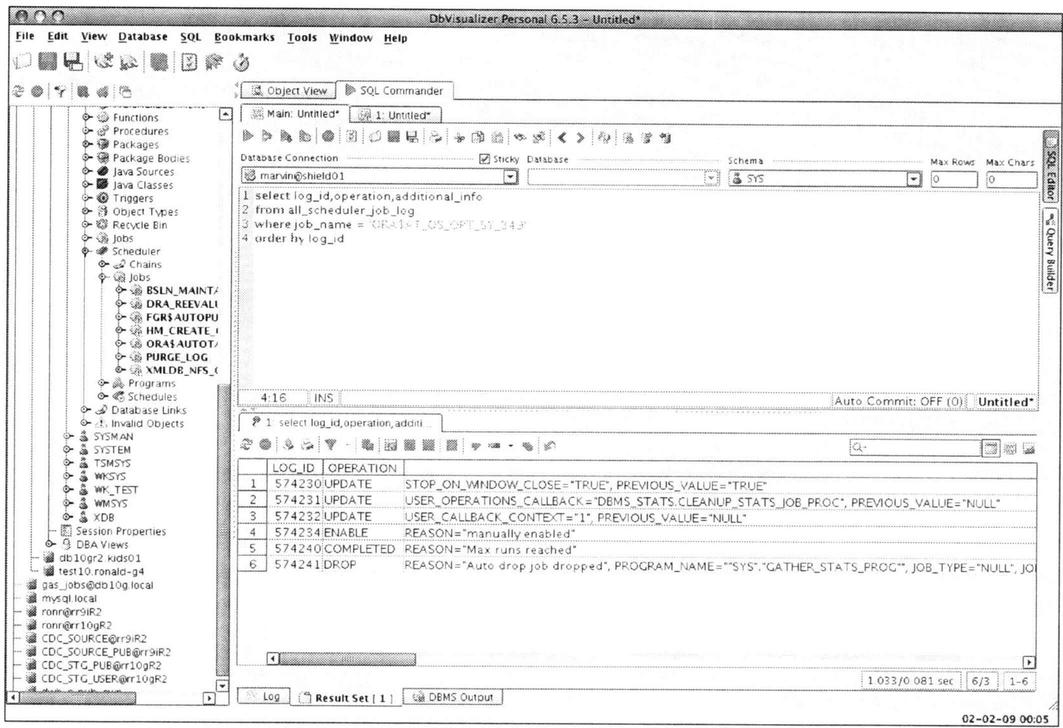

We can take a closer look at the **ADDITIONAL_INFO** column where we see `operation = DROP`.

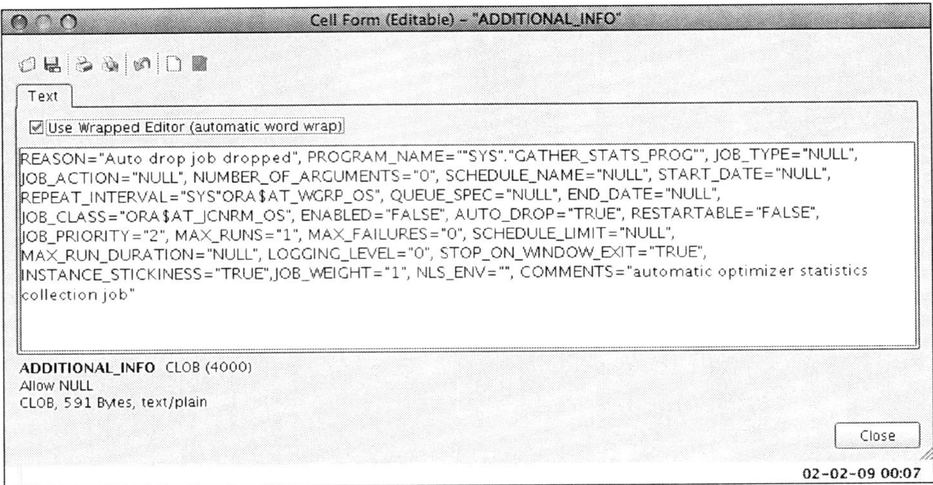

This happens to be one of the jobs that Oracle creates for us to generate optimizer statistics.

In order to see the complete picture, you need to combine both views. Some entries in the log can be a little misleading—especially, the recorded events for chains. These record events look a bit weird as mentioned in *Chapter 2, The Simple Chain*. In the log, we will see an operation named `CHAIN_START` with a `RUNNING` status. Normally, we expect to see the `CHAIN_START` operation with a result: `SUCCEEDED` or `FAILED`.

Log purging

As mentioned before, the log purging is controlled by the log history parameters for the job, the job class, or the Scheduler, depending on the level at which `log_history` is first defined. With the default setting of `30 DAYS` and a job running every second, this means quite a lot of rows in the *`_scheduler_job_log` view, possibly 86,400 per job every day. It is possible to run `dbms_scheduler.purge_log` manually, but why bother? Daily at `03:00`, `purge_log` `job` (from `SYS`) runs `dbms_scheduler.auto_purge`, and it does quite a good job. Sometimes there are complaints about logs that are not purged. A log of a chained job is allowed to be purged only when the chained job is completed. This can pass unnoticed, until one sees logs that are older than expected. In that case, the chain might be stalled, meaning it does not know what to do next based on the defined rules. So, you can force the job to an end. In Chapter 7, *Debugging the Scheduler*, we will see more about making chains run again.

If we want, we can still purge log entries manually using `dbms_scheduler.purge_log`. During development, this can help taking old, failed runs away from the log. Take good care when running it because the default is to clear each and every entry from every log. The following is the definition found in the dbms_scheduler package:

```
-- The following procedure purges from the logs based on the arguments
-- The default is to purge all entries
PROCEDURE purge_log(
  log_history         IN PLS_INTEGER DEFAULT 0,
  which_log           IN VARCHAR2    DEFAULT 'JOB_AND_WINDOW_LOG',
  job_name            IN VARCHAR2    DEFAULT NULL);
```

Many tools use less devastating defaults. The log of the jobs has a value, so why does Oracle have something like "clear all logging" as a default? As always, maintaining logs is something that has to be checked. In this regard, don't forget to check the job class definitions. Did you see the age of the log entries for the `ORA$AT_OS_OPT_SY_349` job? Check out the following screenshot. In the job class for this job (`ORA$AT_JCNRM_OS`), we can see why these types of logs will be kept for a while.

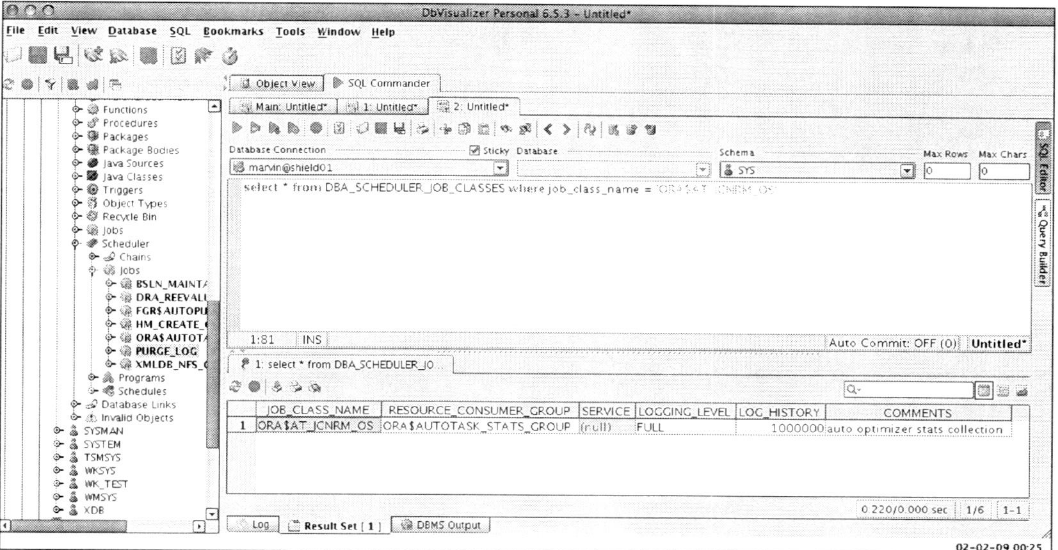

The `log_history` is kept for 1,000,000 days. This must be a reason enough to check all job class definitions as follows:

```
SQL> select job_class_name, logging_level, log_history from
DBA_SCHEDULER_JOB_CLASSES;
```

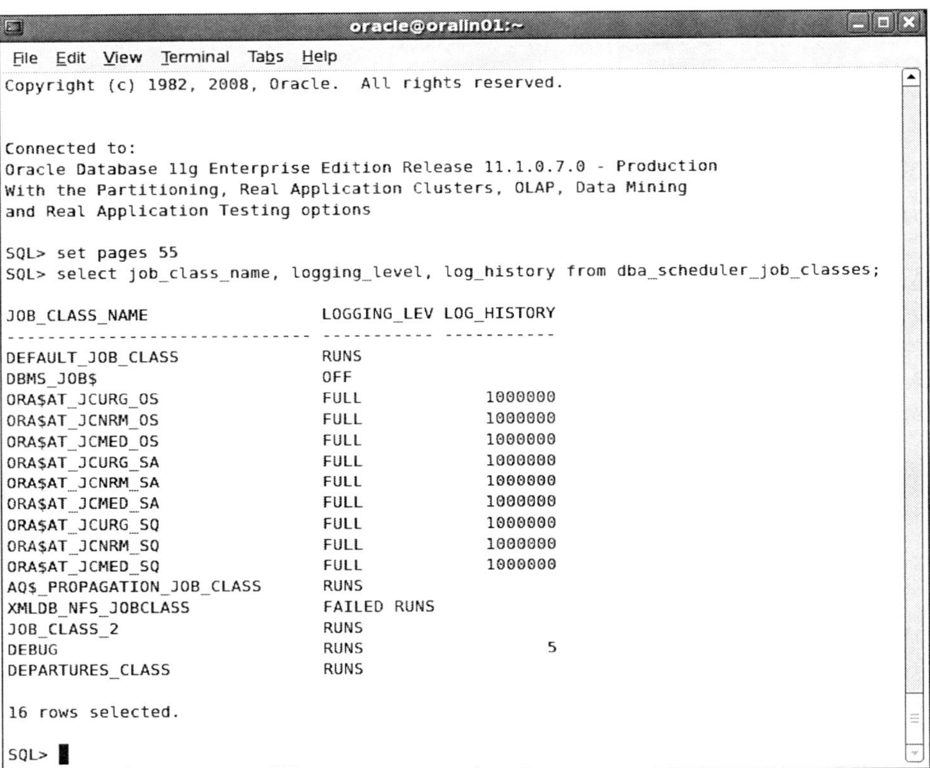

Just in case you think you can do with less than 1 million days of log history, use the following code that changes the `log_history` to 120 days:

```
begin
  dbms_scheduler.set_attribute('sys.ORA$AT_JCNRM_OS',
                                'log_history',120);
end;
```

Manufacturers of data storage won't like this, because now our databases will not grow as fast as before reducing the `log_history`. When it comes to logging, never take anything for granted. Check the definition of the job and job classes as both can surprise you. Setting a logging level to `full` will cost a little extra disk space, but correcting the `log_history` for the Oracle-created automatic jobs will compensate for that. Having the ability to check back what the job definition was after it was dropped can be very valuable.

Summary

In this chapter, we have seen:

- The privileges needed to create regular jobs
- The privileges needed to create external jobs
- The privileges needed to execute jobs
- The risk of granting the `create any job` privilege
- The privileges needed to do maintenance on the Scheduler system
- Where the logging goes
- How to get rid of the log entries—either manually or automatically
- How to completely disable the Scheduler for maintenance
- How to disable the scheduler on database start
- How the `restartable` job attribute works
- How we can define `job_priority`
- How the `job_priority` is used only with the same `job_class` and `start_date`
- How to use the Schedule limit
- How to specify job over the `max_run_duration` event
- How to use the job log to find the definition of a deleted job
- How to check the log retention
- Which tables to check for growth when using Scheduler logging

In the next chapter, we will be looking at managing resources.

4 Managing Resources

We use Oracle's Resource Manager to manage resources. If a system contains only a few jobs, it might not be worth setting this up. However, for any system where thousands of jobs run concurrently with online users, setting this up makes absolute sense. Resource Manager is the key to Oracle Instance Consolidation—one of the more extreme cost optimization techniques available that is often neglected. Online users don't want to be slowed down because of long-running batches. At the same time, they are waiting for the results of these batches; so the batches need to run as quickly as they can. Traditionally, administrators would often make plans for daily usage by online users and separate plans for nightly usage. In our current 24-hour global economy, this no longer makes sense and is unnecessary. If Resource Manager does its job the way it should, there is no longer a need to switch to a nightly plan where the batches have more resources. If there are no online users, or only a few (compared to potentially thousands), the batch jobs will automatically get all the remaining resources.

Let's see how we can fit Scheduler jobs into a resource plan.

Resource consumer group

As we saw in Chapter 3, a job class is mapped on a resource consumer group. So, it makes sense to start defining resource consumer groups now.

First, think about how you want to control the various tasks and how you want them to interact with each other—or even better, how to not interact with each other. Which jobs should get more resources than other jobs? Which users should get a higher priority over the others, and why?

As most users in a database will be regular online users, we can keep them in a default group that gets the second-highest priority. For those few users who tend to mess up the system, we can create a separate group and isolate them from the rest. Resource Manager can guarantee resources for particular resource consumer groups.

The resources not used at priority level 1 will be redistributed at priority level 2, and the remaining resources will be divided further. This can go on for eight priority levels. Take a look at this screenshot:

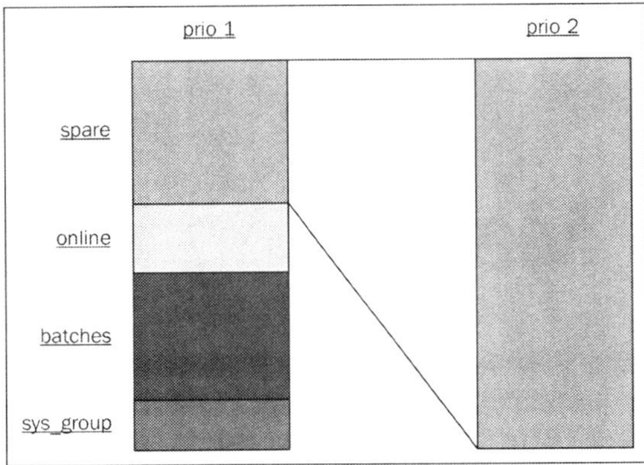

The image above shows that about 30% of the CPU resources are not assigned to priority level 1. These resources can then be redistributed to priority level 2.

For the jobs we are going to manage, we will simply create a group for each type of job. For now, we'll keep it simple and there will be only four groups of jobs. They are as follows:

- `Batch_sub_1s`: For short-running jobs with little or no impact on the system
- `Batch_sub_1m`: For jobs with more impact and which run for up to one minute
- `Batch_sub_1h`: For jobs running for up to one hour
- `Batch_long`: For jobs running for more than one hour

The measures we need to use to divide the jobs vary from system to system. The expected runtime can be a useful indicator, but a resource consumer group list based on departments is also an option. It might well be that a setup that makes good sense in one system is a nightmare in another.

With Resource Manager, we can divide the system's CPU power over the resource consumer groups in an instance. When multiple instances are running on the same server, they will all fight each other because Resource Manager does not balance the load across instances (as it works only within an instance), the same as they would do without Resource Manager. As a rule of thumb, there should be only one instance on a server, so that we don't have to face this problem. At the moment, this is the most powerful option. It ensures that when a system is getting low on CPU power, each group receives its fair share of CPU cycles to do its work.

Before Oracle 11g, there was only the round-robin way of scheduling, where every job received its turn to use the CPU. In 11g, Oracle introduced another option—**run-to-completion**—which gives more emphasis on the already longer-running jobs. This is exactly the opposite of how a Unix operating system works.

In Unix, the longer-running jobs get less CPU. The idea is that if a job is a long-running one, it won't be a part of an interactive process where a terminal user is waiting. In the database, the run-to-completion option might be useful because in the long run, it shortens the usage of undo segments used for the read-consistent view of the job. This is true especially when the batch has to work along with a few hundred online users who are working on the same data. Also, don't forget about locking. As locks are held longer, there is more chance that they will block other users.

Creating resource consumer groups

In this example, we will create a few resource consumer groups. The key to divide the jobs is the expected runtime.

First, create the resource consumer groups.

In Oracle 11g, `cpu_mth` is deprecated and we should use `mgmt_mth` instead.

As many of you are still using 10g, we'll stick to the deprecated method. It is still maintained for backward compatibility. The Resource Manager, like other modern processes, works on an area where it assembles its configuration before submitting it to the database. In Resource Manager, this area is called the **pending area**. Make sure that only a valid configuration is submitted by the Resource Manager. Its use is shown in the following code:

```
--/
BEGIN
  dbms_resource_manager.clear_pending_area();
  dbms_resource_manager.create_pending_area();
  dbms_resource_manager.create_consumer_group
    (
      consumer_group     => 'batch_sub_1s',
      comment            => 'sub second running jobs',
      cpu_mth            => 'ROUND-ROBIN'
    );
```

```
    dbms_resource_manager.create_consumer_group
      (
        consumer_group     => 'batch_sub_1m',
        comment            => 'sub minute running jobs',
        cpu_mth            => 'ROUND-ROBIN'
      );
    dbms_resource_manager.create_consumer_group
      (
        consumer_group     => 'batch_sub_1h',
        comment            => 'sub hour running jobs',
        cpu_mth            => 'ROUND-ROBIN'
      );
    dbms_resource_manager.create_consumer_group
      (
        consumer_group     => 'batch_long',
        comment            => 'long running jobs',
        cpu_mth            => 'ROUND-ROBIN'
      );
    dbms_resource_manager.submit_pending_area();
  END;
  /
```

The result can be seen in the **DBA_RSRC_CONSUMER_GROUPS** view as shown in the following screenshot:

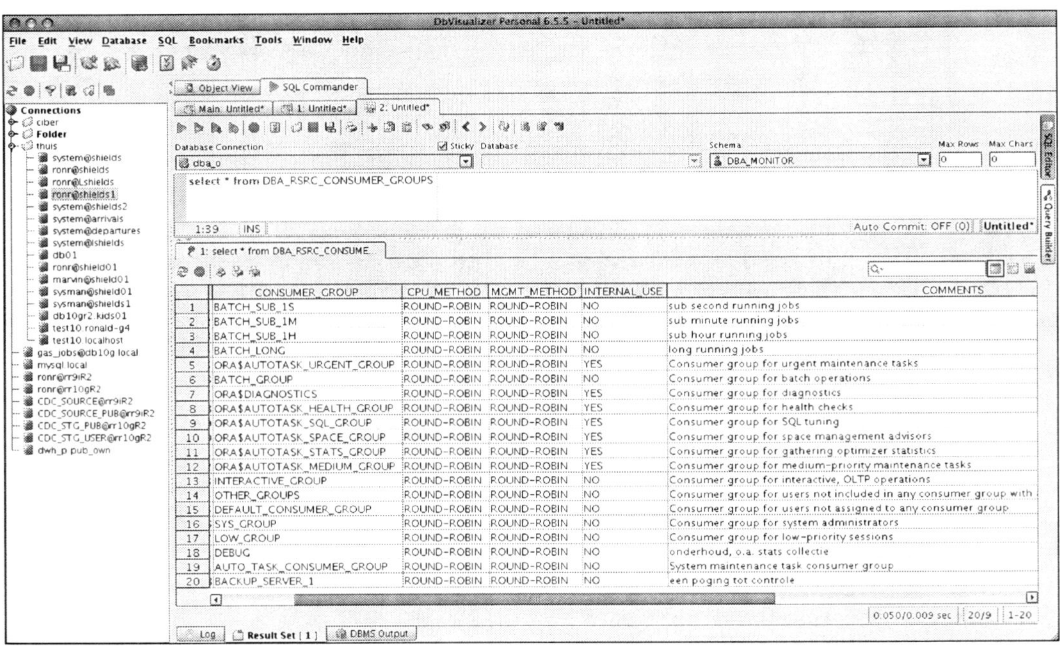

The job owner is not only `marvin`, but also the individual who executes the job. We want `marvin` to be able to use the prepared resource consumer groups. If `marvin` wants to use these groups, we have to grant him the privilege to switch consumer group using the **DBMS_RESOURCE_MANAGER_PRIVS** package. In the `DBA_TAB_PRIVS` view, you will see that `marvin` has the `execute` privilege on the resource groups. Giving an execute privilege on a resource consumer group is not the same as granting the privilege to switch the consumer group. To enable `marvin` to switch to the created resource consumer groups, he needs the appropriate privileges granted to him, as shown in the following piece of code:

```
--/
begin
  dbms_resource_manager_privs.grant_switch_consumer_group
    (
      consumer_group    => 'batch_sub_1s',
      grantee_name      => 'marvin',grant_option => true
    );
  dbms_resource_manager_privs.grant_switch_consumer_group
    (
      consumer_group    => 'batch_sub_1m',
      grantee_name      => 'marvin',
      grant_option      => true
    );
  dbms_resource_manager_privs.grant_switch_consumer_group
    (
      consumer_group     => 'batch_sub_1h',
      grantee_name       => 'marvin',
      grant_option       => true
    );
  dbms_resource_manager_privs.grant_switch_consumer_group
    (
      consumer_group     => 'batch_long',
      grantee_name       => 'marvin',grant_option => true
    );
end;
/
```

User `marvin` can now switch to all the batch resource consumer groups that we just created. A user has to be able to switch to a resource consumer group in order to use it. If you want a user to always use a resource consumer group, make sure that you give the user a *default* resource consumer group. A session can be active for only one resource consumer group at a time. However, we can make a session switch to a different group.

These are the resource consumer groups. The connection between a job and a resource consumer group is the job class.

Class

The class definition identifies the resource consumer group to which the job belongs, so we are not required to use Resource Manager. However, for the processes we want to manage, we have to use Resource Manager and couple them to a `job_class` that has a resource consumer group mapping. Here we define the job classes and map them to a previously defined group:

```
--/
begin
  DBMS_SCHEDULER.CREATE_JOB_CLASS
    (
      JOB_CLASS_NAME              => 'sub_1s',
      LOGGING_LEVEL               => DBMS_SCHEDULER.LOGGING_FULL,
      LOG_HISTORY                 => 5,
      RESOURCE_CONSUMER_GROUP     => 'batch_sub_1s'
    );
  DBMS_SCHEDULER.CREATE_JOB_CLASS
    (
      JOB_CLASS_NAME                => 'sub_1m',
      LOGGING_LEVEL                 => DBMS_SCHEDULER.LOGGING_FULL,
      LOG_HISTORY                   => 5,
      RESOURCE_CONSUMER_GROUP       => 'batch_sub_1m'
    );
  DBMS_SCHEDULER.CREATE_JOB_CLASS
    (
      JOB_CLASS_NAME                => 'sub_1h',
      LOGGING_LEVEL                 => DBMS_SCHEDULER.LOGGING_FULL,
      LOG_HISTORY                   => 5,
      RESOURCE_CONSUMER_GROUP       => 'batch_sub_1h'
    );
  DBMS_SCHEDULER.CREATE_JOB_CLASS
    (
      JOB_CLASS_NAME                => 'longer',
      LOGGING_LEVEL                 => DBMS_SCHEDULER.LOGGING_FULL,
      LOG_HISTORY                   => 5,
      RESOURCE_CONSUMER_GROUP       => 'batch_long'
    );
end;
/
```

`Marvin` also needs the `execute` privileges on the created job classes. So use the following line of code:

```
grant execute any class to marvin;
```

This line of code will enable `marvin` to use all the defined classes. User `marvin` can now use not only the job classes that we defined, but also the job classes defined by others in the database. If you want your jobs to use a certain resource consumer group, you need to define a job class that maps to that resource consumer group.

In our example, the jobs `TEST01` and `TEST02` typically run every subsecond, so we can put them in the `SUB_1S` job class. We can modify an existing job, but only after it has been disabled. If the enabling of any job fails, there can be several possible reasons for that: one is that the privileges are missing; another is that the job dependencies have become invalid. In the following code, we tie the jobs `TEST01` and `TEST02` to the job class `sub_1s`.

```
--/
BEGIN
  dbms_scheduler.disable('TEST01' );
  dbms_scheduler.set_attribute
    (
      name          => 'TEST01',
      attribute     => 'job_class',
      value         => 'SUB_1S'
    );
  dbms_scheduler.enable( 'TEST01' );
  dbms_scheduler.disable('TEST02' );
  dbms_scheduler.set_attribute
    (
      name          => 'TEST02',
      attribute     => 'job_class',
      value         => 'SUB_1S'
    );
  dbms_scheduler.enable( 'TEST02' );
END;
/
```

In the same system, TEST03 and TEST04 run for more than one second, but less than a minute. Therefore, we put them in sub_1m as shown here:

```
--/
BEGIN
  dbms_scheduler.disable('TEST03' );
  dbms_scheduler.set_attribute
    (
      name       => 'TEST03',
      attribute  => 'job_class',
      value      => 'SUB_1M'
    );
  dbms_scheduler.enable( 'TEST03' );
  dbms_scheduler.disable('TEST04' );
  dbms_scheduler.set_attribute
    (
      name       => 'TEST04',
      attribute  => 'job_class', value => 'SUB_1M'
    );
  dbms_scheduler.enable( 'TEST04' );
END;
/
```

Plan

Now that we have some background about Resource Manager, let's look at an example scenario. Like most successful actions, let's start by making a plan. In this case, it's a Resource Manager's plan. Here, we define how resources are divided among the different users or processes. We will also make a plan with room for administrative users (the DBA has to solve problems), normal online users, and the four classes of batches. Each class will have a maximum or total resource usage allocated to it. This means that the low-impact class can have more jobs running than those in the heavy-impact class. For some jobs, it does not make sense to start when all the resources that the job needs are not available. For instance, a report needs to be run that performs excellently when using 64 pq slaves, but becomes a nightmare when it runs on only four slaves. It will clearly be better to wait for the resources instead of starting on time. Entering a Resource Manager plan on the command line is a tedious job. We will use DB Console to get the code.

In DB Console, go to **Server** | **Resource Manager** | **Plans**.

For 10g, Resource Manager is on the **Administration** tab.

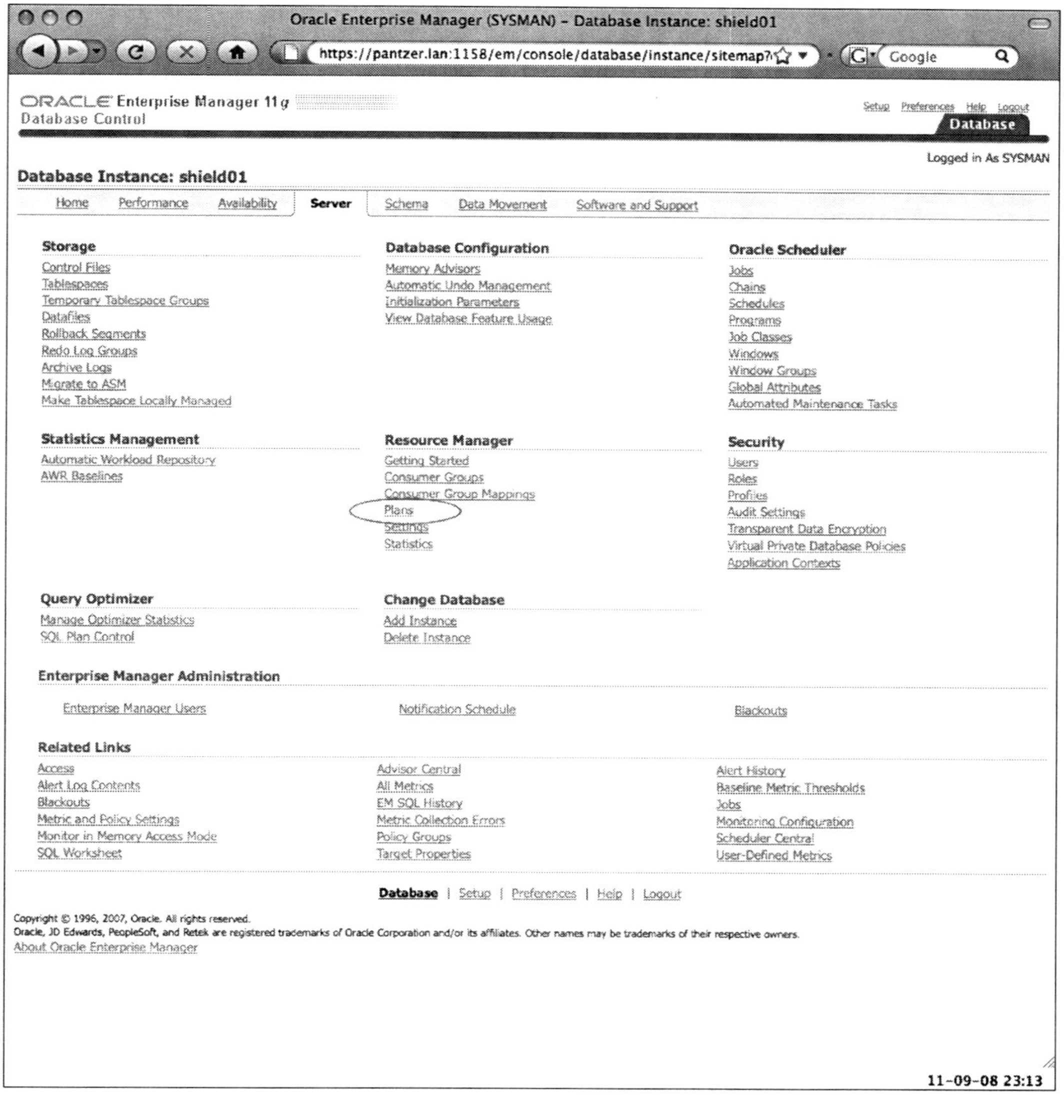

This brings us to the plan overview, where the **Create** button is found on the righthand side.

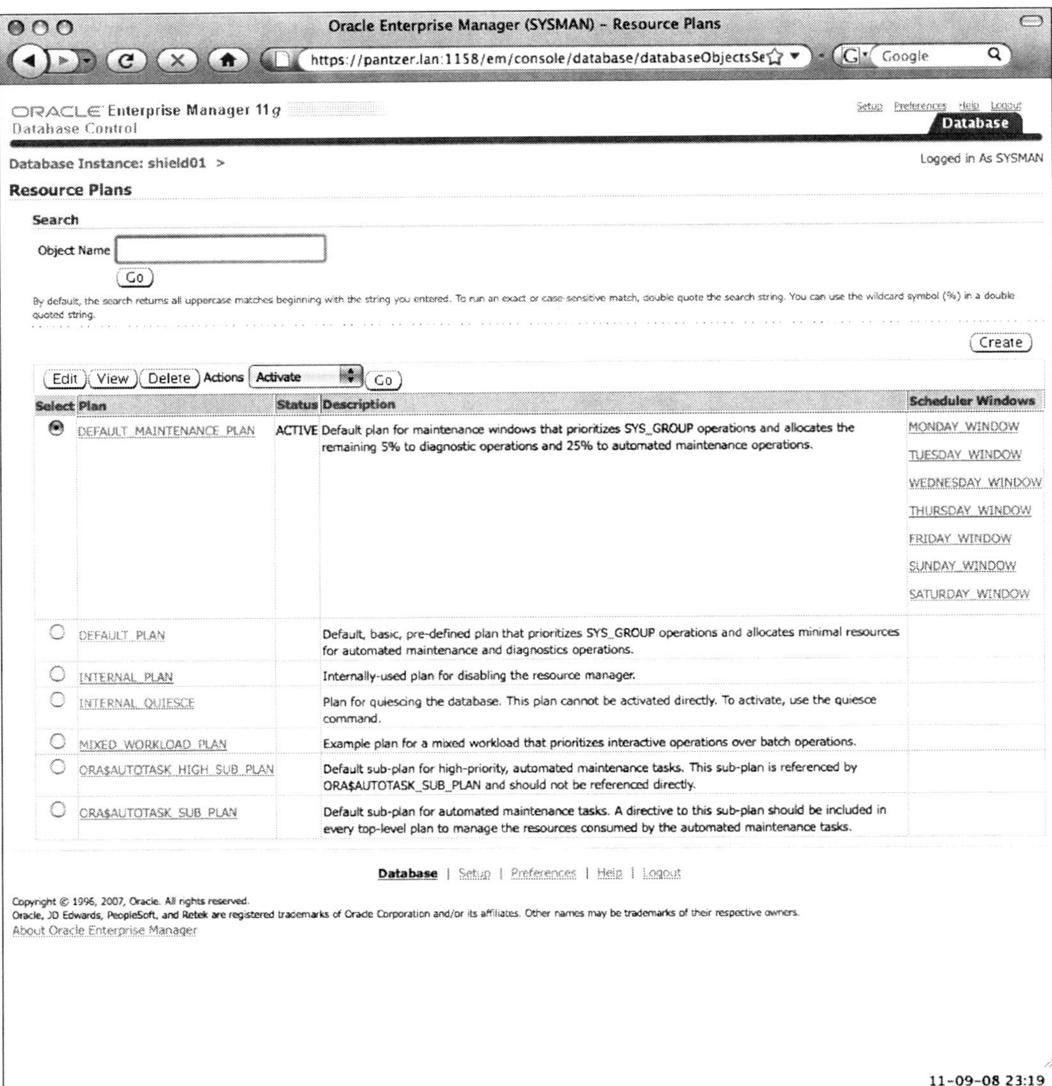

Hit the **Create** button and you will see:

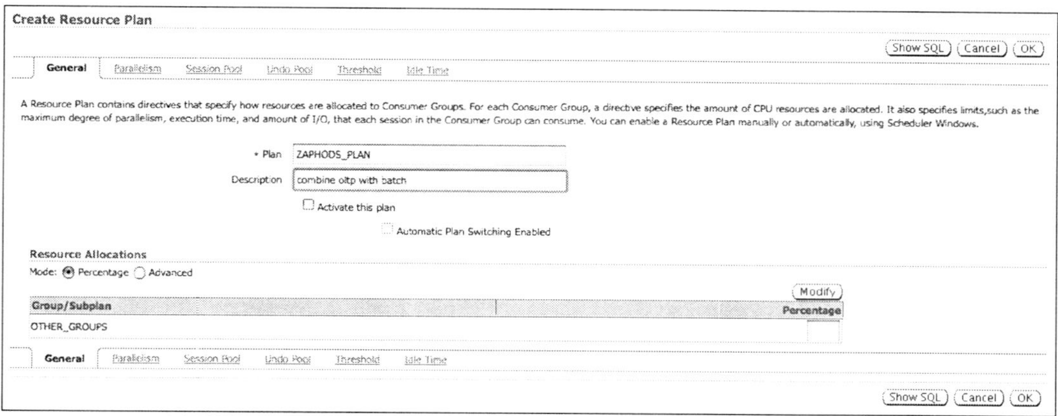

As you can see, the required group **OTHER_GROUPS** is already present. Give the plan a name and provide a comment that describes your plan (optional). The **Modify** button brings us to the screen where we can select which resource consumer groups we want to add in the plan.

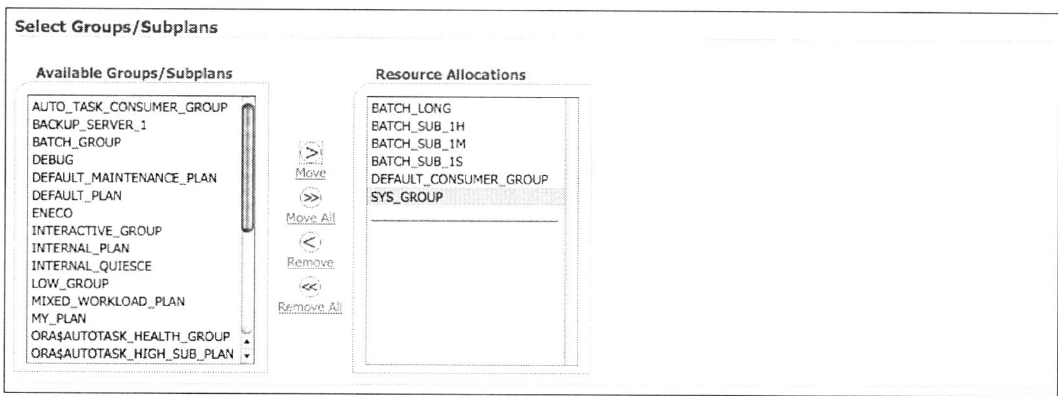

If the list is complete, select the **OK** button that brings us back to the previous screen again, this time with the selected resource consumer groups.

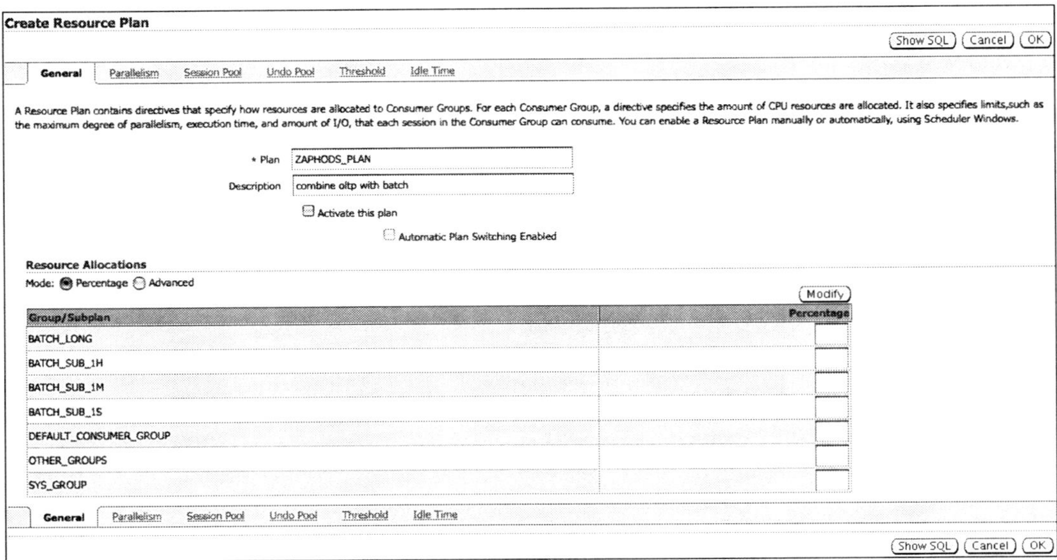
Create Resource Plan

Show SQL | Cancel | OK

General | Parallelism | Session Pool | Undo Pool | Threshold | Idle Time

A Resource Plan contains directives that specify how resources are allocated to Consumer Groups. For each Consumer Group, a directive specifies the amount of CPU resources are allocated. It also specifies limits,such as the maximum degree of parallelism, execution time, and amount of I/O, that each session in the Consumer Group can consume. You can enable a Resource Plan manually or automatically, using Scheduler Windows.

* Plan: ZAPHODS_PLAN

Description: combine oltp with batch

Activate this plan

Automatic Plan Switching Enabled

Resource Allocations

Mode: Percentage | Advanced

Modify

Group/Subplan	Percentage
BATCH_LONG	
BATCH_SUB_1H	
BATCH_SUB_1M	
BATCH_SUB_1S	
DEFAULT_CONSUMER_GROUP	
OTHER_GROUPS	
SYS_GROUP	

General | Parallelism | Session Pool | Undo Pool | Threshold | Idle Time

Show SQL | Cancel | OK

Here we can give each group a maximum allowed percentage of resources to be used. We want more advanced control to give priority scheduling.

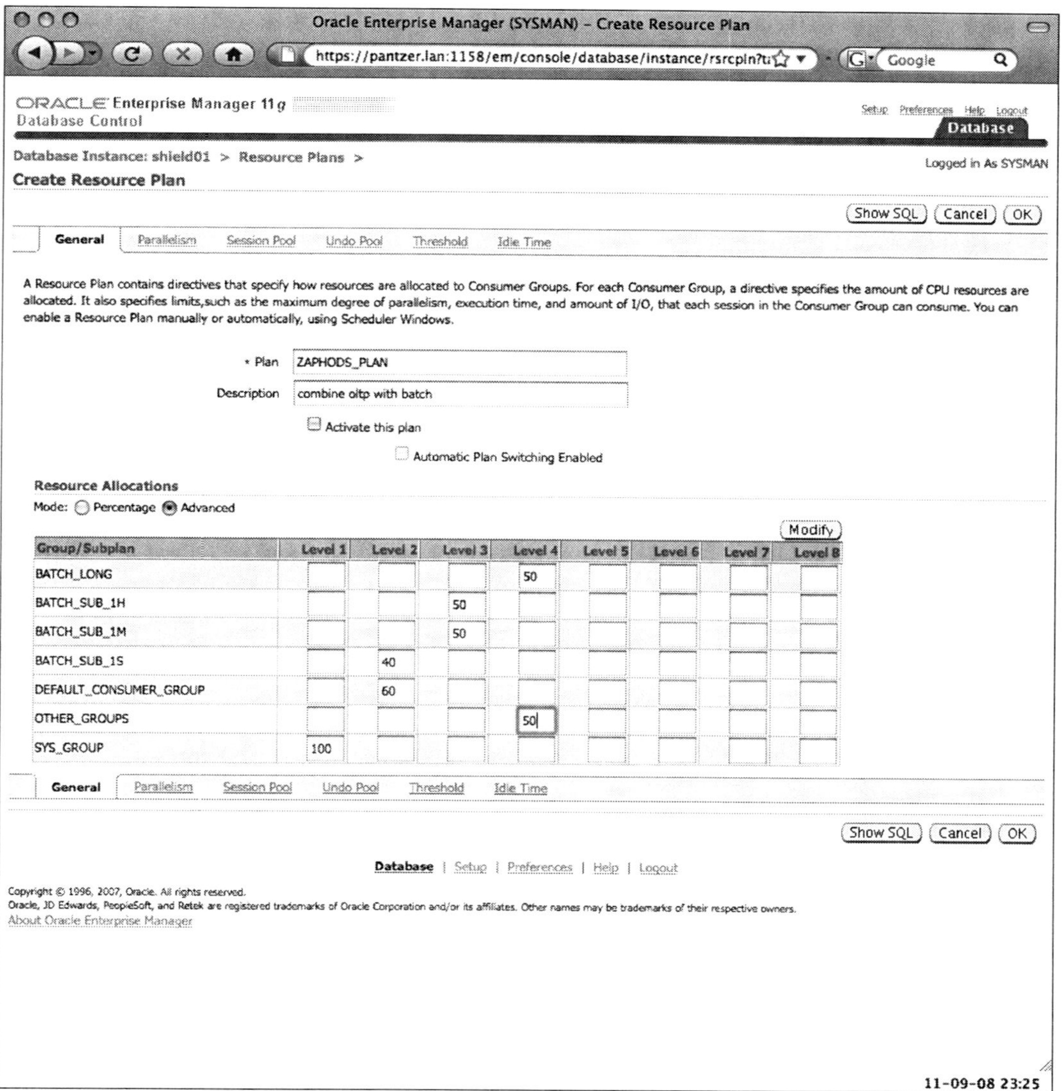

Now, switch to the **Advanced** resource allocation and enter the CPU spreading you want to apply by following this:

1. Give first priority to the **SYS_GROUP**. They are the friendly guys who'll help to get the system running again when problems arise. They need these resources to help others.

2. Second priority is given to the quick, snappy batches and the default consumer group. In this system, most users will initially be in **DEFAULT_CONSUMER_GROUP**. Only users with special needs or users who tend to blow up the system by running bad SQL get special treatment. The normal users get 60% of the resources, leaving 40% for the quick batches. Don't forget that on this second level we get the CPU resources that are not used on the first level.
3. On the third level are the medium jobs that should last for up to an hour. They are granted 50% of the resources.
4. Last, but not the least, are the longer-running batches and the other groups. Users who don't fall into any of the previously mentioned groups automatically fall in to this **OTHER_GROUPS**. They get resources when the higher prioritized users leave cycles for others to utilize.

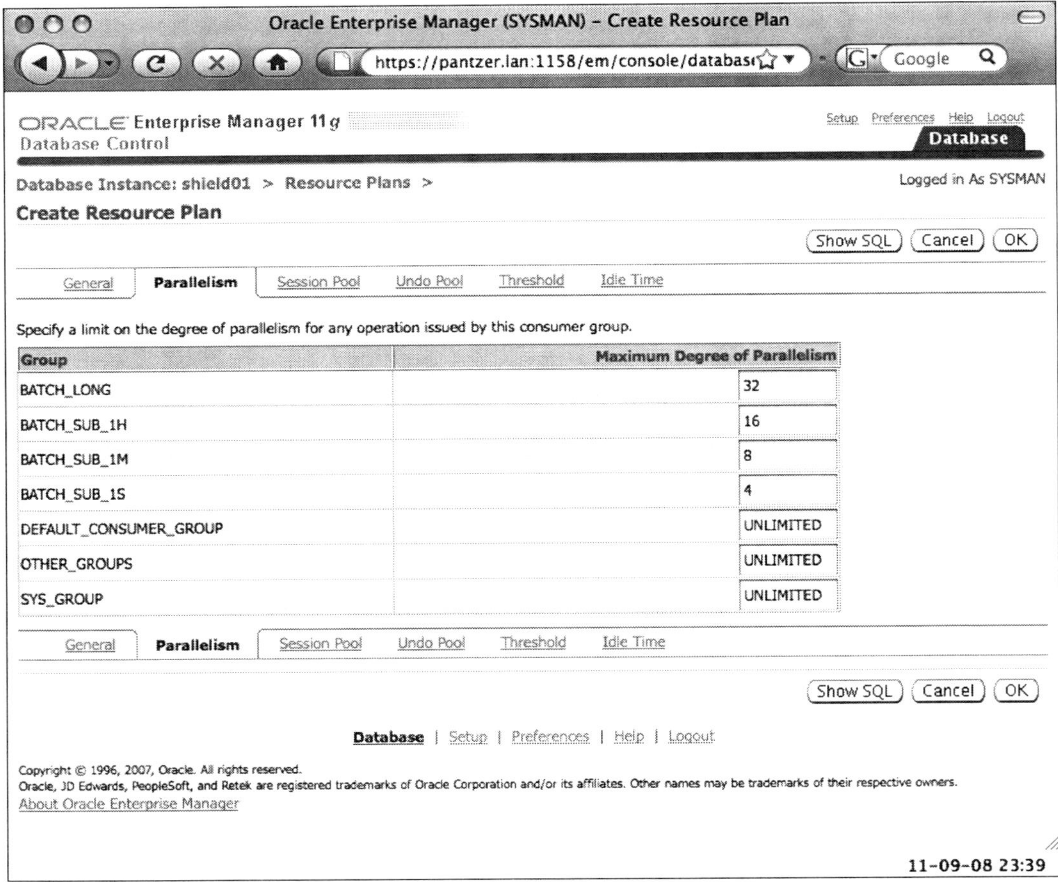

We don't want the normal online users to use parallelism, and keep it limited only to the batch groups. The majority of the online users are supposed to run quick and snappy queries that don't need parallelism. The session pool gives room for two long-running (active) jobs and up to 10 (active) users in the default group. This can be seen in the next screenshot:

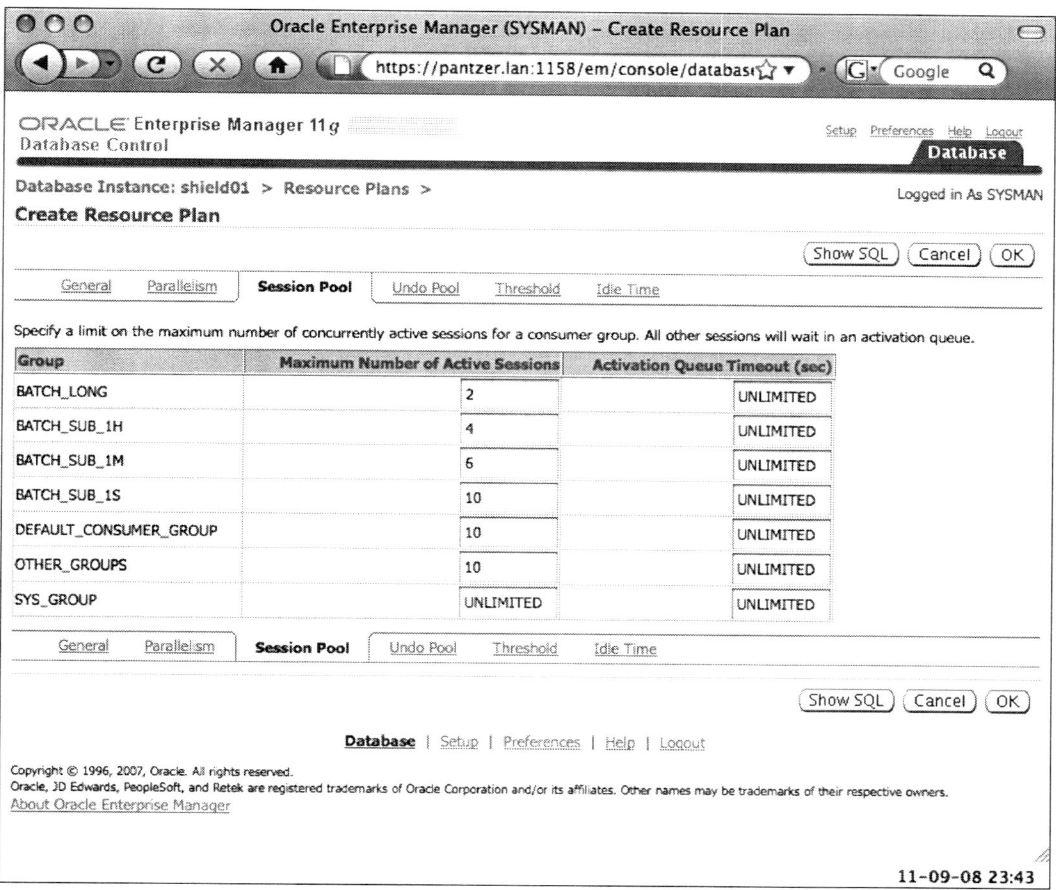

Using thresholds, we can define actions that the Resource Manager has to perform when a limit is exceeded. We have the ability to re-assign a job originally submitted in **BATCH_SUB_1S** to a resource group for longer-running jobs, if it didn't finish within the expected time. Another valid action could be to interrupt the running SQL or kill the session.

In order to avoid further complications, we leave the thresholds in the default state, **UNLIMITED** as you can see here:

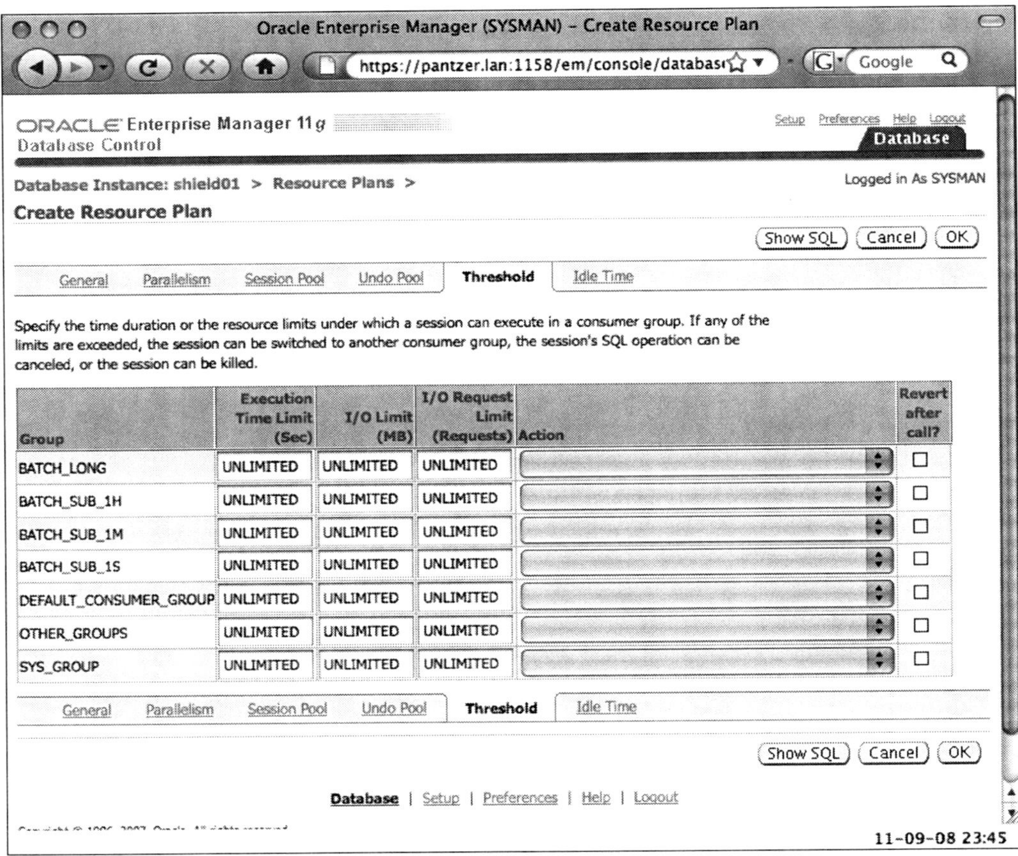

The **Threshold** can be used to make any changes to the job. The change can vary from killing the job to switching it to a different group. For now, we won't use this; we'll leave it to default values, and do the same for **Idle Time**.

The idea behind this change of the job's resource consumer group is that it removes unwanted load from the system. If the job exceeds the specified runtime limit, and we know for sure that the jobs in the resource group in question can never exceed this threshold when it runs in a healthy way, we can terminate the job to free resources for other jobs. The other option is to put the job in a different resource consumer group where it will receive other limits. How the job should be treated is very application-specific. Maybe it is wise to give the job more priority to prevent it from keeping objects or rows locked for longer than needed. This may result in the job getting a lower priority, and so other processes will be able to get more. This also means that the job will run even longer, keep its locks longer, and get slower because it is likely that it has to visit more undo blocks because of the mutation applied by other processes to construct the read-consistent view.

It is also possible for the Resource Manager to check the expected runtime of SQL and not start the SQL when the prognosis shows that the expected runtime is longer than allowed for SQL. This will hardly make sense for the Scheduler, but in a system where online users can run ad hoc SQL, this could be very valuable.

The **Show SQL** button reveals the code that is generated for us.

Window

Windows are all around us. In this context, a **window** specifies a period in time. In Oracle Resource Manager, we can use windows to trigger the start of jobs at a window's opening time, and stop jobs at its closing time. A window also has a Resource Manager plan that activates when the window opens.

Now, all we need to do is to activate this plan. If everything is working as intended, it should be possible to have many jobs running at the same time without losing performance for the normal users. As Oracle has an enabled maintenance plan that is coupled to all weekdays, you might find yourself wondering why your plan is not active anymore—the day after activating the Zaphod's plan. This is because the Zaphod's plan is not yet coupled to a window. Oracle has already defined the windows in which they intend to run standard maintenance tasks. For now, we will leave it that way and create a window called `prod` that is open 24 hours a day. This means we need to schedule the automated tasks that Oracle includes in the database to some other means of scheduling, that is, other than just a window.

One option might be to create a few windows for every day and tie the Zaphod's plan to all of them. In doing so, it is possible to have jobs activated and deactivated by the opening or closing of a particular window.

The same can be achieved by coupling a job to a schedule and using the `max_run_duration` in the job definitions.

There are some subtle differences between the two choices. A closing window can terminate a running job, whereas the `max_run_duration` defined in the job can 'only' raise an event. The event handler can choose to do whatever it wants with the job that raised the event. So be careful with the option that Oracle gives to terminate a running job by closing a window. There are many problems when a job does not terminate in a natural way. Using a schedule requires a little more setup, but it gives more control.

Window groups

By default, Oracle includes a few window groups to combine the days of the week in a maintenance plan. Although it looks pretty, the benefits are uncertain. As only one window can remain open at any given time, using windows in a sensible way requires a lot of planning; and in the end, there will be combinations of windows and schedules making it harder to understand what made a job start (or stop). The restriction of only one open window at any given time makes it hard to use. It would be more convenient to have the ability to keep multiple windows open at the same time. To stick to the predefined days of the week schedules, why not have the window *Monday* open along with the window *morning*? For scheduling, a job is tied to a window.

Monitoring

In this case, monitoring is about monitoring the usage of the resource consumer groups. In DB Console, this can be found in the **Resource Manager** column where we also found the location to create plans; but this time, we have to look at the **Statistics** entry. We can find an overview of what is happening in the database in there. The following screenshot is taken from a database that is using Resource Manager:

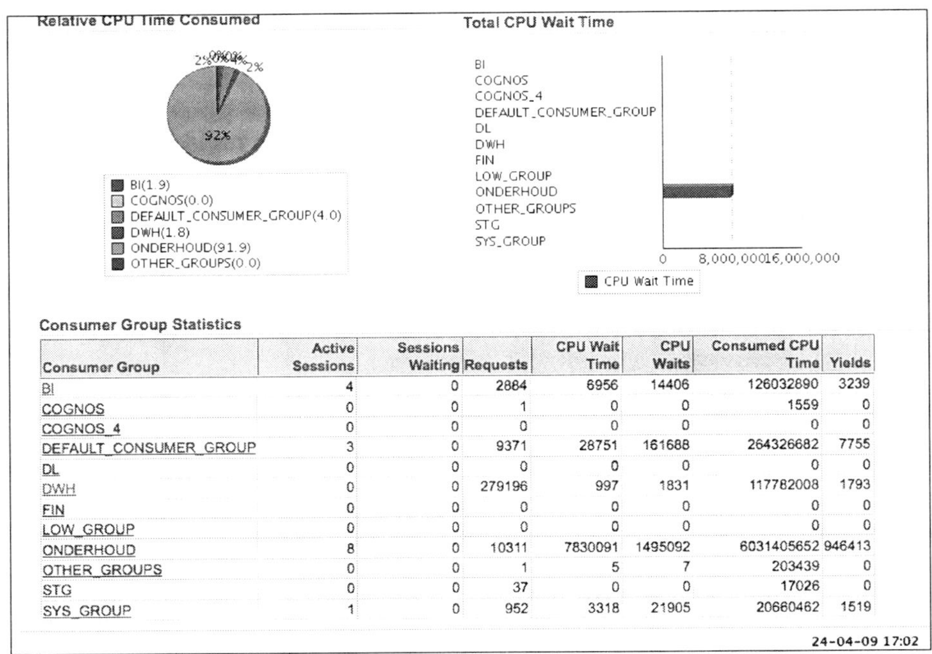

Consumer Group Statistics

Consumer Group	Active Sessions	Sessions Waiting	Requests	CPU Wait Time	CPU Waits	Consumed CPU Time	Yields
BI	4	0	2884	6956	14406	126032890	3239
COGNOS	0	0	1	0	0	1559	0
COGNOS_4	0	0	0	0	0	0	0
DEFAULT_CONSUMER_GROUP	3	0	9371	28751	161688	264326682	7755
DL	0	0	0	0	0	0	0
DWH	0	0	279196	997	1831	117782008	1793
FIN	0	0	0	0	0	0	0
LOW_GROUP	0	0	0	0	0	0	0
ONDERHOUD	8	0	10311	7830091	1495092	6031405652	946413
OTHER_GROUPS	0	0	1	5	7	203439	0
STG	0	0	37	0	0	17026	0
SYS_GROUP	1	0	952	3318	21905	20660462	1519

This shows that the system is currently running happily.

At the moment, there are no sessions waiting. We can also see that some sessions have been waiting (see the **CPU Waits** column). Even worse, Resource Manager has actively taken away the turn from the processes to give the CPU resources to other processes (**Yields**). When Resource Manager is actively interfering with processes, we can see this in the **Top Actions** overview in DB Console or Grid Control. The following screenshot shows the waits for Scheduler, which usually means that Resource Manager is capping processes to stay within their CPU quantum:

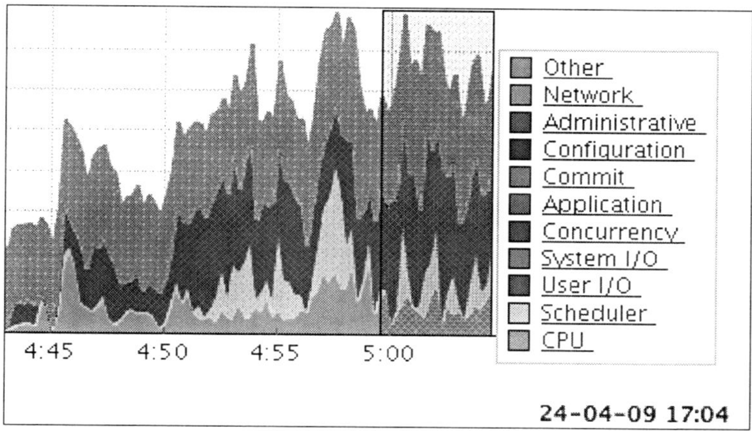

The graphical tools are just reading some views to get their data, and so can we. There are lots of views in the database that we can use. To quickly find which views are available, we can run the following query:

```
select view_name from dba_views where view_name like '%RSRC%' or
view_name like '%RESOURCE%' order by 1;
```

This returns 44 rows in a regular 11gR1 database.

To instantly find which users have privileges for what resource consumer group, we can use this:

```
select * from DBA_RSRC_CONSUMER_GROUP_PRIVS;
```

To find what is the default resource consumer group for a user, check this out using:

```
select * from DBA_RSRC_GROUP_MAPPINGS;
```

In the DBA_RSRC_PLANS view, we can find which Resource Manager plans are defined and in the DBA_RSRC_PLAN_DIRECTIVES view, we can see how the resources are divided. Effectively, it is the DBA_RSRC_PLAN_DIRECTIVES view that is populated when you configure a Resource Plan in DB Console or Grid Control. This is shown in the following screenshot:

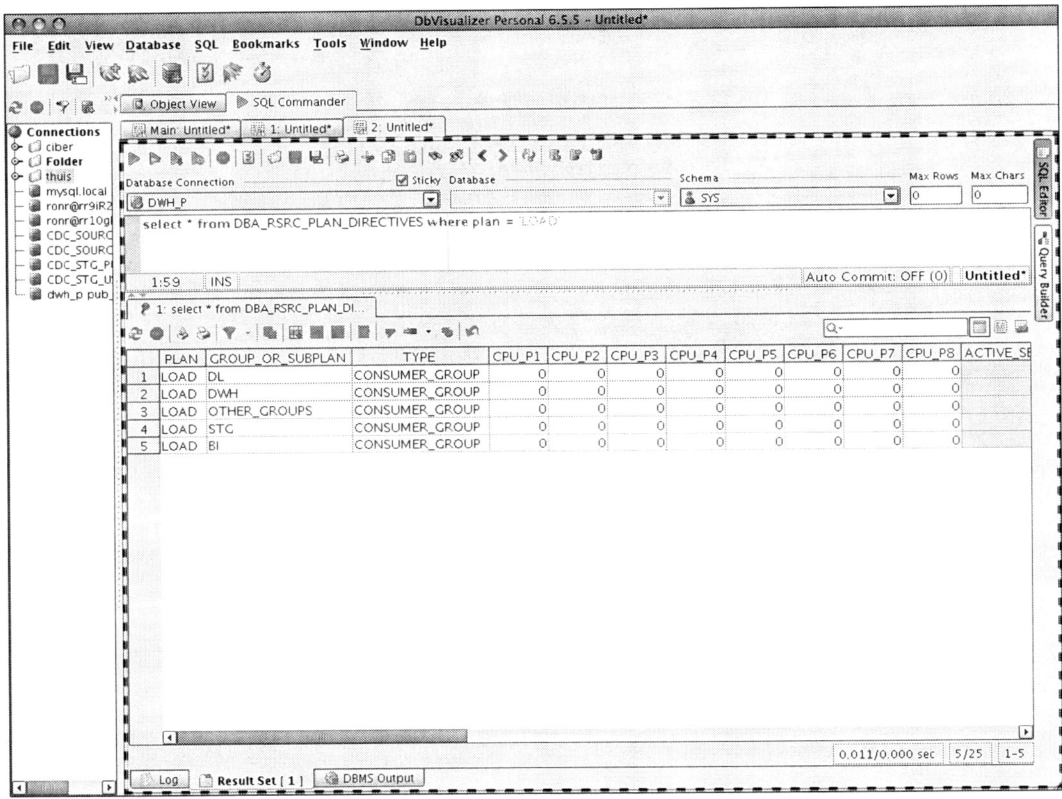

In this case, there is no control on the CPU usage. However, there are a few more columns as shown in the following screenshot:

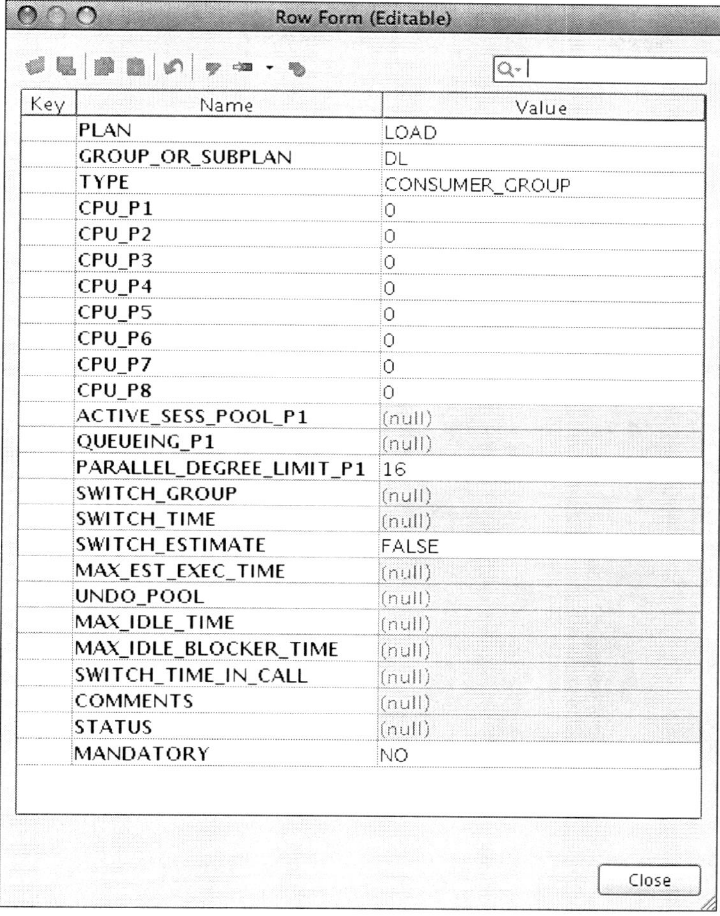

Row Form (Editable)

Key	Name	Value
	PLAN	LOAD
	GROUP_OR_SUBPLAN	DL
	TYPE	CONSUMER_GROUP
	CPU_P1	0
	CPU_P2	0
	CPU_P3	0
	CPU_P4	0
	CPU_P5	0
	CPU_P6	0
	CPU_P7	0
	CPU_P8	0
	ACTIVE_SESS_POOL_P1	(null)
	QUEUEING_P1	(null)
	PARALLEL_DEGREE_LIMIT_P1	16
	SWITCH_GROUP	(null)
	SWITCH_TIME	(null)
	SWITCH_ESTIMATE	FALSE
	MAX_EST_EXEC_TIME	(null)
	UNDO_POOL	(null)
	MAX_IDLE_TIME	(null)
	MAX_IDLE_BLOCKER_TIME	(null)
	SWITCH_TIME_IN_CALL	(null)
	COMMENTS	(null)
	STATUS	(null)
	MANDATORY	NO

Close

For this resource consumer group, the only limitation is the degree of parallelism.

For monitoring the usage, the following view is the most interesting:

```
select * from GV$RSRC_CONSUMER_GROUP;
```

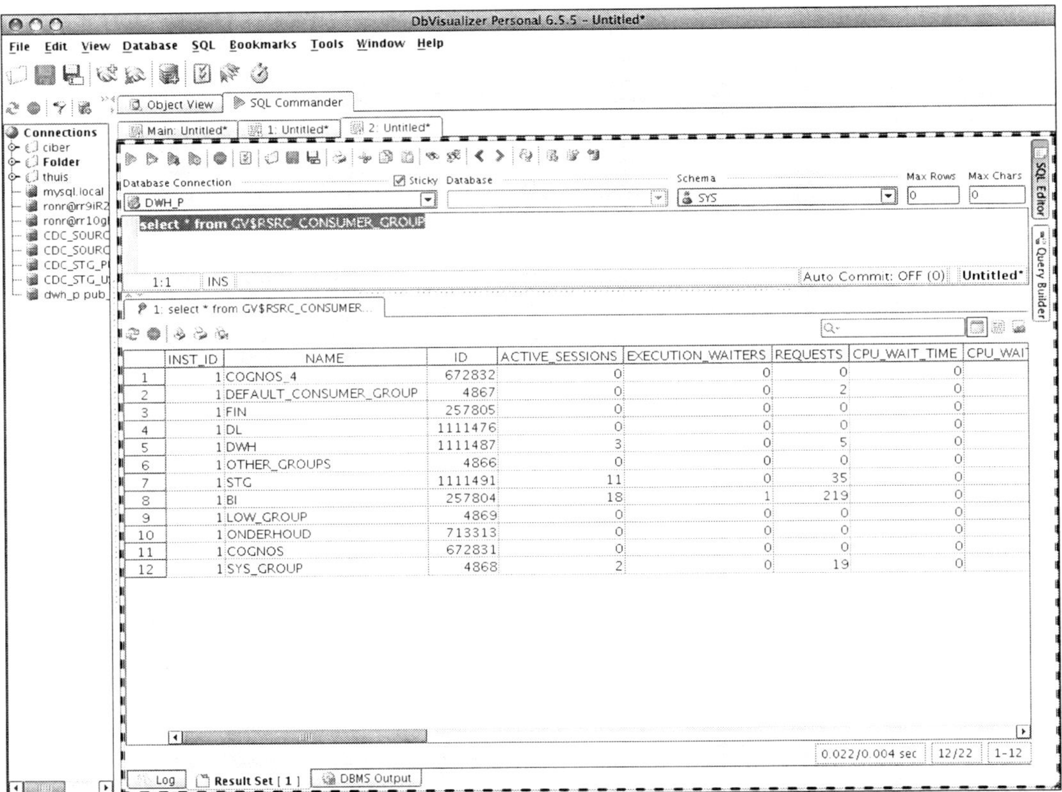

In this case, we can see that currently there are several jobs waiting. We cannot say whether this waiting is good or bad without knowing what is happening in the database. If you have generated a few thousand jobs in an enabled state, with a `start_date set` to `NULL`, they are all available to be picked up by the Scheduler. You don't want them to run all at once; more likely, you want them to enter the system gradually. In that case, the number of jobs waiting for execution will grow. This column does not specify the total number of jobs that are ready to run in that job class. However, more processes than you have configured are running in this resource consumer group.

In the `GV$RSRC_SESSION_INFO` view, we can see the per-session statistics. Join it with `v$session` to find who is doing what in your instance. Also, see the following screenshot:

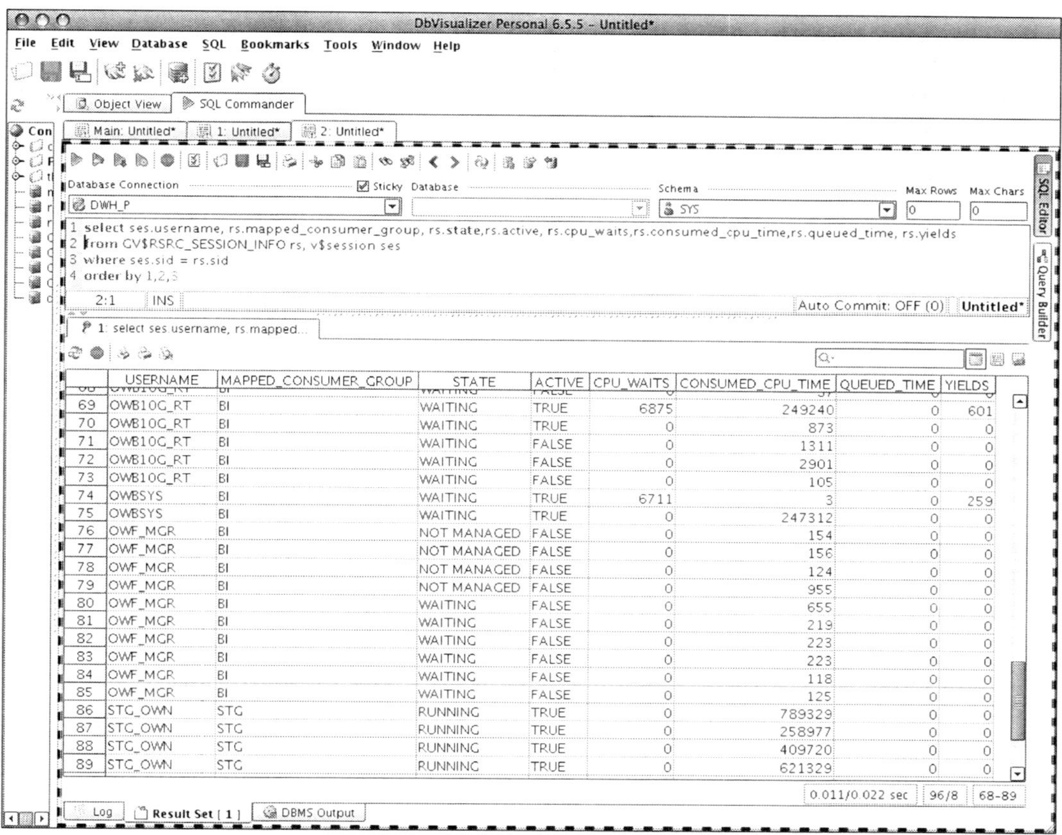

Depending on what you want to see, there are enough views that can help you to find what you are looking for. This should give a good starting point to dig further.

Problems with Resource Manager

There are a few things to keep in mind when you want to make real use of the Scheduler and want it to be controlled by Resource Manager. Sometimes it so happens that a system is idle, which means it's not using much CPU, and still your jobs are not started. Or it could also be that all of a sudden the jobs stop getting started without any modification of jobs or resource plans at all. These are nasty situations. To start with, make sure that every patch for Resource Manager is applied. For Oracle 10.2.0.4, start with the patch for `bug 7482069`, which is a collection of fixes for Resource Manager and is generic for all platforms.

Also, check the alert log during instance start and also check if the NUMA setting fits your system. By default, Oracle enables NUMA optimization in 10.2.0.4. This can have side effects that are not always positive, especially when your system does not happen to be a NUMA system. **NUMA** stands for **Non Uniform Memory Architecture**, which essentially means that unlike most systems, each CPU has its own memory (and not a shared one) on a system bus. If you see that your NUMA settings are enabled, you can disable them by setting the `_enable_NUMA_optimization=FALSE` and `_db_block_numa = 1`:

```
alter system set "_enable_NUMA_optimization" = false;
alter system set "_db_block_numa" = 1;
```

Sometimes, the job system can get back to life by closing a window or switching back to the `internal_plan`, which essentially means disabling Resource Manager. This is no solution, but it can help in times of trouble.

When nothing helps, it could make sense to use `oradebug` to make a trace of the `cjq0` process. This trace can help Oracle development to pinpoint the real problem and help you solve the cause of the problems. This can be done using SQL*Plus as follows:

`ps -ef|grep ora_cjq0_${ORACLE_SID}`

Make a note of the process ID (PID) of the `cjq0` process of your instance using the following code:

```
sqlplus "/ as sysdba"
oradebug setospid PID_of_cjq0_found_using_ps
oradebug tracefile_name
```

This line of code lists the filename of the trace file:

```
oradebug Event 27402 trace name context forever, level 37
```

This line of code enables the trace:

```
oradebug Event 27402 trace name context off
```

As a result, the trace is disabled.

The trace file grows rather quickly. Stop the trace as soon as you catch the problem—a job that does not start, is under the control of the Resource Manager, and has plenty of resources available—and upload it to Oracle support.

There are a few problems with the Resource Manager, and they do not always show up. Start using it and see how you can control the load. Start with simple tasks and see how the jobs are gradually consumed by the database. It is real fun to see this happen.

At the time of writing, there is a bug that relates to `job_weight`, and to which currently there is no fix. In the short term, I advise you to avoid using `job_weight` because it can result in jobs not being started at all.

This is where the Oracle Scheduler is way ahead of other schedulers. In third-party schedulers, controlling a job load based on CPU usage of the system is very hard, if possible at all. Some implementations open a queue when the system is below a certain level and allow each and every queued job to start running at once. This will, in effect, kill the system before it is able to close the queue again because the CPU usage is above the threshold. Oracle prevents this from happening by using the `internal_plan`. It treats all the sessions equally, but with a custom Resource Manager plan you can give more priority to the more important processes of users.

Problems that Resource Manager solves

Resource Manager is not without its own problems, but it does solve others' problems and is absolutely worth investigating. The use of Resource Manager is a strategic decision and belongs to a global design system where we put one instance of a database on one server. We won't combine multiple instances on a server. This is called **instance consolidation**. From the clients, we should address service names and not instance names to connect to the database. If we follow these rules, we can make the best use of Resource Manager. Resource Manager can solve the following issues:

- Guarantee sessions a minimum amount of CPU resources
- Distribute load among groups of users or processes
- Control the degree of parallelism for sessions
- Control the number of active sessions in a session pool
- Free the system from unwanted processes that consume more than expected resources (runaway processes)
- Prevent unwanted long-running operations from being started at all
- Control session idle times, making a difference between blocking sessions and non-blocking sessions

Using the Resource Manager instead of the operating system, we get better use of the operating system's resources. This can be explained by the fact that the Oracle server knows much better when it is smart to take a process from the run queue in comparison with the operating system. For example, a process that holds a latch does not have to be swapped out because a latch is supposed to be held for only a brief period of time. When a process is taken from the run queue, it takes ages before it is back to being able to use the CPU. This can cause a major slowdown of the whole application.

Another thing that the operating system cannot possibly know is that an idle session blocks another session. The database knows not only this, but also knows for how long that session has been idle. This gives the database—Resource Manager—the ability to terminate a session if it is idle for a given period of time, or to terminate when it is blocking other session. This makes the application run more smoothly.

In a database where ad hoc queries are being used, it could be wise to put those users who run ad hoc queries in a dedicated resource consumer group. Here the Resource Manager uses an estimate before the query is started and can decide to run (or not) the query based on the limits that are applied to the resource consumer group. In the same kind of database, limiting the degree of parallelism can be a good idea because this can prevent the over-utilization of the pq processes that are defined for the database. Over-utilization is never good and effectively slows down the whole application.

Resource Manager can make processes wait for resources and have them run when the needed resources are available, which allows the process to complete much more quickly. In many situations, the hardware is scaled up so that Resource Manager can solve the performance problems in a very elegant and cost-effective way.

Summary

Resources should be managed using the Resource Manager. When jobs are controlled by individual schedules, a lot can be done manually by making sure that plenty of resources are always available.

When jobs are controlled by a window, it is very important to have a good Resource Manager plan in place. Otherwise, all the jobs that have been submitted will flood the system at window open time—causing lots of waits and, most likely, lots of trouble. The goal for the Resource Manager is to make the jobs go in the fastest possible way through the system. Other things we have seen are:

- How to create a resource consumer group
- How to grant privileges to switch a resource consumer group to a user
- How to couple a `job_class` to a resource consumer group
- How to couple a `job_class` to an existing job
- How to create a Resource Manager plan using DB Console
- How to control the number of active sessions to be equal to the number of jobs in a Resource Manager plan using the session pool
- How to control the maximal degree of parallelism that we allow for a resource consumer group
- Why we should apply patch `7482069` when we are using Oracle 10.2.0.4, and want to do some serious work with Resource Manager

In the next chapter, we will be getting out of the database using Oracle 11gR1's newly introduced remote scheduler agent.

5 Getting Out of the Database

In the previous chapters, we have mainly focused on the existing `dbms_scheduler` functionality—things that are not new in Oracle 11g. In this chapter, this is going to change. Here, we will get our hands on the most important addition to the Scheduler—the **remote job agent**. This is a whole new kind of process, which allows us to run jobs on machines that do not have a running database. However, they must have Oracle Scheduler Agent installed, as this agent is responsible for executing the remote job. This gives us a lot of extra power and also solves the process owner's problem that exists in classical local external jobs. In classical local external jobs, the process owner is by default *nobody* and is controlled by `$ORACLE_HOME/rdbms/admin/externaljob.ora`. This creates problems in installation, where the software is shared between multiple databases because it is not possible to separate the processes. In this chapter, we will start by installing the software, and then see how we can make good use of it. After this, you will want to get rid of the classical local external jobs as soon as possible because you will want to embrace all the improvements in the remote job agent over the old job type.

Security

Anything that runs on our database server can cause havoc to our databases. No matter what happens, we want to be sure that our databases cannot be harmed. As we have no control over the contents of scripts that can be called from the database, it seems logical *not* to have these scripts run by the same operating system user who also owns the Oracle database files and processes. This is why, by default, Oracle chose the user *nobody* as the default user to run the classical local external jobs. This can be adjusted by editing the contents of `$ORACLE_HOME/rdbms/admin/externaljob.ora`.

On systems where more databases are using the same `$ORACLE_HOME` directory, this automatically means that all the databases run their external jobs using the same operating system account. This is not very flexible. Luckily for us, Oracle has changed this in the 11g release where remote external jobs are introduced. In this release, Oracle decoupled the job runner process and the database processes. The job runner process, that is the job agent, now runs as a remote process and is contacted using a **host:port** combination over TCP/IP.

The complete name for the agent is remote job agent, but this does not mean the job agent can be installed only remotely. It can be installed on the same machine where the database runs, and where it can easily replace the old-fashioned remote jobs. As the communication is done by TCP/IP, this job agent process can be run using any account on the machine. Oracle has no recommendations for the account, but this could very well be *nobody*. The operating system user who runs the job agent does need some privileges in the `$ORACLE_HOME` directory of the remote job agent, namely, an execution privilege on `$ORACLE_HOME/bin/*` as well as read privileges on `$ORACLE_HOME/lib/*`. At the end of the day, the user has to be able to use the software. The remote job agent should also have the ability to write its administration (log) in a location that (by default) is in `$ORACLE_HOME/data`, but it can be configured to a different location by setting the `EXECUTION_AGENT_DATA` environment variable.

In 11g, Oracle also introduced a new object type called `CREDENTIAL`. We can create credentials using `dbms_scheduler.create_credential`. This allows us to administrate which operating system user is going to run our jobs in the database. This also allows us to have control over who can use this credential. To see which credentials are defined, we can use the `*_SCHEDULER_CREDENTIAL` views. We can grant access to a credential by granting `execute` privilege on the credential. This adds lots more control than we ever had in Oracle 10gR2. Currently, the Scheduler Agent can only use a username-password combination to authenticate against the operating system.

The jobs scheduled on the remote job agent will run using the account specified in the credential that we use in the job definition. Check the *Creating job* section to see how this works. This does introduce a small problem in maintenance. On many systems, customers are forced to use security policies such as password aging. When combining with credentials, this might cause a credential to become invalid.

Any change in the password of a job runtime account needs to be reflected in the credential definition that uses the account.

As we get much more control over who executes a job, it is strongly recommend to use the new remote job agent in favor of the classical local external jobs, even locally. The classical external job type will soon become history.

A quick glimpse with a wireshark, a network sniffer, does not reveal the credentials in the clear text, so it looks like it's secure by default. However, the job results do pass in clear text. The agent and the database communicate using SSL and because of this, a certificate is installed in the `${EXECUTION_AGENT_DATA}/agent.key`. You can check this certificate using Firefox. Just point your browser to the host:port where the Scheduler Agent is running and use Firefox to examine the certificate.

There is a bug in 11.1.0.6 that generates a certificate with an expiration date of 90 days past the agent's registration date. In such a case, you will start receiving certificate validation errors when trying to launch a job. Stopping the agent can solve this. Just remove the `agent.key` and re-register the agent with the database.

The registration will be explained shortly.

Installation on Windows

We need to get the software before the installation can take place. The Scheduler Agent can be found on the Transparent Gateways disk, which can be downloaded from Oracle technet at `http://www.oracle.com/technology/software/products/database/index.html`.

There's no direct link to this software, so find a platform of your choice and click on **See All** to get the complete list of database software products for that platform. Then download the **Oracle Database Gateways** CD. Unzip the installation CD, and then navigate to the setup program found in the `toplevel` folder and start it.

The following screenshot shows the download directory where you run the **setup** file:

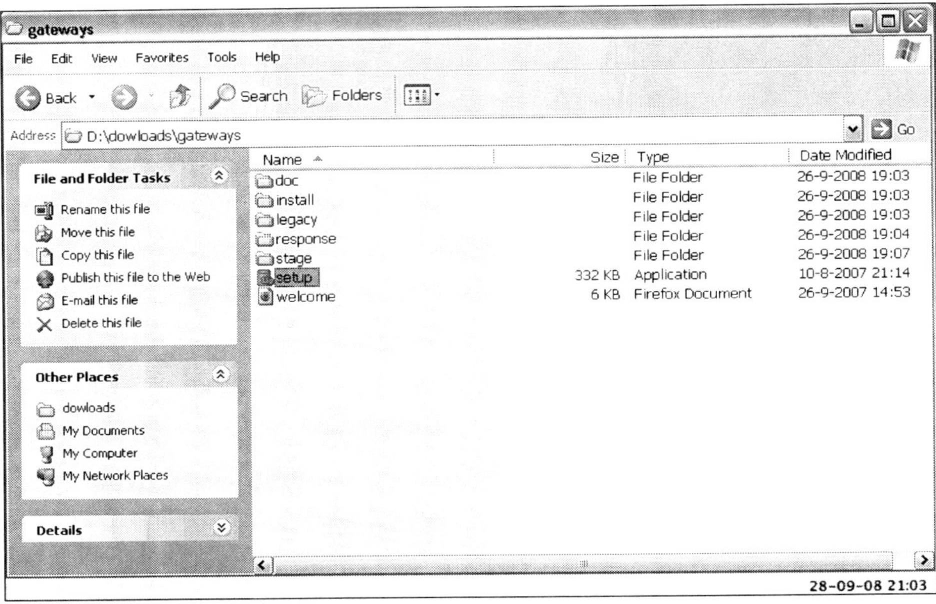

After running the setup, the following **Welcome** screen will appear. The installation process is simple.

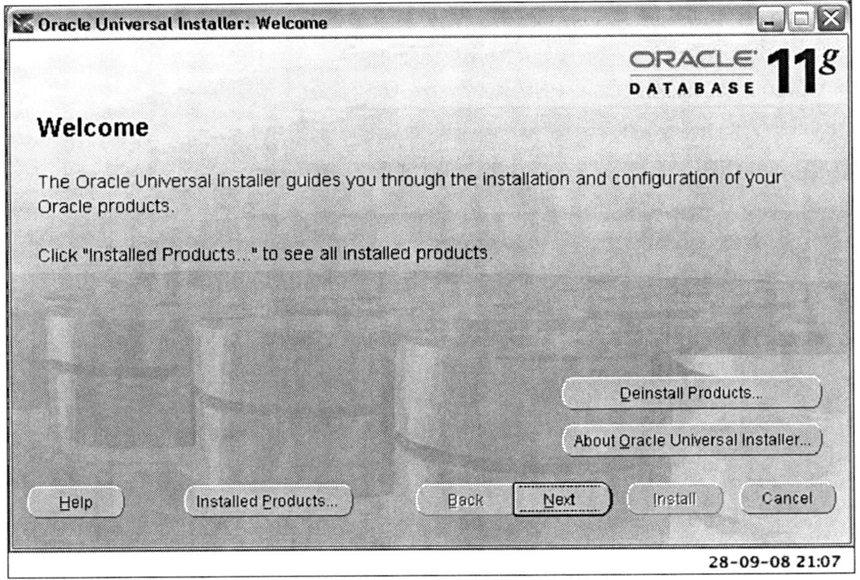

Click on the **Next** button to continue to the product selection screen.

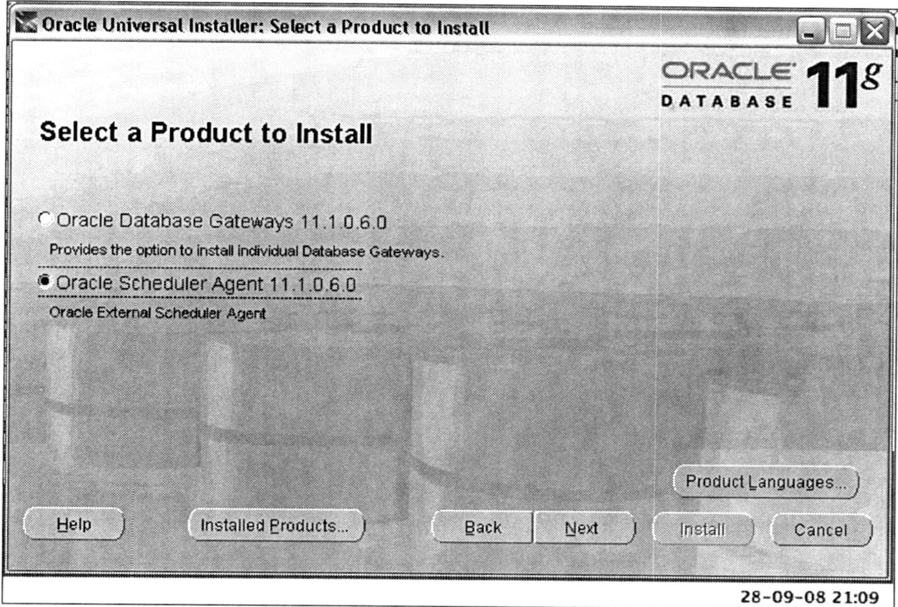

Select **Oracle Scheduler Agent 11.1.0.6.0** and click on the **Next** button to continue. Enter **Name** and **Path** for `ORACLE_HOME` (we can keep the default values).

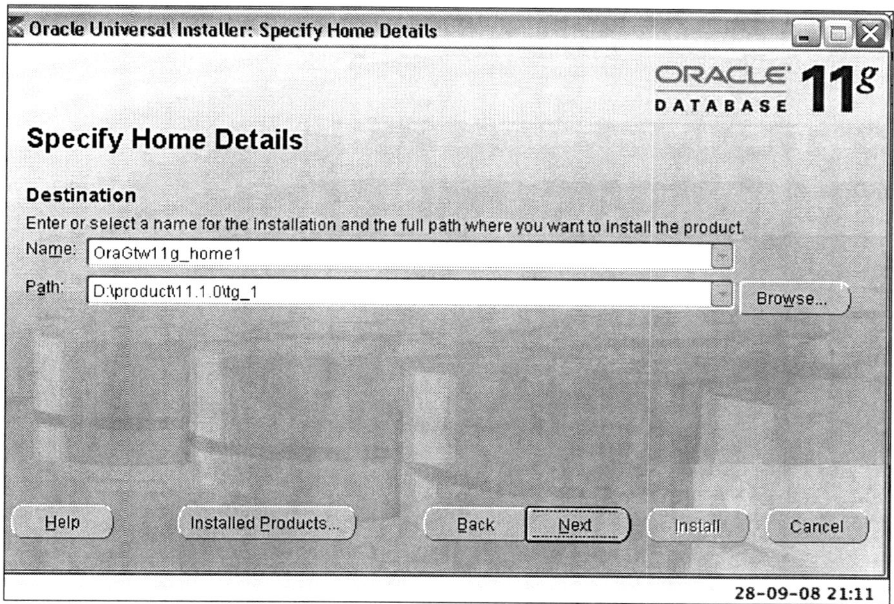

Now click on **Next** to reach the screen where we can choose a port on which the database can contact the agent.

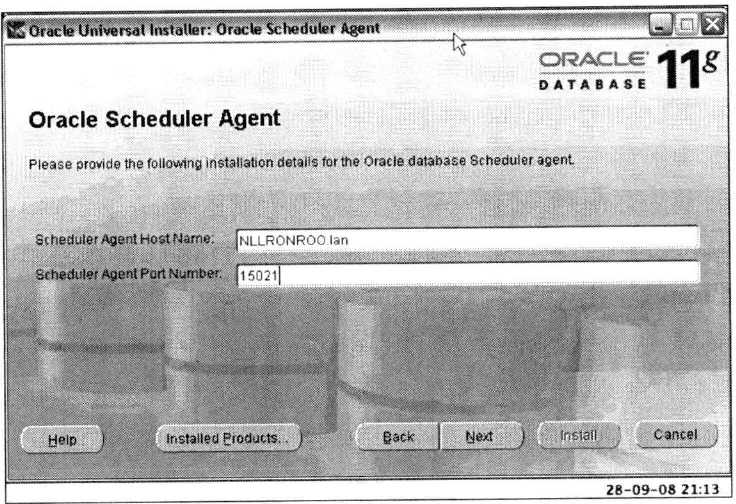

I chose `15021`. On Unix systems, pick a port above `1023` because the lower ports require root privileges to open. The port should be unused and easily memorizable, and should *not* be used by the database's listener process. If possible, keep all the remote job agents registered to the same database and the same port. Also, don't forget to open the firewall for that port. Hitting the **Next** button brings us to the following **Summary** screen:

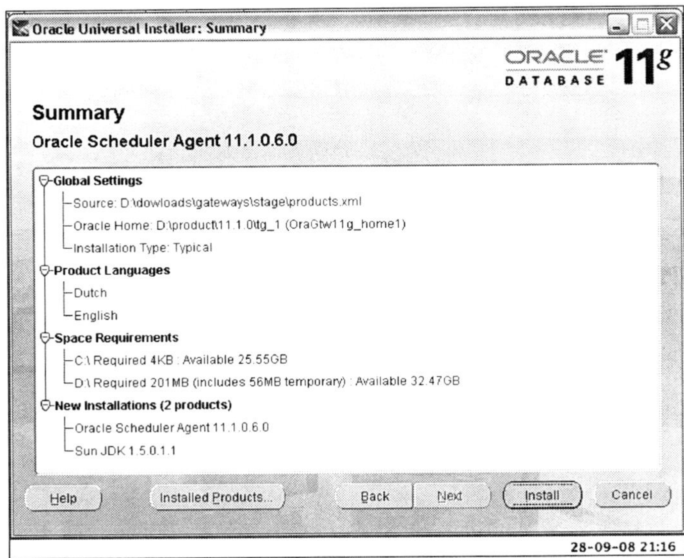

We click on the **Install** button to complete the installation. If everything goes as expected, the **End of Installation** screen pops up as follows:

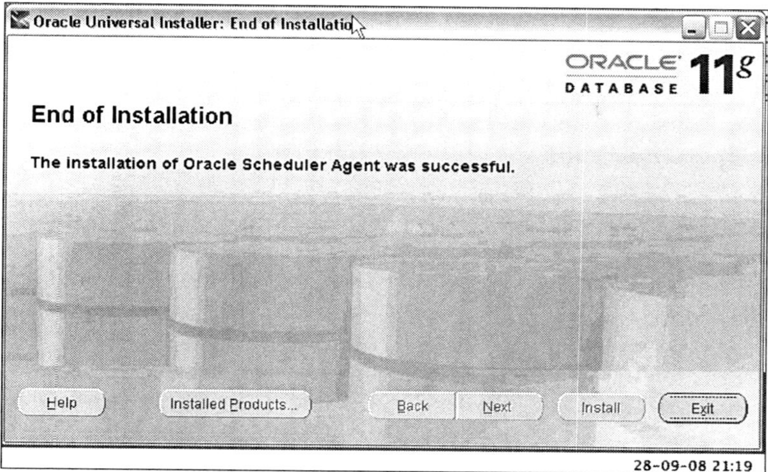

Click on the **Exit** button and confirm the exit.

We can find **Oracle Execution Agent** in the services control panel. Make sure it is running when you want to use the agent to run jobs.

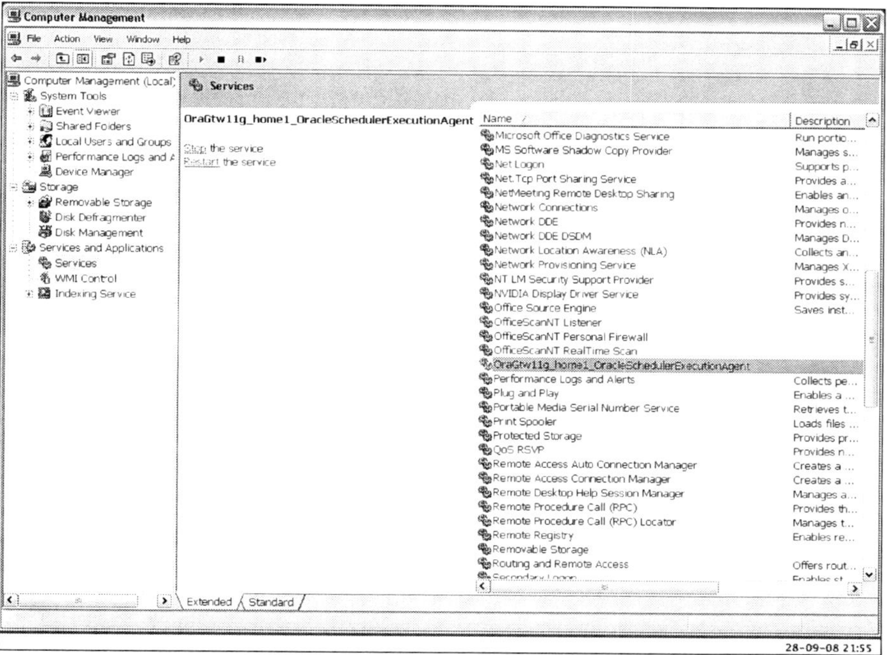

Installation on Linux

Having downloaded and unzipped the installer, navigate to the `gateways` directory and start the installer with `./runInstaller`. Now we will get the same screens as we did for the Windows installation. The only difference, apart from the slashes pointing in the right direction, is the pop up asking to run `root.sh` at the end of the installation. Running `root.sh` sets `setuid` root on the `$ORACLE_HOME/bin/jssu` executable to the `setuid` root.

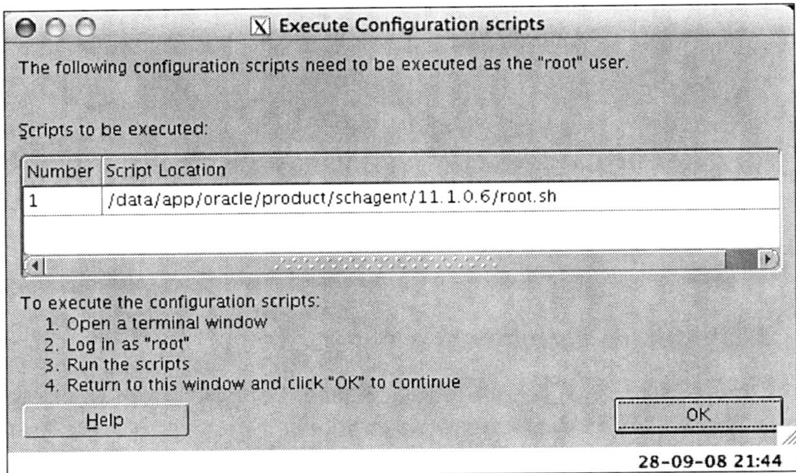

Run `root.sh` as requested and finish the installation. The `root.sh` only sets `setuid` root on the `$ORACLE_HOME/bin/jssu` executable using the following code:

```
# jssu must be setuid and owned by root
if [ -f $ORACLE_HOME/bin/jssu ]; then
        $CHOWN root $ORACLE_HOME/bin/jssu
        $CHMOD 4750 $ORACLE_HOME/bin/jssu
fi
```

Put a `schagent:/data/app/oracle/product/schagent/11.1.0.6:N` tag in `/etc/oratab` and use `oraenv` to set the environment for the agent as follows:

```
oracle@pantzer:/data/app/oracle — ssh — 96×27
[oracle@pantzer oracle]$ . oraenv
ORACLE_SID = [shield01] ? schagent
The Oracle base for ORACLE_HOME=/data/app/oracle/product/schagent/11.1.0.6 is /data/app/oracle
[oracle@pantzer oracle]$ ls -l $ORACLE_HOME/bin/jssu
-rwsr-x--- 1 root oracle 21836 Aug  1  2007 /data/app/oracle/product/schagent/11.1.0.6/bin/jssu
[oracle@pantzer oracle]$
16-02-09 21:44
```

In the listing mentioned in the screenshot above, it is clearly visible that `jssu` has the `setuid` root privileges. This also means that the `root.sh` has been successfully run. The `setuid` root privilege connotes that the executable can use the privileges of the owner of this executable, which is `root` in this case.

For Linux, Mac OS X, and AIX, the default location for `oratab` is `/etc/`; and for Solaris, it is `/var/opt/oracle/`. Check the platform-dependent installation manual for the default location on your platform.

Upgrading the remote job agent

It's a good idea to apply any new updates published by Oracle. If you are still using the 11.1.0.6 agent, you will see some problems that are fixed by the 11.1.0.7 upgrade. The upgrade of the agent is not very difficult once you know that the same patch set should be applied as that for the database server installation. This is not very well documented, but this is how it works—start the installer found in the patch set, and then select the agent's `ORACLE_HOME` to upgrade.

The upgrade process is quick and easy till the last part—the execution of the root shell. In the 11.1.0.7 patch, you are asked to run the `root.sh`. Run it as `root` and check the properties of `${ORACLE_HOME}/bin/jssu`. This file should have the `setuid` root privileges to function correctly. The `root.sh` that we are requested to run contains the following:

```
#!/bin/sh
/data/app/oracle/schagent/11.1.0.7.0/install/root_schagent.sh
```

The `root_schagent.sh` file contains an error that prevents the setting of the `setuid` root on the `jssu` file. The `root_schagent.sh` file begins with this:

```
#!/bin/sh
ORACLE_HOME=%ORACLE_HOME%
```

This is fine for a Windows system, but not for a Unix or Linux system. In these systems, we expect the following:

```
#!/bin/sh
ORACLE_HOME=$ORACLE_HOME
```

Change the `root_schagent.sh` file accordingly. Make sure that `ORACLE_HOME` is defined and run the `root.sh` again. Now the `setuid` root bits should be in place.

Silent install of the remote job agent

When you decide to use the remote job agent, there will be a lot of installation work. We can use the interactive installer as described before, but this can also be done in a much faster way by using the **silent install** option. This will work best when the machines on which you are installing have uniform installation. First, decide what the `ORACLE_HOME_NAME` and `ORACLE_HOME` locations will be. This is the standard for all silent Oracle installations. For the agent, we also need `HOST_NAME` and `PORT` where the agent will listen at the time of installation. We can easily change that later, as most of us prefer to do. Here we will see the installation of the base release followed by the patch.

Base release

For the base release, use the same Gateways CD that we used in the interactive installation. Just change the current directory to the `gateways` directory where you can see the `runInstaller` executable. The base release is 11.1.0.6. We will immediately upgrade it to the latest possible release, which (at the time of writing this) is 11.1.0.7; so we are going to put the base release in the `11.1.0.7.0` directory. If you are not planning to do this upgrade, it would make more sense to install the base release in a `11.1.0.6.0` directory with an adjusted `ORACLE_HOME_NAME` of the `schagent111060`.

```
export s_HOST_NAME=pantzer.lan
export s_PORT=15021
./runInstaller -silent -responseFile $PWD/response/schagent.rsp
ORACLE_HOME_NAME=schagent111070
ORACLE_HOME=/data/app/oracle/schagent/11.1.0.7.0
s_nameForDBAGrp=dba n_configurationOption=3
FROM_LOCATION="$PWD/stage/products.xml"
s_hostName=${s_HOST_NAME} s_port=${s_PORT}
```

When the installer is ready, run the `root.sh` script as is usually done after an installation. After this, check that `jssu` has the `setuid` root privileges.

```
ls -l /data/app/oracle/schagent/11.1.0.7.0/bin/jssu
```

Patch to the latest available level

The Scheduler is improving rapidly, so it is preferable to perform the upgrades at regular intervals. We use the same source of installation for the agent as we do for the database software upgrade. Again, start in the same working directory as that of the interactive installation where you can see the `runInstaller` executable.

Since 11.1.0.7, Oracle asks during the installation whether (or not) you want to be notified by email when a new security patch is released. Normally, we would already have this notification in place. So during the installation, we will most likely decline this using:

```
./runInstaller -silent -responseFile $PWD/response/patchset.rsp
ORACLE_HOME_NAME=schagent111070
ORACLE_HOME=/data/app/oracle/schagent/11.1.0.7.0
DECLINE_SECURITY_UPDATES=true
```

This starts the installer and performs the upgrade of the previously installed `ORACLE_HOME`. There is a problem in the script that is called from the `root.sh`, which is generated for us. We should fix this using the following before running the `root.sh` script:

```
cat /data/app/oracle/schagent/11.1.0.7.0/install/root_schagent.sh
|sed "s/%ORACLE_HOME%/$ORACLE_HOME/" >/tmp/rs$$
cp -p /tmp/rs$$
/data/app/oracle/schagent/11.1.0.7.0/install/root_schagent.sh
rm /tmp/rs$$
```

Now run the `root.sh` as we normally do. It is important that `jssu` has the `setuid` root privileges, so check them using:

```
ls -l /data/app/oracle/schagent/11.1.0.7.0/bin/jssu
```

This should look as follows:

```
-rwsr-x---  1 root dba 29497 Sep 11  2008
/data/app/oracle/schagent/11.1.0.7.0/bin/jssu
```

Preparing the database for remote agent usage

There are a few things to check and do before we can use the remote job agent. The following steps will be explained in detail:

1. Verify that XDB is installed.
2. Set HTTP port, if not set.
3. Install the remote job agent objects.
4. Set the registration password.

Verifying the XDB installation

In order to use a remote Scheduler, the database needs to have XML database installed.

Check this by verifying `dba_registry` for the existence and validity of the `comp_id 'XDB'` as follows:

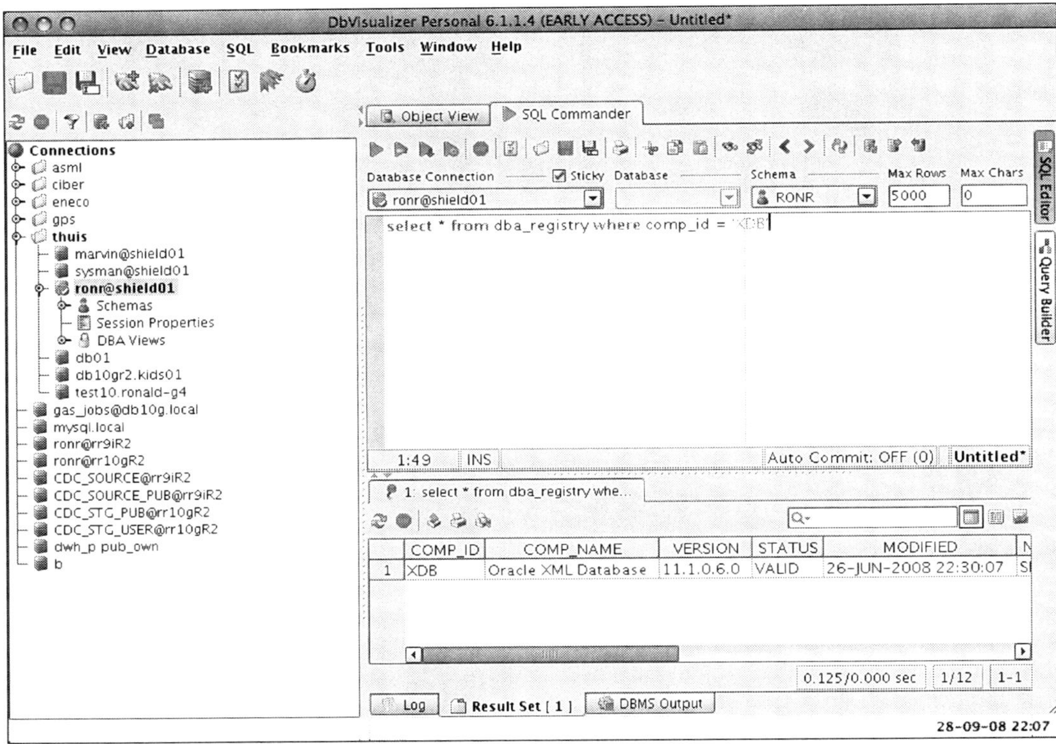

In this case, the XML Database is installed and valid.

Setting the HTTP port

The agent uses the database's HTTP port to contact the database. Check which port is in use and set a port if needed. As with the agent, make sure that the port is above `1023`, as the lower ports are reserved for the root. There is not much to say about which port is good or bad, but don't take the port that the remote job agent is listening on. As we poor humans have trouble remembering simple numbers, it might be convenient to pick `15021` for the agents and `16021` for the database.

Other Oracle products, such as Application Express, use the database HTTP port. When setting this port, ensure that all of the uses are taken into account.

Check the port with this:

```
SELECT DBMS_XDB.gethttpport FROM dual;
```

If needed, set the port with this:

```
--/
begin
  DBMS_XDB.sethttpport(16021);
end;
/
```

The agent can contact the database on port `16021` to make sure that it is not messed up by any firewalls. Now, create the database objects used by the Scheduler Agent.

Creating remote Scheduler objects

You can create the `remote_scheduler_agent` user in the database and a few lines of code using the following:

```
sqlplus '/ as sysdba' @?/rdbms/admin/prvtrsch.plb
```

This creates `dbms_isched_remote_access` in the `SYS` schema; and the `restrict_access` function, and the `register_agent` and `submit_job_results` procedures in the `remote_scheduler_agent` schema.

Setting registration password

We can set a password that the agent needs to use at the time of registration using the following:

```
--/
begin
  DBMS_SCHEDULER.set_agent_registration_pass
                  ('very_difficult_password');
end;
/
```

This password will only be used to register the agent. After the registration, an SSL certificate will be used to authenticate the agent.

Configuring a remote agent

The remote agent's configuration is simple. It has to be registered as a target for the database. The registration has to be done manually using the schagent utility found in `$ORACLE_HOME/bin`.

On Linux, I added a pseudo `ORACLE_SID` (schagent) to the `oratab` file (`schagent:/data/app/oracle/product/schagent/11.1.0.6:N`). We can use that and `oraenv` to set the right environment variables for us—this was nice and easy.

```
  1  begin
  2  DBMS_SCHEDULER.set_agent_registration_pass('very_difficult_password');
  3* end;
SQL> /

PL/SQL procedure successfully completed.

SQL>
                                                         16-02-09 22:04
```

Now that we know the registration password, we can use it to register the agent from the machine on which the agent works for us. There is no need to keep a record for this password. It is only used during the registration process and we can change it whenever we want. The following screenshot shows the registration of the agent:

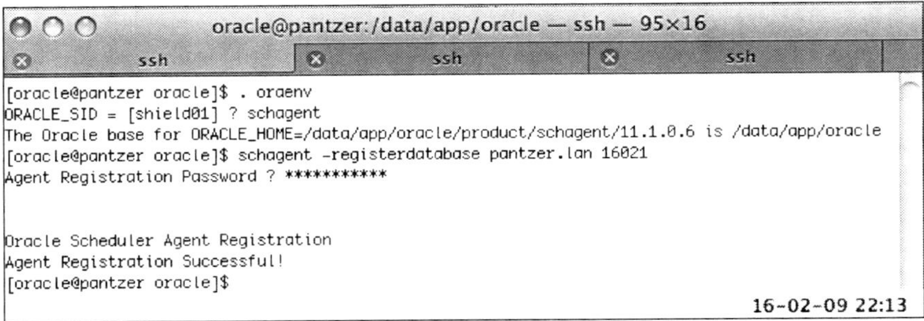

On Windows, the screen output should look like this:

```
C:\WINDOWS\system32\cmd.exe
Microsoft Windows XP [versie 5.1.2600]
(C) Copyright 1985-2001 Microsoft Corp.

M:\>d:

D:\>cd product\11.1.0\tg_1\bin

D:\product\11.1.0\tg_1\bin>schagent -registerdatabase pantzer.lan 16021
Agent Registration Password ? *very_difficult_passwor*
*
Oracle Scheduler Agent Registration
Agent Registration Successful!

D:\product\11.1.0\tg_1\bin>_
```

From now on, the agents should be useable.

Troubleshooting

In case of problems with the installation, check if the port is reachable with telnet to the host and port, for example `telnet pantzer.lan 16021`. This should give a clear screen as a response—definitely not "connection refused" (wrong machine/port or service is not running) or no response at all (firewall)..If you get the response "connection refused", check whether the agent is running or not. If the agent is not running, start it using `schagent -start` and try again. If the agent was running, check the port that the agent is using in the agent configuration file.

The agent configuration file is found in `$ORACLE_HOME/schagent.conf` and in my system contains the following:

```
# This is the configuration file for the Oracle Scheduler Agent.
#
# The agent will look first for schagent.conf in {EXECUTION_AGENT_DATA}
# and then in {EXECUTION_AGENT_HOME}. It will only use whichever is
# found first and throw an error if none is found.
#
# You can change these values to suit your environment.

# network port to listen on for requests (between 1 and 65536)
PORT=15021

# host name of the host the agent is running on. If this is not
# specified, the resolved name of the local address will be used
HOST_NAME = NLLRONROO.lan

# maximum number of jobs to run simultaneously (between 1 and 1000)
MAX_RUNNING_JOBS=5

# if this is set to TRUE, the agent will reject put_file requests
DISABLE_PUT_FILE=FALSE

# if this is set to TRUE, the agent will reject get_file requests
DISABLE_GET_FILE=FALSE

# if this is set to TRUE, the agent will reject job execution requests
DISABLE_JOB_EXECUTION=FALSE
# the agent will reject any attempt to use any user on this list.
# This list should be comma-separated and is case-insensitive.
DENY_USERS=root,administrator,guest
```

```
# if this list is not empty, the agent will only allow use of a user
# on this list. This list should be comma-separated and is
# case-insensitive.
# ALLOW_USERS=

# types of logging to do. Zero or more of the following options:
# OVERVIEW, WARNINGS, ALL, ERROR_STACKS, MILLISECONDS
LOGGING_LEVEL=OVERVIEW,WARNINGS
```

The first thing that comes to my mind when a registration has been done is: "How can I check this?" Unfortunately, there appears to be no way to check the status of the agent's registration—not even in the database. It would be very convenient to have an Oracle view that gives an oversight of which agents are talking with the database. I filed an enhancement request (`7462577`) for this. So with a little luck, we can check the status of remote agents in the near future. What we can do is see if the agent is running on the host and check the log file as follows:

```
> ps -ef|grep schagent
oracle    4739 31910  0 15:30 pts/2    00:00:00 grep schagent
oracle   25272     1  0 Mar04 ?        02:48:52 /data/app/oracle/schagent/11.1.0.7.0/jdk/jre
/bin/java -cp /data/app/oracle/schagent/11.1.0.7.0/lib/schagent.jar -DEXECUTION_AGENT_HOME=/
data/app/oracle/schagent/11.1.0.7.0 -DEXECUTION_AGENT_DATA=/data/appdata/oracle/schagent/DBA
_O oracle.scheduler.agent.ExecutionAgent
```

Or we can check a specific agent's process as follows:

```
> ps -fp`cat ${EXECUTION_AGENT_DATA}/agent.pid`
UID        PID  PPID  C STIME TTY          TIME CMD
oracle   25272     1  0 Mar04 ?        02:48:52 /data/app/oracle/schagent/11.1.0.7.0/jdk/jre
```

Or we can check the `logfile` of the agent as follows:

```
> tail -1 ${EXECUTION_AGENT_DATA}/agent.log
2009.04.29 03:07:57 CEST Job terminated successfully. Duration: 30.073 seconds
```

Multiple agents on the same host

The remote agent is a very powerful tool and is easy to deploy. We can use a separate installation for every agent that we want to have running on a host. With a little modification of the `$ORACLE_HOME/bin/schagent` code, we can easily configure multiple agents on a single host using the same software tree.

The contents of `$ORACLE_HOME/schagent.conf` suggest that the location of this file and the runtime files can be controlled by the `EXECUTION_AGENT_DATA` environment variable. We need to have this ability when we want to run multiple agents on the same host using the same software tree. If you take a look at `$ORACLE_HOME/bin/schagent`, there will be a little surprise. The `EXECUTION_AGENT_DATA` variable is reset to `NULL`, making the variable useless. I hope this is a bug that can be fixed soon. For now, I entered a *comment* sign before the line that resets the `EXECUTION_AGENT_DATA` variable, which led to an enhancement request (`7560494`). There is a good chance that this will be fixed in the next release. However, it is safe to change the code in `schagent` from:

```
!/bin/sh

# set this if you change your Agent home
EXECUTION_AGENT_HOME="/data/app/oracle/product/schagent/11.1.0.6"

# set this to use a different data directory for the Agent
EXECUTION_AGENT_DATA=""
```

to:

```
!/bin/sh

# set this if you change your Agent home
EXECUTION_AGENT_HOME="/data/app/oracle/product/schagent/11.1.0.6"

# set this to use a different data directory for the Agent
# EXECUTION_AGENT_DATA=""
```

Sometimes an enhancement can be as simple as adding a comment sign as explained above. When using this approach, the runtime files for the agent will be created in the `${EXECUTION_AGENT_DATA}` directory. This includes the `agent.key` file, which is the SSL certificate that the agent uses. The `${EXECUTION_AGENT_DATA}` directory also becomes the data directory. Here, all the administrative and log files that the agent uses to run jobs will be stored. The logging of the jobs run by the agent will be in a log subdirectory. This subdirectory will grow because the agent is not performing any log cleaning at the moment. This is the case with the current release, which is 11.1.0.7. But this will surely improve in the future release of the agent. It seems logical to remove the log files from the agent at the same time when the log is purged from the job log tables in the originating database. The logging of the agent is in `${EXECUTION_AGENT_DATA}/agent.log`.

In this file, you will find the log entries of the agent, including details such as an agent started a job, received a new job, started a new job, and returned a job result to the database.

When using multiple agents on the same host, it is a smart move to adjust the userpart of oraenv. It should also define and export the EXECUTION_AGENT_DATA. Also, it implies that each agent gets its own tag in oratab.

The end of the oraenv script could be like this:

```
#
# Install any "custom" code here
#
EXECUTION_AGENT_DATA=/your/location/${ORACLE_SID}
Export EXECUTION_AGENT_DATA
And the oratab entries:
schagent{ID1}:/your/agents/ORACLE_HOME:N
schagent{ID2}:/your/agents/ORACLE_HOME:N
```

These definitions ensure that the software is taken from the correct location, and having the autostart on N makes sure that the database start procedures ignore the schagent* entries when the system starts. However, you do need to create a startup procedure that starts schagents on your system.

Credentials

To be able run jobs on a remote agent, we have to add the credential_name attribute to the jobs specification. To do this, we must create one first. We can create credentials using DBMS_SCHEDULER.create_credential and remove them with DBMS_SCHEDULER.drop_credential. At the moment, it is not mandatory to use credentials for local external jobs, but Oracle advises us to use them instead of falling back on the (soon to be deprecated) defaults. Using credentials also has documentation benefits. The operating system account that is involved becomes much more obvious, so the advice is to go and start using credentials. I created a normal user jobs, with the password employed, who has to run the jobs.

The attributes for credentials are as follows:

Attributes	Description
username	The username to execute the job
password	Password to authenticate the user, which is stored as unreadable
comments	An optional comment. It can describe what the credential is intended for
database_role	Database role to use when logging in (either SYSDBA, or SYSOPER, or NULL)
windows_domain	The Windows domain to use when logging in

Run the following code connected as your job's owner to create a credential:

```
--/
BEGIN
  DBMS_SCHEDULER.create_credential(
                                       credential_name => 'jobs_cred',
                                       username        => 'jobs',
                                       password        => 'employed'
                                       );
END;
/
```

The creator is the owner of the credentials and users can be given access to them using a `grant execute`:

```
grant execute on jobs_cred to marvin;
```

The defined credentials are shown at `dba | all | user` in the `_scheduler_credentials` views. With Windows, it is important to note that the user specified by the credential must have the `logon as batch job` security policy (same as the jobs user that was used by OEM in the good old days). This policy can be set using the **local security policies** dialog found in the **administrative tools** control panel. Forgetting to set this policy is the most common cause of the Scheduler to OS (and Oracle Enterprise Manager to OS) interaction issues. If for some reason an administrator does not want to grant this privilege, explain to him or her that this privilege is mandatory to be able to use the agent.

Creating job—targeting Unix

There is much similarity between the familiar local external jobs and the new remote external jobs. The main difference is the destination attribute that has to be used for remote external jobs. Here we simply specify the `HOST_NAME:PORT` combination that we used at the agent's installation time. Let's see what happens when we run the first script to see what is in the job's environment:

```
--/
BEGIN
  DBMS_SCHEDULER.create_job(
                            job_name   => 'env',
                            job_type   => 'EXECUTABLE',
                            job_action => '/tmp/test.sh',
                            auto_drop  => FALSE,
                            enabled    => FALSE
                            );
  DBMS_SCHEDULER.set_attribute('env', 'credential_name', 'JOBS_CRED2');
  DBMS_SCHEDULER.set_attribute('env', 'destination', 'pantzer:15021');
  DBMS_SCHEDULER.enable('env');
END;
/
```

As soon as we enable the job, it is executed. In the `schedulerjob_run_details` view, the **ADDITIONAL_INFO** column displays the filename where the agent stored the output for the job as shown in the following screenshot:

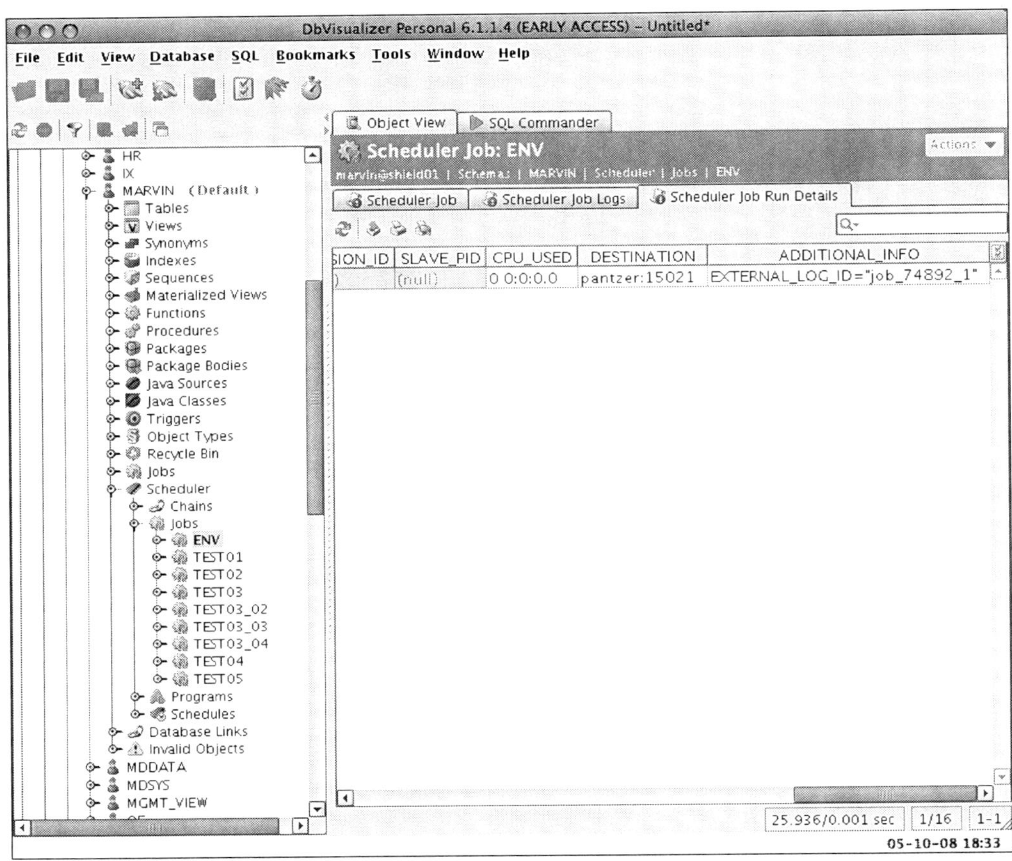

This job output can be found in the agent's `$EXECUTION_AGENT_HOME/data/log/`, `${EXECUTION_AGENT_DATA}/log/`, or `$ORACLE_HOME/data/log/` directory depending on how you configured this. We can go there and check this file, but it is more convenient to have the computer display this information for us. In order to get the output, Oracle has provided us with the `get_file` procedure in `dbms_scheduler`. In the **ADDITIONAL_INFO** column, we get **EXTERNAL_LOG_ID="job_74892_1"**. And `get_file` expects `job_74892_1` with `_stdout` or `_stderr` appended to it, depending on what we want to get. Too bad that Oracle did not offer the filename or whatever input `get_file` needed. Instead, we need to filter the file name from the **ADDITIONAL_INFO** column. The following query separates the `file_name` part from the **ADDITIONAL_INFO** column for the last execution of the job called `ENV`:

```
select * from (SELECT log_id, additional_info,
                      REGEXP_SUBSTR(additional_info,'job[_0-9]*')
               AS external_log_id
               FROM user_scheduler_job_run_details
               WHERE job_name = 'ENV'
               ORDER BY log_id desc)
where rownum = 1;
```

In the `get_file` call, we need to specify a credential that specifies the same operating system account as the one that we used for the job. So why not just use the same credential? We are using it here:

```
--/
DECLARE
  l_clob  CLOB;
  l_additional_info  VARCHAR2(50);
  l_external_log_id  VARCHAR2(50);
BEGIN
  SELECT additional_info, external_log_id
  INTO l_additional_info, l_external_log_id
  FROM (SELECT log_id, additional_info,
               REGEXP_SUBSTR(additional_info,'job[_0-9]*')
        AS external_log_id
        FROM   user_scheduler_job_run_details
        WHERE  job_name = 'ENV'
        ORDER BY log_id DESC)
  WHERE ROWNUM = 1;
  DBMS_OUTPUT.put_line('ADDITIONAL_INFO: ' || l_additional_info);
  DBMS_OUTPUT.put_line('EXTERNAL_LOG_ID: ' || l_external_log_id);
  DBMS_LOB.createtemporary(l_clob, FALSE);
  DBMS_SCHEDULER.get_file
    (
      source_file      => l_external_log_id ||'_stdout',
      credential_name  => 'JOBS_CRED',
      file_contents    => l_clob,
      source_host      => 'pantzer:15021'
    );
  DBMS_OUTPUT.put_line('stdout:');
  DBMS_OUTPUT.put_line(l_clob);
END;
/
```

This gives a quite surprising output:

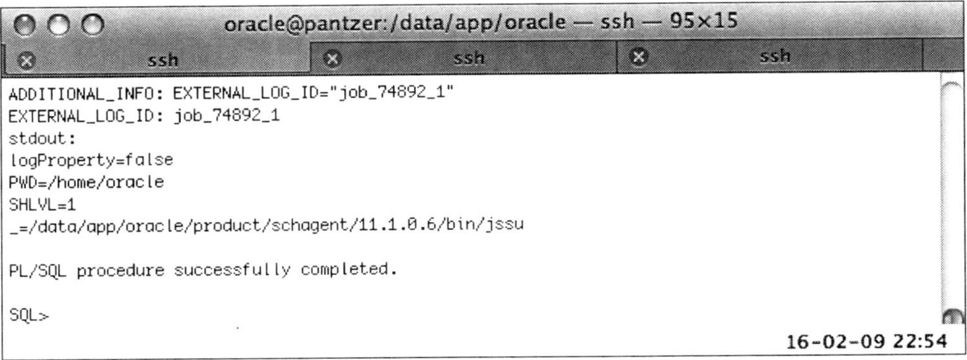

The PWD variable shows the location from where the schagent was started. In this case, it is the home directory of the Oracle user; not the home directory of the user that was specified in the credential or the conventional external job— / (root). My advice is not to use this directory as it is subject to change. After every release of Oracle, we see that less information is passed from the database to the environment of a job. When starting the schagent, the first issue is to change the default directory to the $EXECUTION_AGENT_DATA directory and then start the agent. This makes sure that you always start the agent using the same environment, and also prevents any unwanted mixing up of directories being used by different agents.

```
>cd ${EXECUTION_AGENT_DATA}
>schagent -start
Scheduler agent started
>
```

During the execution of the job, both stdout and the stderr files are created. The latter is deleted at the end of the job when it is empty. If you request the output file from an existing job, but did not generate the requested file, the returned output is empty.

When you request a job file from a job that did not run, Oracle returns ora-01031 : insufficient privileges. This may look strange, but there is a possibility that that you provided the wrong credential. When you specified the wrong credential, it could be possible that the operating system user (specified in the user credential) has no privileges to access the directory in which the log file is stored.

The agent also has a file in which it tries to administer the jobs it knows about. This file is log/job_idss and has enough information to tell us where the job came from, who the job was (both schema and runtime user), and what was executed.

Creating job—targeting Windows

On Windows, everything is almost the same; almost, but not quite. On Unix systems, we can run any script and get the desired results. On Windows, we have to call `cmd.exe` and have it call our script with the script's optional arguments. So the script has to be seen as the second argument for `cmd`. To get a similar test as for Linux, we have to use the following code:

```
--/
BEGIN
  DBMS_SCHEDULER.create_job
    (
      job_name              => 'env_windows',
      job_type              => 'EXECUTABLE',
      number_of_arguments   => 2,
      job_action            => 'C:\windows\system32\cmd.exe',
      auto_drop             => FALSE,
      enabled               => FALSE
    );
  DBMS_SCHEDULER.set_job_argument_value('env_windows',1,'/c');
  DBMS_SCHEDULER.set_job_argument_value('env_windows',2,
                                        'd:\temp\test.cmd');
  DBMS_SCHEDULER.set_attribute('env_windows', 'credential_name',
                                                   'jobs_cred');
  DBMS_SCHEDULER.set_attribute('env_windows', 'destination',
                                     'nllronroo.lan:15021');
  DBMS_SCHEDULER.enable('env_windows');
END;
/
```

The job called `env_windows` uses `cmd.exe` that calls the `d:\temp\text.cmd` script. The agent used to run this code can be found on the `nllronroo` machine at port `15021`.

It generates the following output:

```
C:\WINDOWS\system32>set
ComSpec=C:\WINDOWS\system32\cmd.exe
logProperty=false
OS=Windows_NT
PATHEXT=.COM;.EXE;.BAT;.CMD;.VBS;.JS;.WS
PROMPT=$P$G
SystemDrive=C:
SystemRoot=C:\WINDOWS
```

In this case, the `test.cmd` script was:

```
set
```

This is roughly the equivalent of the `test.sh` script:

```
env
```

Runtime observations of the remote Scheduler

As the remote Scheduler is running more or less independently from the database that sends its jobs to the agent, it is possible that the originating database goes offline while a long-running job is underway. The system is robust enough to survive this. There are several situations to distinguish such as:

- The database goes offline, but then comes back online before the job finishes
- The database goes offline and the job finishes before the database is online again
- The job agent stops before the job ends

In the first situation, where the database is back online before the job finishes, the agent submits the job completion data as if nothing happened at all. Even in the database, the remote job keeps the `RUNNING` status and is handled as if nothing had happened.

In the second situation, the remote job agent tries to submit the job completion data to the database and this time it fails. The data is saved in `pending completion data` and the agent continues normal processing. After one hour, the agent tries to resubmit the data and keeps trying this every hour until it succeeds. In the period following the start of the database, the job keeps its `RUNNING` status till the agent succeeds in submitting the completion data. When the database submits a new job to the agent before the one-hour resubmission interval has passed, the agent does nothing more than start the new job. Here is a little room for improvement. The agent knows that the database is back online and can resubmit the job completion data as soon as it receives a new job from the same database. An enhancement request has been filed for this.

In the third situation, there is a real problem. The job continues its run till it completes. Only, the agent has no way to tell what happened to the job because the agent was down. As soon as the agent is started again, it submits a "stopped by SYS" signal to the database and marks the job as `FAILED`. I must admit that I don't know how this can be improved, other than that I expected the running job to be terminated when the agent is taken offline. Now it is happily doing its job and is getting the possibly incorrect `FAILED` flag. The point is that the agent has no way to tell what really happened.

Resource Manager

At this moment, it is not possible to use Resource Manager for remote external jobs. But this is going to change for sure. We can put the jobs in a job class that has a resource consumer group mapped on it. But for remote external jobs, these definitions are ignored. For regular jobs, we can find the job class that was used when the job ran in the `*_scheduler_job_log` views. For remote external jobs, that column contains a `NULL` value indicating that Resource Manager settings were not applied on them. An enhancement request has been filed for this. The Resource Manager integration for the remote Scheduler Agent needs at least the active session pool. This enables the database to limit the number of parallel jobs submitted to the agent. There is a very limited configuration in the `schagent.conf` file (`MAX_RUNNING_JOBS`). This file is not flexible enough and is invisible to the database administrator.

Summary

In this chapter, we have seen the most important change in Scheduler 11g—the remote external job. It is easy to set up and configure. But at the same time, it seems impossible to see what agent is configured against the database. At the moment, the Resource Manager support is missing.

In this chapter, we saw:

- How robust the agent is
- How easy it is to configure multiple agents on a single host using a single software installation
- How to get remote log files from the agent to the originating database
- How to target a Windows system as a remote platform
- How to target a Unix/Linux system as a remote platform
- How to check the port that the agent is using
- How to check the certificate that the agent is using

In the next chapter, we are going to take a look at Scheduler's event system—how events are generated and how can we act on these events.

6
Events

So far, we have mostly used jobs that ran immediately upon being enabled, or when we called the `run_job` procedure of the `dbms_scheduler` package. Many jobs are *time-based*; they are controlled by a schedule based on some kind of calendar.

However, not everything in real life can be controlled by a calendar. Many things need an action on an ad hoc basis, depending on the occurrence of some other thing. This is called **event-based scheduling**. Events also exist as the outcome of a job. We can define a job to raise an event in several ways—when it ends, or when it ends in an error, or when it does not end within the expected runtime. Let's start with creating job events in order to make job monitoring a lot easier for you.

In this chapter, we will see how events that are generated by a job or a chain step can be intercepted to enable the monitoring of jobs. After that, we will see how we can use events to start a job that is waiting for an event.

Monitoring job events

Most of the time when jobs just do their work as expected, there is not much to monitor. In most cases, the job controller has to fix application-specific problems (for example, sometimes file systems or table spaces get filled up). To make this easier, we can incorporate events. We can make jobs raise events when something unexpected happens, and we can have the Scheduler generate events when a job runs for too long. This gives us tremendous power. We can also use this to make chains a little easier to maintain.

Events in chains

A chain consists of steps that depend on each other. In many cases, it does not make sense to continue to step 2 when step 1 fails. For example, when a *create table* fails, why try to load data into the nonexistent table? So it is logical to terminate the job if no other independent steps can be performed.

One of the ways to handle this is implementing error steps in the chain. This might be a good idea, but the disadvantage is that this quickly doubles the steps involved in the chain, where most of the steps—hopefully—will not be executed. Another disadvantage is that the chain becomes less maintainable. It's a lot of extra code, and more code (mostly) gives us less oversight.

If a job chain has to be terminated because of a failure, using the option of creating an **event handler** to raise a Scheduler event is recommended instead of adding extra steps that try to tell which error possibly happened. This makes event notification a lot simpler because it's all in separate code and not mixed up with the application code.

Another situation is when the application logic has to take care of steps that fail, and has well-defined countermeasures to be executed that make the total outcome of the job a success.

An example is a situation that starts with a test for the existence of a file. If the test fails, get it by FTP; and if this succeeds, load it into the database. In this case, the first step can fail and go to the step that gets the file. As there is no other action possible when the FTP action fails, this should raise a Scheduler event that triggers—for example—a notification action. The same should happen when the load fails.

In other third-party scheduling packages, I have seen these notification actions implemented as part of the chain definitions because they lack a Scheduler event queue. In such packages, messages are sent by mail in extra chain steps. In the Oracle Scheduler, this queue is present and is very useful for us. Compared to 10g, nothing has changed in 11g. An event monitoring package can de-queue from the `SCHEDULER$_EVENT_QUEUE` variable into a `sys.scheduler$_event_info` type variable. The definition is shown in the following screenshot:

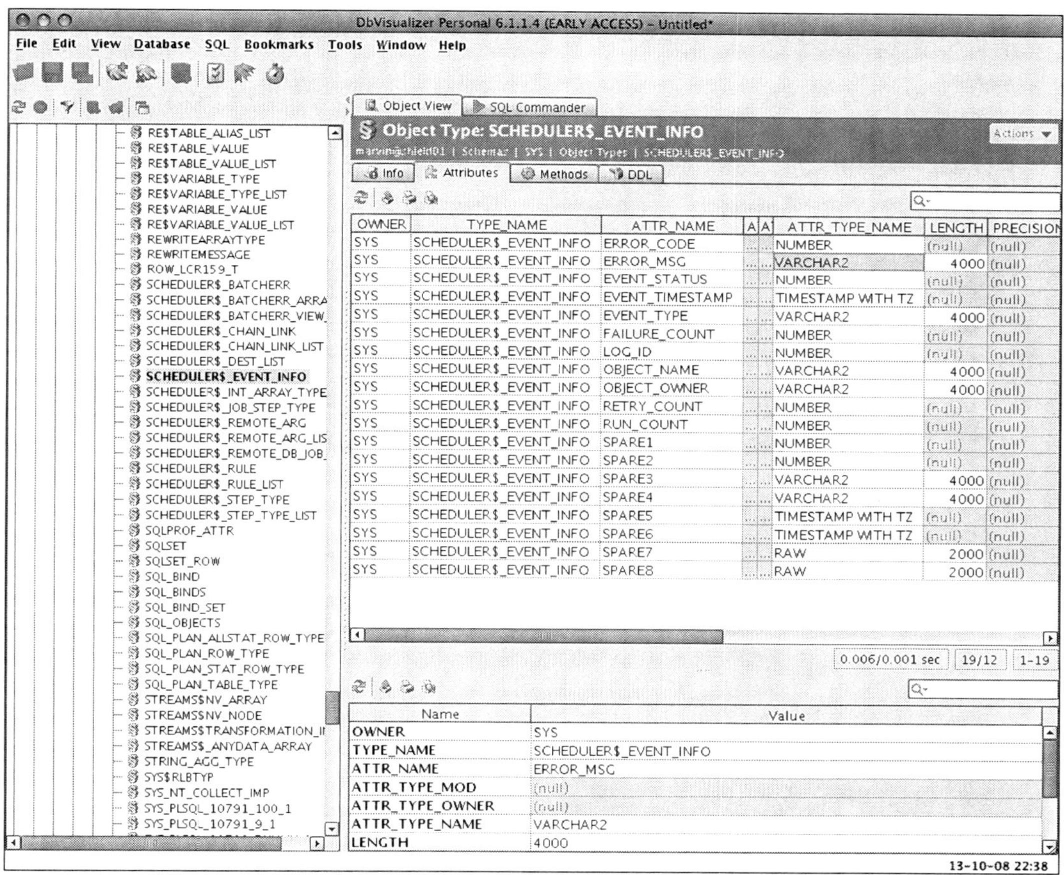

What you can do with an event handler is up to your imagination. The following DB Console screenshot shows the interface that can be used to specify which events to raise:

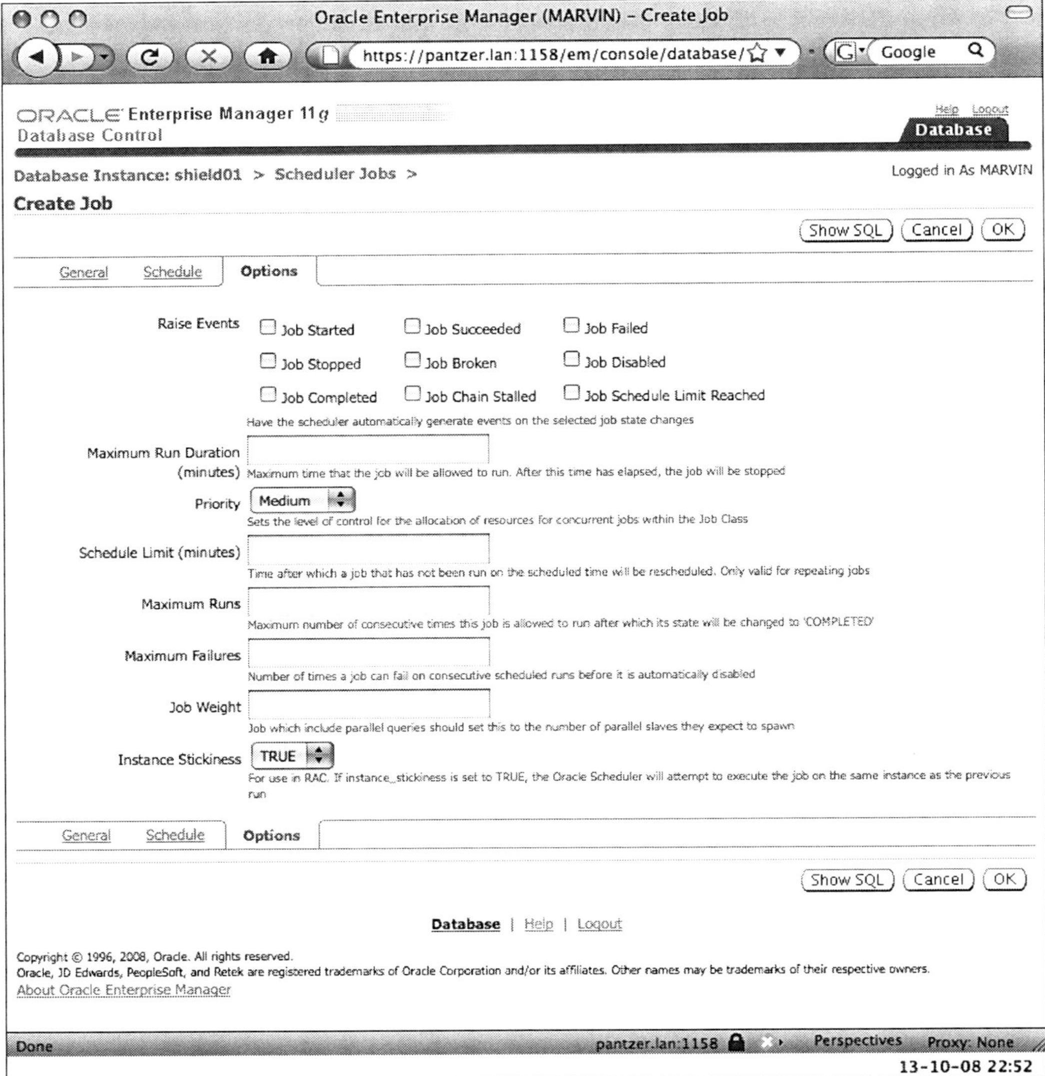

It is easy to generate an event for every possible event listed above and have the handler decide (by the rules defined in tables) what to do. This does sound a little creepy, but it is not very different from having a table that can be used as a lookup for the job found in the event message where—most of the time—a notification mail is sent, or not sent. Sometimes, a user wants to get a message when a job starts running; and most of the time, they want a message when a job ends.

In a chain, it is especially important to be able to tell in which step the event happened and what *that* step was *supposed* to do. In the event message, only the job name is present and so you have to search a bit to find the name of the step that failed.

For this, we can use the `LOG_ID` to find the step name in the `SCHEDULER_JOB_LOGS` (`user/dba/all_SCHEDULER_JOB_LOG`) view, where the step name is listed as `JOB_SUBNAME`. The following query can be used to find the `step_name` from the `dba all_scheduler_log` view, assuming that the event message is received in `msg`:

```
select job_subname from all_scheduler_job_log where
log_id = msg.log_id;
```

To enable the delivery of all the events a job can generate, we can set the `raise_events` attribute to a value of:

```
dbms_scheduler.job_started + dbms_scheduler.job_succeeded +
dbms_scheduler.job_failed + dbms_scheduler.job_broken +
dbms_scheduler.job_completed + dbms_scheduler.job_stopped +
dbms_scheduler.job_sch_lim_reached + dbms_scheduler.job_disabled +
dbms_scheduler.job_chain_stalled
```

Or in short, we can set it to: `dbms_scheduler.job_all_events`.

There are many things that can be called events. In the job system, there are basically two types of events: events caused by jobs (which we already discussed) and events that makes a job execute.

Event-based scheduling

On many occasions, a calendar will do fine for scheduling jobs. However, there are situations that require an immediate action and which cannot wait for the next activation based on a calendar. An example might be of a user who logs on to the database and then, using a logon trigger, more actions are executed.

Another example could be a situation in which we want a backup server to be utilized to the maximum, but not beyond that. We schedule all the backups independent of each other and have each backup raise an event when ready, which tells the system that another backup can go ahead. By letting the backup jobs wait for an event that essentially flags "there is backup capacity available now", we make sure that a backup does not take longer than needed. We also make sure that the backup system is pushed to the highest throughput.

When we just use a preset date and time to start the backups, chances are that more backups are running at the same time (possibly caused by the growth of one or more databases, which is potentially causing their backups to be longer than anticipated). On the other hand, when we make sure that more backups are never ever run at the same time, we will likely have lots of idle time in the backup system.

This is a reason enough to learn how we can make good use of events. However, there are a few things we need to do. It essentially comes down to:

- Creating a queue and defining a payload for that queue
- Having a process that puts the message on the queue
- Coupling one or more job definition(s) to the queue

Again, this gives a kind of control that is hard to find in third-party scheduling packages.

Event messages are placed on an event queue and this is handled by AQ. So we need to call the AQ packages and for that we require `DBMS_AQ` and `DBMS_AQADM`. In the days before Oracle 10g, we needed to set the `AQ_TM_PROCESSES` parameter to a non-zero value to work. Since Oracle 10g, this is no longer the case and we can leave the `AQ_TM_PROCESSES` value to zero.

First, make sure we can use AQ.

```
select grantee, privilege, table_name
from dba_tab_privs
where table_name in ( 'DBMS_AQ', 'DBMS_AQADM')
and grantee = 'MARVIN';
/
```

The expected output is as shown in the following screenshot:

```
SQL> select grantee, privilege, table_name
from dba_tab_privs
where table_name in ( 'DBMS_AQ', 'DBMS_AQADM')
and grantee = 'MARVIN'
/
  2    3    4    5
GRANTEE                        PRIVILEGE                                TABLE_NAME
------------------------------ ---------------------------------------- ------------------------------
MARVIN                         EXECUTE                                  DBMS_AQ
MARVIN                         EXECUTE                                  DBMS_AQADM

SQL>
```

If this query does not show **MARVIN** having the **EXECUTE** privileges on both `DBMS_AQ` and `DBMS_AQADM`, we need to give them to our user.

As a DBA, execute the following:

```
grant execute on dbms_aq    to marvin;
grant execute on dbms_aqadm to marvin;
grant select on dba_aq_agents to marvin;
grant create type to marvin;
alter user marvin quota unlimited on users;
--/
begin
  dbms_aqadm.grant_system_privilege ('ENQUEUE_ANY', 'marvin', FALSE);
  dbms_aqadm.grant_system_privilege ('DEQUEUE_ANY', 'marvin', FALSE);
  dbms_aqadm.grant_system_privilege ('MANAGE_ANY', 'marvin', TRUE);
end;
/
```

This makes sure that `marvin` has enough privileges to be able to create and use queues. Now connect as `marvin`, create an object type that we can use to put a message on the queue, and read from the queue later on.

```
connect marvin/panic
create or replace type bckup_msgt as object ( msg varchar2(20) )
/
```

This defines a type consisting of one msg field of 20-character length. This is the type we will be using in the queue for which we create a queue table next:

```
--/
begin
  dbms_aqadm.create_queue_table
    (
      queue_table              => 'bckup_qt',
      queue_payload_type       => 'bckup_msgt',
      multiple_consumers       => TRUE
    );
  dbms_aqadm.create_queue
    (
      queue_name               => 'bckup_q',
      queue_table              => 'bckup_qt'
    );
  dbms_aqadm.start_queue ( queue_name => 'bckup_q' ) ;
end ;
/
```

This creates a queue table called bckup_qt, which contains messages defined by bckup_msgt. After that, bckup_q starts immediately.

The following objects show up in the schema, which are created to support the queue table:

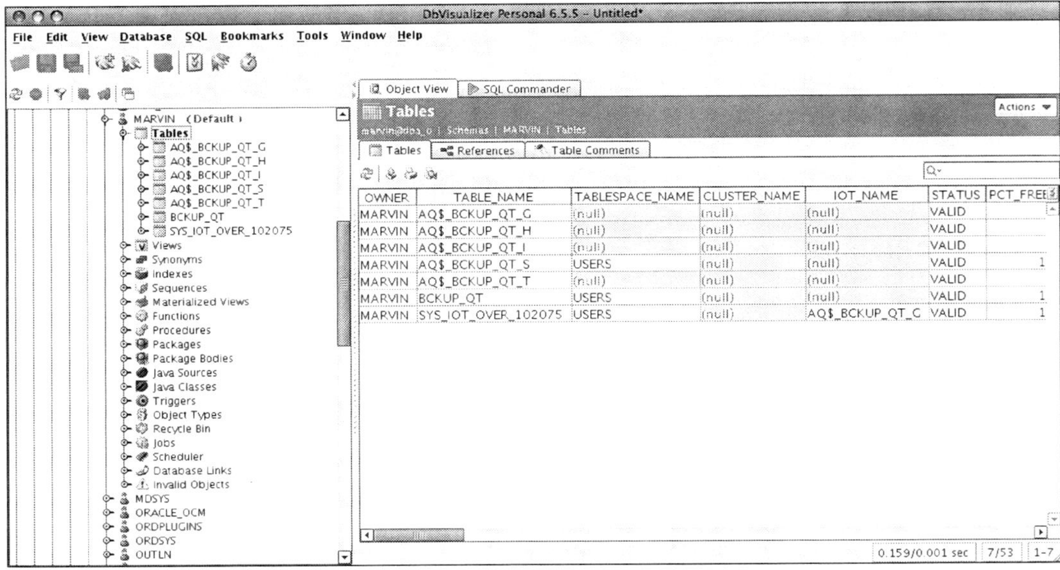

This also explains why **MARVIN** needs quota on his default tablespace.

The queue definitions part is ready. Now, we can tie a job to the queue. First, create a job as follows:

```
--/
BEGIN
 sys.dbms_scheduler.create_job
  (
  job_name             => '"MARVIN"."BCKUP_01"',
  job_type             => 'EXECUTABLE',
  job_action           => '/home/oracle/bin/rman.sh',
  event_condition      => 'tab.user_data.msg=''GO''',
  queue_spec           => '"MARVIN"."BCKUP_Q"',
  start_date           => systimestamp at time zone 'Europe/Amsterdam',
  job_class            => '"LONGER"',
  comments             => 'backup a database',
  auto_drop            => FALSE,
  number_of_arguments => 1,
  enable               => FALSE
  );
 sys.dbms_scheduler.set_attribute
  (
  name                 => '"MARVIN"."BCKUP_01"',
  attribute            => 'raise_events',
  value                => dbms_scheduler.job_started +
                          dbms_scheduler.job_succeeded +
                          dbms_scheduler.job_failed +
                          dbms_scheduler.job_broken +
                          dbms_scheduler.job_completed +
                          dbms_scheduler.job_stopped +
                          dbms_scheduler.job_sch_lim_reached +
                          dbms_scheduler.job_disabled +
                          dbms_scheduler.job_chain_stalled
  );
 sys.dbms_scheduler.set_job_argument_value
  (
  job_name             => '"MARVIN"."BCKUP_01"',
  argument_position    => 1,
  argument_value       => 'db_01'
  );
 DBMS_SCHEDULER.SET_ATTRIBUTE
  (
  name                 => '"MARVIN"."BCKUP_01"',
  attribute            => 'destination',
  value                => 'pantzer:15021'
  );
```

```
DBMS_SCHEDULER.SET_ATTRIBUTE
    (
      name          => '"MARVIN"."BCKUP_01"',
      attribute     => 'credential_name',
      value         => '"MARVIN"."JOBS_CRED2"'
    );
END;
/
```

This is just a simple remote external job that calls an RMAN script with an argument for the database to back up. As the backup will take longer than a few seconds, it looks obvious to put it in the `job_class` called `LONGER` that we defined a while ago. The queue that is coupled to this job is the queue we defined before. It is `bckup_q` as defined by the `queue_spec` parameter. As soon as the `GO` message appears in the payload of the queue, *all* of the jobs that listen to this queue and those waiting for this `GO` message will get started. The code listed for the `MARVIN` job can also be put together using DB Console. In the following **Schedule** screen, select **Event** as **Schedule Type**:

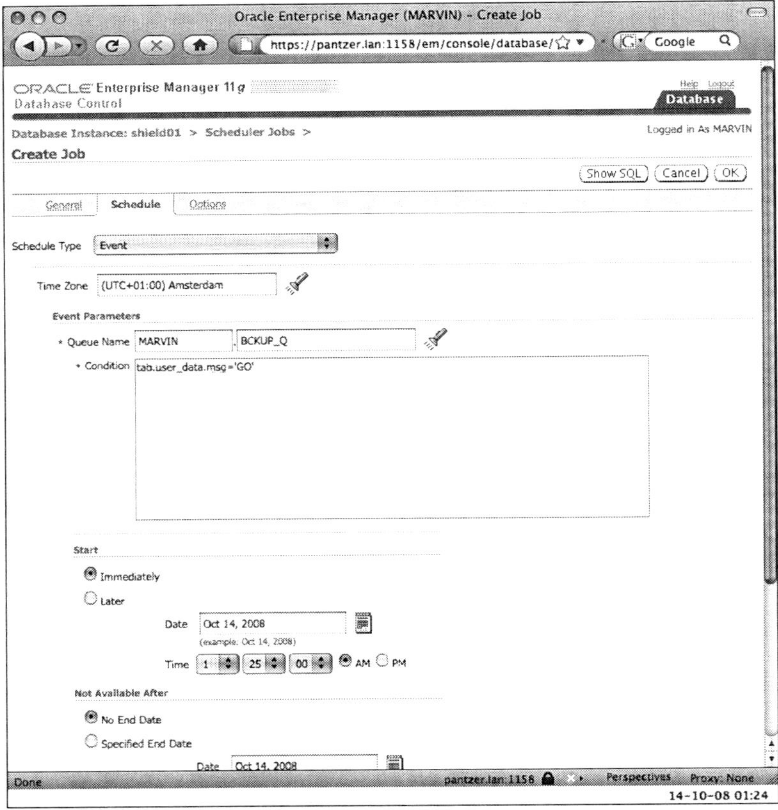

As the job was not **Enabled**, it now looks like the following:

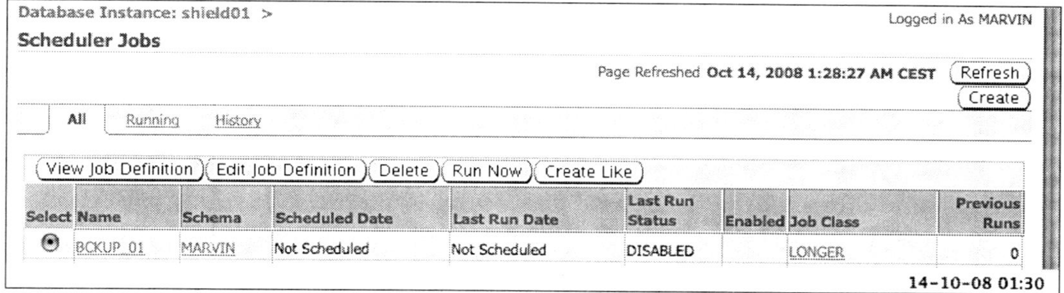

So, let's enable the job:

```
--/
BEGIN
  sys.dbms_scheduler.enable( '"MARVIN"."BCKUP_01"' );
END;
/
```

This produces the following:

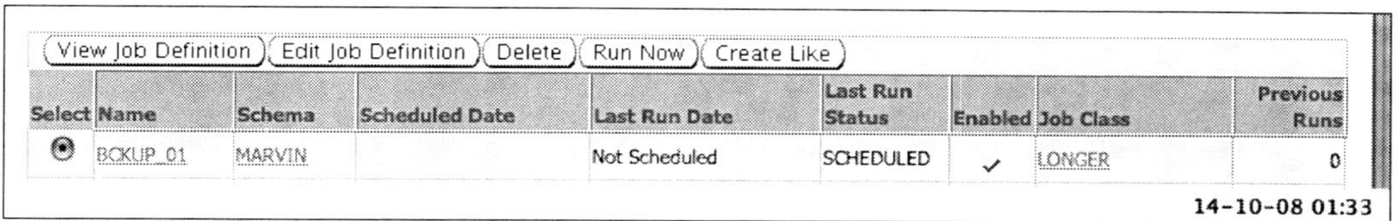

The job is currently scheduled, but not on a date. All we need to do now is have someone put a `GO` message in the `bckup_q`.

```
--/
declare
  my_msgid RAW(16);
  props dbms_aq.message_properties_t;
  enqopts dbms_aq.enqueue_options_t;
begin
  sys.dbms_aq.enqueue('marvin.bckup_q', enqopts, props,
                      marvin.bckup_msgt('GO'), my_msgid);
end;
/
commit;
```

The result is that *all* of the jobs waiting for the `GO` message are started at the same time. With the health of the backup system in mind, it would be wiser to query the jobs view, find the backup job that was scheduled first, and give that job its specific event. In that case, the `BCKUP_01` job will wait for the message **BCKUP_01**; and `BCKUP_02` will wait for the message "BCKUP_02".

Another option is that Oracle can allow us to define an event that is delivered to exactly one waiting job at a time. An enhancement request has been filed for this. It will make this kind of waiting a bit easier because normal queuing behavior is then saved. This means that things such as job priorities will be honored. When we define a separate event for every job, we have manual control but we cannot influence the selection order of the jobs in the queue, for example, by raising the priority of a job.

When a backup is ready, the backup system can handle the next backup. We can utilize the `enqueue` operation by putting our next `GO` message into the queue in the epilogue of the backup script. However, what will happen if the script crashes? The next backup will never be released. Again, a smarter location for this code would be in an event handler routine that just waits for termination messages from the Scheduler event queue. As soon as it sees the termination of a backup, it can decide to call in the next one by giving that waiting job a signal at its location.

Summary

This chapter gave you a quick look at the two basic types of events that play a role in the Scheduler: the event generated by status changes in a running job and the event that causes a job to run. Both are very important factors in the power of the Scheduler. The objects that we have discussed in the chapter are:

- How we can schedule time-based and event-based jobs
- How jobs can generate events
- How jobs can wait for events to get the job running
- How to listen to events
- How to generate events
- How to get the payload of an event (de-queue)
- How to find the step name that caused the event to happen
- Why we need quota when using a user event queue
- What privileges we need to be able to use scheduler events
- What is the advantage of monitoring jobs using the event system
- Which events a job can cause
- How to write a short form containing all possible events

Scheduler is an impressive tool that enables us to build complex systems. In the next chapter, we will see a few tricks to help you when debugging it.

7
Debugging the Scheduler

As we all know, Murphy was an optimist. He said that if anything can possibly go wrong, it will. So, we can apply Murphy's Law to our Scheduler world and create a new law—"If anything can act differently from what is expected, and things probably will, start checking the system." There are a few files in the system that are critical for the working of the Scheduler, and their working is more critical for external jobs than for jobs that stay inside the database. Let's look at some of these critical files across platform versions—there have been lots of changes since the initial 10.2.0.1 release. Then, we will step through a few issues that might surprise even scripters who are familiar with the platform. Whenever an Oracle release is important, it will be listed separately.

Unix—all releases

Something that has not been made very clear in the Oracle Scheduler documentation is that redirection cannot be used in jobs (<, >, >>, |, &&, ||). Therefore, many developers have tried to use it. So, let's keep in mind that we cannot use redirection, not in 11g as well as older releases of the database.

The scripts must be executable, so don't forget to *set* the execution bits. This might seem like knocking down an open door, but it's easily forgotten.

The user (who is the process owner of the external job and is `nobody:nobody` by default) should be able to execute the `$ORACLE_HOME/bin/extjob` file. In Unix, this means that the user should have execution permissions on all the parent directories of this file. This is not something specific to Oracle; it's just the way a Unix file system works. Really! Check it out. Since 10gR1, Oracle does not give execution privileges to others. A simple test for this is to try starting SQL*Plus as a user who is neither the Oracle installation user, nor a member of the DBA group—but a regular user. If you get all kinds of errors, then it implies that the permissions are not correct, assuming that the environment variables (`ORACLE_HOME` and `PATH`) are set up correctly.

The `$ORACLE_HOME/install/changePerm.sh` script can fix the permissions within `ORACLE_HOME` (for 10g). In Oracle 11g, this again changed and is no longer needed. The Scheduler interprets the return code of external jobs and records it in the `*_scheduler_job_run_details` view. This interpretation can be very misleading, especially when using your own exit codes. For example, when you code your script to check the number of arguments, and code an `exit 1` when you find the incorrect number of arguments, the error number is translated to **ORA-27301: OS failure message:No such file or directory** by Oracle using the code in `errno.h`. In 11g, the Scheduler also records the return code in the `error#` column. This lets us recognize the error code better and find where it is raised in the script that ran, when the error codes are unique within the script.

When Oracle started with Scheduler, there were some quick changes. Here are the most important changes listed that could cause us problems when the definitions of the mentioned files are not exactly as listed:

- **10.2.0.1**: `$ORACLE_HOME/bin/extjob` should be owned by the user who runs the jobs (process owner) and have `6550` permissions (`setuid` process owner). In a regular notation, that is what `ls -l` shows, and the privileges should be `-r-sr-s---`.
- **10.2.0.2**: `$ORACLE_HOME/rdbms/admin/externaljob.ora` should be owned by root. This file is owned by the Oracle user (the user who installed Oracle) and the Oracle install group with `644` permissions or `-rw-r--r--`, as shown by `ls -l`. This file controls which operating system user is going to be the process owner, or which user is going to run the job. The default contents of this file are as shown in the following screenshot:

```
oracle@pantzer:/data/app/oracle/product/rdbms/11.1.0.6 — ssh — 80×38
[oracle@pantzer 11.1.0.6]$ cat rdbms/admin/externaljob.ora
# $Header: externaljob.ora 16-dec-2005.20:47:13 rramkiss Exp $
#
# Copyright (c) 2005, Oracle. All rights reserved.
# NAME
#   externaljob.ora
# FUNCTION
#   This configuration file is used by dbms_scheduler when executing external
#   (operating system) jobs. It contains the user and group to run external
#   jobs as. It must only be writable by the owner and must be owned by root.
#   If extjob is not setuid then the only allowable run_user
#   is the user Oracle runs as and the only allowable run_group is the group
#   Oracle runs as.
#
# NOTES
#   For Porters: The user and group specified here should be a lowly privileged
#                user and group for your platform. For Linux this is nobody
#                and nobody.
# MODIFIED
#     rramkiss   12/09/05 -  Creation
#
##############################################################################
# External job execution configuration file externaljob.ora
#
# This file is provided by Oracle Corporation to help you customize
# your RDBMS installation for your site.  Important system parameters
# are discussed, and default settings given.
#
# This configuration file is used by dbms_scheduler when executing external
# (operating system) jobs. It contains the user and group to run external
# jobs as. It must only be writable by the owner and must be owned by root.
# If extjob is not setuid then the only allowable run_user
# is the user Oracle runs as and the only allowable run_group is the group
# Oracle runs as.

run_user = nobody
run_group = nobody
[oracle@pantzer 11.1.0.6]$
                                                              17-02-09 22:21
```

`$ORACLE_HOME/bin/extjob` must be the `setuid` root (permissions `4750` or `-rwsr-x---`) and executable for the Oracle install group, where the `setuid` root means that the root should be the owner of the file. This also means that while executing this binary, we temporarily get root privileges on the system.

`$ORACLE_HOME/bin/extjobo` should have normal `755` or `-rwxr-xr-x` permissions, and be owned by the normal Oracle software owner and group. If this file is missing, just copy it from `$ORACLE_HOME/bin/extjob`.

On AIX, this is the first release that has external job support.

- **11g release**: In 11g, the same files as in 10.2.0.2 exist with the same permissions. But `$ORACLE_HOME/bin/jssu` is owned by root and the Oracle install group with the `setuid` root (permissions `4750` or `-rwsr-x---`).

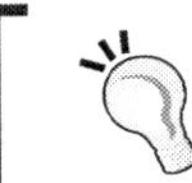

It is undoubtedly best to stop using the old 10g external jobs and migrate to the 11g external jobs with credentials as soon as possible.

The security of the remote external jobs is better because of the use of credentials instead of falling back to the contents of a single file in `$ORACLE_HOME/`, and the flexibility is much better. In 11g, the process owner of the remote external jobs is controlled by the credential and not by a file.

Windows usage

On Windows, this is a little easier with regard to file system security. The `OracleJobscheduler` service must exist in a running state, and the user who runs this service should have the `Logon as batch job` privilege.

A `.bat` file cannot be run directly, but should be called as an argument of `cmd.exe`, for example:

```
--/
BEGIN
  DBMS_SCHEDULER.create_job
    (
      job_name              => 'env_windows',
      job_type              => 'EXECUTABLE',
      number_of_arguments   => 2,
      job_action            => 'C:\windows\system32\cmd.exe',
      auto_drop             => FALSE,
      enabled               => FALSE
    );
  DBMS_SCHEDULER.set_job_argument_value('env_windows',1,'/c');
  DBMS_SCHEDULER.set_job_argument_value('env_windows',2,
                                    'd:\temp\test.bat');
end;
/
```

This job named `env_windows` calls `cmd.exe`, which eventually runs the script named `test.bat` that we created in `d:\temp\`. When the script we want to call needs arguments, they should be listed from argument number `3` onwards.

Bugs

In addition to the permissions on these files, there also happen to be bugs in the Scheduler. If you ever plan to use chains, apply the patch for bug `5705385`. It should be fixed in 11.1.0.7 and 10.2.0.5, and is available as one-off patch for 10.2.0.3 and 10.2.0.4. This bug causes the situation in which a running chain exists without a running job. If you don't have this patch and you start a job that is running a chain, it ends successfully. The next run terminates upon startup. The third start will have the chain running again and the fourth run will again terminate upon startup.

By definition, no running chain can exist when there is no running job that runs the chain. Without this fix, the situation is a little different; a chain can exist in `*_SCHEDULER_RUNNING_CHAINS` without a job in `*_SCHEDULER_RUNNING_JOBS`.

Starting the job again cleans this situation up. In case you cannot apply this patch, it is possible to use the job event queue to trigger the detection of this situation and have it cleaned up again. Let's see how this happens:

```
procedure kick_chain_without_job
is
cursor bugs is
  select job_name, chain_name, start_date
  from user_scheduler_running_chains c
  where not exists (select 'x'
                    from user_scheduler_running_jobs j
                    where j.job_name= c.job_name)
  and start_date=(select min(start_date)
                  from user_scheduler_running_chains rc
                  where c.chain_name = rc.chain_name)
  order by start_date;
r bugs%rowtype;
begin
  open bugs;
  fetch bugs into r;
  if bugs%found
  then
    loop
    -- insert into event_log (dat_sys,error_msg,object_name,
                                                object_owner)
       -- values (sysdate,'kick '||r.job_name||' to
                             end',r.job_name,owner);
      dbms_scheduler.run_job (r.job_name,false);
      fetch bugs into r;
      if bugs%notfound
      then
        exit;
```

```
        end if;
      end loop;
    end if;
    close bugs;
  end kick_chain_without_job;
```

This code was called from the general event catcher routine and was able to deal with this specific bug. The code checks for all occurrences of a job in the buggy state and gives them a little kick. The result is that the situation is as it was intended to be—the job is not running, the chain is not running, and when the job is started again, it really does start.

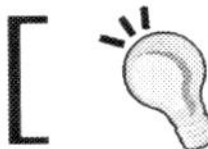

Whenever available, it is advisable to implement the patch 5705385.

Again, in 10gR2, there is a problem when using Resource Manager. The combination of Oracle Scheduler and Oracle Resource Manager should make a very powerful team because this would enable us to schedule jobs whenever we want, without having to worry about the load on the system. In the Resource Manager, we configure how we want to prioritize jobs, depending on where the resource consumer groups are mapped on. At the moment, the scheduling stops after a few hundred jobs have been processed; and there seems to be no way to get these jobs running other than disabling Resource Manager by activating the default Resource Manager plan, `internal_plan`. This can happen when you use the `job_weight` attribute for the jobs. The `job_weight` attribute is used as a multiplier when selecting a job to be executed. For unknown reasons, the Scheduler stops selecting jobs when the active session pool is relatively small. At first sight, the usage of `job_weight` may seem a smart choice. However, the problem is that the usage is not clearly defined, and in the end we can better forget about this attribute.

In 10gR2, it does happen every now and then that locks block the `cjq0` process. This job is the job queue coordinator, so it does have an impact. A workaround for this is to kill the `cjq0` process. It will automatically get restarted.

Also, on all the releases and platforms until version 11.1.0.7, `alertlog` messages may appear about restarting the dead `cjq0` process with `ORA-07445` and `ORA-0600` errors, if the call stack is for:

- `ORA-7445` [`kslgetl()`]: `kslgetl kkjqspl kkjcjexe kkjssrh ksbcti ksbabs ksbrdp`
- `ORA-7445` [`kkjqfre()`]: `kkjcjpr kkjssrh ksbcti ksbabs ksbrdp`
- `ORA-600` [`ksl_invalid_latch`], [`kslges`]: `kslges kslgetl kkjqspl kkjcjexe kkjssrh ksbcti ksbabs ksbrdp`

This can very well be the bug `7147411` that is fixed in 11.1.0.7. If you are hit by this bug, apply the patch for it. It is also available for 10g.

Another funny bug is the one in which the `cjq0` process ends up in a loop if any other database exists with the same name as the active window. In that case, the solution is to rename or drop that object and bounce the database. You can use the following query to check if you have this problem:

```
select object_name, object_type
from dba_objects
where exists (select window_name
        from dba_scheduler_windows
        where window_name = object_name and object_type <> 'WINDOW');
```

If this query returns rows, take the mentioned action. The problem is one of the effects of the bug `5911728`. The other symptom is that you get `ORA-01422` when you try to drop a chain that has the same name as another database object. To prevent this, make sure that all your chain names and chain rule names are unique within the database. This problem is fixed in 10.2.0.5 and 11gR2.

Sometimes it can happen that in `alertlog` you see `ORA-0600` when starting the `cjq0` process. The `cjq0` process does start, but the error is strange and should normally not occur. This is the bug `7649136` that is fixed in 10.2.0.5 and 11gR2. The problem is a very rare condition with special timing involved where the `NULL` pointer happens to pass through.

When you are switching a window, the `cjq0` process may get `ORA-1000`—that is, `ORA-01000: maximum open cursors exceeded`. This could very well be the bug `8285404` that is fixed in 11gR2 with a few backports available for 11.1.0.7.

In 11.1.0.7, there still are some support procedures in `dbms_scheduler` that are not working as expected, especially on remote external jobs. Most of these problems are solved in 11gR2 and for most problems, a backport is available. When calling `copy_job`, you can get an exception instead of a copy of the job if it happens to be a remote external job. When the copy does take place, it is not a complete copy; everything that has to do with the fact that it is a remote external job is left uncopied.

The definition of a job allows us to temporarily disable a job by setting the `end_date` attribute to a date in the future. If `end_date` is set and it is crossed, the job is disabled. To re-enable the job, set a new start date and ensure that the `end_date` is `NULL` or set it further in the future than the current system date. The `NULL` case does not work. Setting the `end_date` to a date very far in the future is a reasonable workaround for this.

In all the releases so far, there are problems with reading job events from the Scheduler event queue. The problem is that some events are repeatedly read from the queue. When building a system that reacts upon events, this is very awkward. The bug in question is `7593937`; the patch is available for a backport to 11.1.0.7 and is fixed in 11gR2.

Remote external jobs do get an SSL certificate when they register to the database that they are supposed to perform work for. In the current (11.1.0.6) Scheduler Agent, there is a little bug that generates a certificate that expires after 90 days. A workaround is to re-register the agent. The problem is fixed in 11.1.0.7. If you are running the 11.1.0.6 agent, you will have to upgrade it and re-register the agent. The upgrade procedure is explained in *Chapter 5, Getting Out of the Database*.

All of the bugs I found were generic for all the platforms. This list is certainly not a complete list, but it will be usable for many readers who are planning to use the Scheduler. The intention of this list is not to scare people away from the Scheduler, but more to show that problems are solved by Oracle development when we provide them with a case.

Job environment

Don't make any assumptions about the environment your job runs in. Oracle has made lots of changes with regards to the environment the job gets when it is launched outside the database. In 9i, there is a Java method that enables us to start a job on the operating system that has lots of information in the environment. This environment got poorer with each upgrade. In earlier releases, ORACLE_HOME, PATH, and ORACLE_SID were defined and PWD was in $ORACLE_HOME/dbs. In 10g, these three variables disappeared. In 11gR1, the current directory of processes scheduled (using the remote external job agent), is the current directory at the time the agent started. So, you should not rely on any variable in the environment.

Before you start using external jobs, think about how the job should define its own environment. Don't forget about the **ulimits**, they also tend to change between releases. Even something as simple as a change in the stack size (`limit -s`) can have surprising consequences for some programs. The same is true for the working directory. In Oracle 9i, the working directory was `$ORACLE_HOME/dbs`. In 10g, this changed to root (/) and in 11g, we are back in the directory from where we started the remote job agent. Don't be surprised if this changes back to root in a future release.

To see what environment your script has to cope with, a simple test script could be helpful. Things to include here are:

```
echo hostname is:
/bin/hostname
echo ulimits are:
ulimit -a
echo the environment is:
/usrbin/env
echo connected user is:
/usr/bin/id
```

Checks to do in the database

If a job does not run, check the enabled state of the job, the chain, and the program(s) it uses. Jobs can become invalid during normal object invalidation actions such as changing objects on which the job depends.

Check the chain definition. In `dbms_scheduler`, there is now a procedure that analyzes a chain, and then deposits the results in a `pl_sql` table and server output. This can be very useful and some example code is shown as follows:

```
--/
declare
rl sys.scheduler$_rule_list := sys.scheduler$_rule_list();
stl sys.scheduler$_step_type_list := sys.scheduler$_step_type_list();
spl sys.scheduler$_chain_link_list:= sys.scheduler$_chain_link_list();
begin
  select SYS.SCHEDULER$_RULE(rule_name, condition, action)
  bulk collect into rl
  from user_scheduler_chain_rules
  where chain_name = 'YOUR_CHAIN_TO_CHECK';
  select SYS.SCHEDULER$_step_type(step_name, step_type)
  bulk collect into stl
  from user_scheduler_chain_steps
  where chain_name = 'YOUR_CHAIN_TO_CHECK';
  dbms_scheduler.analyze_chain(
                              chain_name  => 'YOUR_CHAIN_TO_CHECK',
                              rules       =>   rl, steps    =>   stl,
                              step_pairs  => spl
                              );
  for i in spl.first .. spl.last
  loop
    dbms_output.put_line(i||':'||spl(i).first_step_name||
                        ''||spl(i).second_step_name);
  end loop;
end;
/
```

The following screenshot shows sample output of this code:

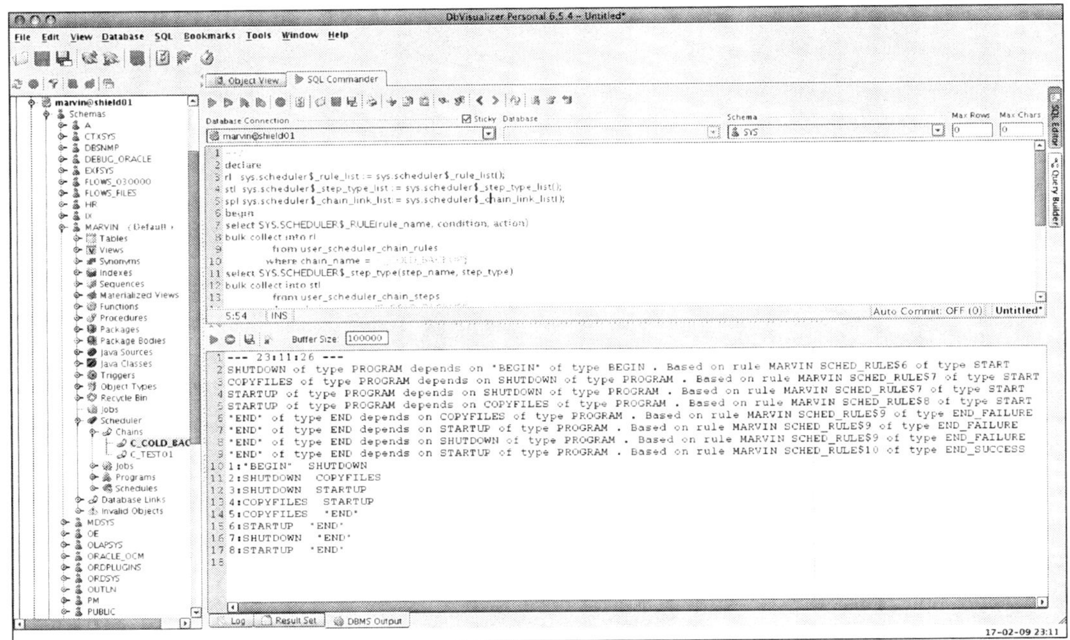

The output shows where the chain could start and what the next steps could be. Sometimes, a chain rule cannot be evaluated immediately because a *condition* is not (yet) true. In such a case, the chain will stall and never reach an end. This status can be read from the `*_scheduler_running_chains` view and it could very well be the case that only a manual intervention can help the chain into the next step. In a case where a condition might become true after a step ends, the chain rules will only be evaluated again if the evaluation interval for that chain is set manually by calling the `evaluate_running_chain` procedure. It is OK to do this during development and debugging, but normally one is expected to use `evaluation_interval` in the `create_chain` procedure, or set this attribute using the `alter_chain` procedure.

When things get bad, and a forced or timed evaluation does not enable us to achieve our goal, there is an even more powerful tool that can help. It is the `alter_running_chain` procedure. Using this procedure, we can set the state of a job step to whatever we want. Again, this is nice for development and debugging, but normally one would expect the rules to be complete enough to handle all the situations. Here is an example showing the use of this procedure:

```
--/
dbms_scheduler.alter_running_chain('JOB','step_03',
                                   'state', 'SUCCEEDED');
/
```

This is useful if step_03 failed and there was no rule for this possible occurrence. We can also start the following step without bothering with step_03 at all:

```
--/
dbms_scheduler.alter_running_chain('JOB','step_04', 'state',
                                                    'RUNNING');
/
```

Here we just made step_04 running and we kept the status of step_03 as it was. This is very powerful, so use it with care. Otherwise, before you know it your problems would have grown instead of getting solved like you had hoped. Without knowing the other rules of the chain, you might not get what you wanted to achieve. What should be the end result of step_03 that has a failed status and step_04 that has a success status? Check the rules for the chain you are messing with.

A little more difficult are the situations in which a chain runs another chain. In this case, the job_name has to be built up from the parent_job_name until the sub[_sub,...]_job_name (to identify the chain) has to be altered.

Let's take an example. A job JOB01 starts a chain CH01. The chain gets its own job that runs the chain, which is the same as that for normal job steps. This sub_job_name can be found in *_scheduler_running_chains. In order to manipulate a step in the chain CH01, we need to specify it as owner.job_name.job_subname for alter_running_chain to work on the right chain. In this case, it would look as: JOB01.CH01

As always, test your jobs, test your chains, and make sure that every possible result of every chain step can be handled by the accompanying set of chain rules. When all the rules and the mentioned patches are in place, there is not much to worry about.

If a job stops being started and it is supposed to run under the resource control, you might get the job running by effectively disabling the Resource Manager by enabling internal_plan. This assumes that the job still has the status SCHEDULED.

In a **Real Application Clusters** (**RAC**) database, if a job is not running when expected, check in which instance the job ran for the last time and check if the **instance stickiness** has been used. If the instance_stickiness job attribute has been defined, Scheduler will only run the job when the instance where the job ran the last time is running. According to the Scheduler documentation, the job will be run by another instance if the instance to which the job sticks is not able to run the job for a significant time. And, the problem is that there is no definition given for the term "significant".

The checks listed here should normally get you up and running again but the list is not complete. No living creature can ever meet every possible problem, so over time this list will evolve. When development continues working on the issues, we can expect this list to shrink in the later releases.

Summary

Debugging jobs is no more difficult than debugging normal PL/SQL or scripts. Especially for the scripts that run as external jobs, don't forget the limitations of the environment definitions. Scripters used to scripting for cron know how to handle a "poor" environment. I hope this chapter gave enough tools to start debugging. The next chapter is about a real-life scenario. The things learned here should be very useful in real life. In this chapter, we saw:

- How the file privileges for external jobs should be:
  - In Unix systems using various releases of Oracle
  - In Windows systems
- What the `externaljob.ora` file looks like
- Normal Unix redirection cannot be used in jobs
- Windows scripts should be called using `cmd.exe`
- A list of Scheduler bugs with solutions or workarounds
- How to analyze a job chain using PL/SQL
- How to solve a stalled chain
- How to address a chain step
- How to prevent a stalled chain situation
- What to check in the database when unexpectedly a job does not run
- How to check the environment of a job
- How to cope with problems of the `cjq0` process
- How to get such a job running again

In the next chapter, we will see a few completely worked out examples of how to use the Scheduler in real life.

8 The Scheduler in Real Life

In this chapter, we will see how we can incorporate Oracle Scheduler into real-life scenarios and solve various problems in a variety of ways. The scenarios themselves are not really important, but they are real enough to show the power of Oracle Scheduler.

One of the first things to consider when thinking about what to schedule in the Scheduler database is the statistics collection. This is the collection of the optimizer statistics in the database. The challenge here is to have the statistics run whenever they are needed, without slowing down the business application that is supposed to run on the database.

Another thing to consider is running the backups. For the backups, we can use the remote external job agent. Here, we can use the Scheduler Agent and see how to use the Scheduler events to react on the results of a job. This can be seen as an advanced form of chaining where we do not build a chain as an object definition, but as a chain defined by events that call for actions.

Statistics collection

From Oracle 10g onwards, Oracle has included a job that automatically collects optimizer statistics for us. So, there is no real need to make such a process again. It might look like inventing a different-colored wheel, but it can be useful if you want more control on how the statistics are collected.

For this, we will make a simple package named `sched_stats`. As many readers are more than likely to be still using Oracle 10g, the code that we will use is compatible for Oracle 10g as well as 11g. The package has the following four procedures:

- `schedule_run`
- `run`
- `statob`
- `Drop_jobs`

The schedule_run procedure

The Schedule_run procedure creates the job that is actually scheduled on a twice-daily basis and has all the parameters with defaults that can be overridden:

```
procedure schedule_run
( jobclass    in varchar2 default 'DEFAULT_JOB_CLASS',
  jobname     in varchar2 default 'run_stats',
  sjobprefix  in varchar2 default 'stats_',
  repinterval in varchar2 default'FREQ=DAILY;BYHOUR=5,17;BYMINUTE=4',
  pctchange   in number   default 5);
```

This procedure simplifies the scheduling of the generation run. The result of schedule_run procedure can be replaced by a Grid Control session in which we create a job that calls the run procedure. The schedule_run procedure is most useful when deploying the sched_stats package and the job in many databases using a standard script.

The run procedure

The run procedure generates a single job for every object that is to be analyzed and whenever possible, it uses the cascade option. So in the end, it is possible that when analyzing a table, the indexes that belong to that table are also analyzed. For the partitioned tables, the run procedure generates a job for every partition that needs new statistics, and not for the table by itself. This can save a lot of time. Sometimes a partitioned table has global indexes. If this is the case, such an index has to be analyzed on its own and not as a cascade of the table because we do not make global statistics for the table.

For larger objects, we use a larger degree of parallelism than for small objects. For objects that have no statistics at all, we generate a job with top priority where the other jobs have normal priority. The interface for the run procedure is as follows:

```
procedure run ( stale_pct in number,
                sjob_class  in varchar2 default 'DEFAULT_JOB_CLASS',
                sjob_prefix in varchar2 default null);
```

The job that is generated by the run procedure is of a type PL/SQL and it calls the statob procedure. This procedure makes the actual call to dbms_stats to collect the requested statistics for the specified object. The statob procedure will be detailed next.

The statob procedure

The statob procedure performs the actual analyze the task and is called by the generated jobs. The interface to statob is as follows:

```
procedure statob ( owner in varchar2,
                   object_type    in varchar2,
                   object_name    in varchar2,
                   partition_name in varchar2,
                   psample_pct    in number,
                   pdegree        in number);
```

If you leave all of the defaults in place, it is called by the stats_NNNN jobs that are generated by the run procedure. Every object that is selected by the run procedure will be processed by a job of its own that calls this statob procedure with the parameters it needs.

The drop_jobs procedure

At this point, we may suddenly decide that we do not want the generated jobs to run anymore. In this case, we can call the drop_jobs procedure that drops all the generated jobs that are not running, using the following code:

```
procedure drop_jobs ( sjobprefix in varchar2 default 'stats');
```

In case we don't want the already generated jobs to run, we can call the sched_stats package using the following code:

```
begin
  sched_stats.drop_jobs;
end;
/
```

And this code will take care of removing all generated STATS_NNNN jobs that are not already running. However, this assumes you left all the defaults in place.

Generating the jobs

As mentioned before, the run procedure generates jobs. The jobs get a name that is generated by combining a self-chosen prefix that defaults to STATS, with a sequence number added to it in a call to dbms_scheduler.generate_job_name. This ensures that all the generated job names are unique. The run procedure checks the DBA_TAB_MODIFICATION view and uses this information combined with ALL_TABLES, ALL_TAB_PARTITONS, and ALL_TAB_STATISTICS views to find table or partitions that should be analyzed. A table or partition should be analyzed if more than stale_pct of its rows have been modified, added, or deleted.

A table or partition should not be analyzed if the statistics are already locked for different reasons. One reason for this may be that it enables us to manage the statistics for the locked table by hand (and not by an automated procedure), which works well for most tables.

> Some tables have very irregular behaviors. For instance, during a batch run, a table can be empty while the generation of the `stats` process takes place. After that, the application will see the statistics where the table seems to be empty; whereas in reality, it already has millions of rows loaded. If this is the case, the statistics for such a table have to be managed by the application and should be locked to prevent them from being analyzed by the generic procedures. The problem is that when the optimizer sees that a table has no rows, it will make an execution plan that is different than when it sees that there are a hundred million rows in place. In such a situation where the application has a very big variation in the number of rows during a run, it is smarter to have the application generate the statistics at the appropriate moments.

Let's dive into some pieces of the code to explore how we can generate the jobs.

Firstly, for every table or partition that is selected, we create a separate job with a name that is defined by a given prefix of `sjob_prefix`. The `sjob_prefix` is the prefix that we give during the `schedule_run` procedure call, and the default is `stats_`. The code that generates the job names is:

```
begin
        l_job_name := dbms_scheduler.generate_job_name (sjob_prefix);
```

`generate_job_name` generates a unique job name with the specified prefix followed by a serial number. If the prefix is `STATS_`, the generated name could be `STATS_1` or `STATS_2009`, depending on how often a job name has been generated this way.

As we can only specify a stored procedure as a valid `job_type` and not a package procedure, the generated job is of the type `PLSQL_BLOCK`.

In the PL/SQL block, we will call the `statob` procedure with the parameters needed. The parameters for the `statob` procedure are `owner`, `object_name`, `object_type`, and optionally, `partition_name`. The parallel degree is to be used for sampling and the percentage of the table is to be used for sampling the table. For these kinds of short-lived jobs, we specify `auto_drop = true`, which ensures that the job is dropped at the end of the run. The job class defines how the job will be handled by the Resource Manager and when the job log entries will be purged. The following snippet of code is used to create the job using the generated name and passing it the arguments that eventually will be passed to `dbms_stats`:

```
dbms_scheduler.create_job(job_name => l_job_name,
  job_type => 'PLSQL_BLOCK',
  job_action => 'begin'||'sched_stats.statob('''||i.table_owner||''',
                                          '''||i.table_name||''',
                                      '''||i.partition_name||''',
                                          '||''||i.degree||');
                 end;',
  comments => 'gather stats for '||
  i.table_owner||'.'||i.table_name||' '||i.partition_name,
  job_class => sjob_class,
  auto_drop => true,
  enabled => false);
```

In this PL/SQL block, we simply call the second procedure of the package, STATOB, as it does the actual analysis of the specified table or partition.

If a table or a partition is selected to be analyzed, the segmentsize controls the degree of parallelism that is used to perform the analysis of the object. Jobs have the job_weight attribute. According to the manual, this attribute can be used to do the advanced things involving parallelism. It can be very tempting to use it and assign it the same value as the degree that we use to analyze the object we are working on. It might look like a good idea, but the definition is very vague and when used, it can very well happen that the jobs to run stop being selected. Don't use it until the correct usage is clearly defined.

It does not make much sense to keep these generated jobs for future use, so it is a good idea to make these jobs auto_drop. This means that the job is dropped automatically when it is executed as follows:

```
dbms_scheduler.set_attribute (
                              name        => l_job_name,
                              attribute   => 'auto_drop',
                              value       => true
                              );
```

The job log entries are saved, purged, and controlled by the JOB_CLASS definition or by the global Scheduler attributes.

There is no further schedule. We will just start the job as soon as possible by enabling the job like this:

```
dbms_scheduler.enable (name => l_job_name);
```

When you submit lots of jobs this way, you will notice that after having created a few, the first jobs start running before the generation of the other jobs has completed. How many jobs run together depends on how the active Resource Manager plan is defined. If no Resource Manager plan is active, the number of concurrent jobs will be close to the number of CPUs in the system.

Performing the analysis

The statob procedure performs the actual analysis. I guess there is no need to explain that dbms_stats should be used for this as you all are familiar with the dbms_stats package. Check the "PL/SQL Packages and Types Reference" and "Concepts" manuals for more information. The selection that generates the list of tables and partitions is made in such a way that it only generates the partition statistics for the partitioned tables, and not the global statistics. If all of the partitions of a table have statistics, the table has its statistics derived from the partitions. This is recognizable by the GLOBAL_STATS column of the table that has NO when it falls back to the aggregated partition statistics and YES when the table has been analyzed by itself. The granularity parameter controls for what parts (default, partition, subpartition, or global) of the table the statistics are gathered. In the code, we use the granularity partition. granularity=global means that the statistics are gathered for the complete table. granularity=partition means that only the specified partition is to be analyzed and this is mostly much quicker than analyzing the whole table. Here is the code that is used to call the dbms_stats.gather_table_stats procedure:

```
else
    -- partitioned table, only do the specified partition
    execute immediate 'begin dbms_stats.gather_table_stats'||
                                                 '(ownname => :owner'||
                                                 ',tabname => :table_name'||
                                                ,partname=>:partition_name'||
                                              ',granularity=>''partition'''||
                                                 ',cascade => true'      ||
                                                 ',degree  => :pdegree'  ||
                                                 '); end;'
    using owner, table_name, partition_name, pdegree;
end if;
END statob;
```

Handling the tables that are not partitioned is slightly simpler as no partname and granularity are needed.

Generating the scheduled run

The schedule_run procedure creates a scheduled job that calls the run procedure at the specified STIME on which the statistics collection should start passing the stale_pct, sjob_class, and sjob_prefix to the run procedure as shown in the previous code. We can have this job scheduled just before the batches start at 17:00 hours and near the end of the batch window at 05:00 hours in the morning. This makes sure that the batches get accurate statistics when they start and also guarantees that the online users get accurate statistics when the batches are ready.

The job that is generated by SCHEDULE_RUN has just one moment on the day that it runs. It is easy to change this to whatever you want by modifying the job procedures of dbms_scheduler. When deploying this code to many databases, it should be customized to meet your specific needs.

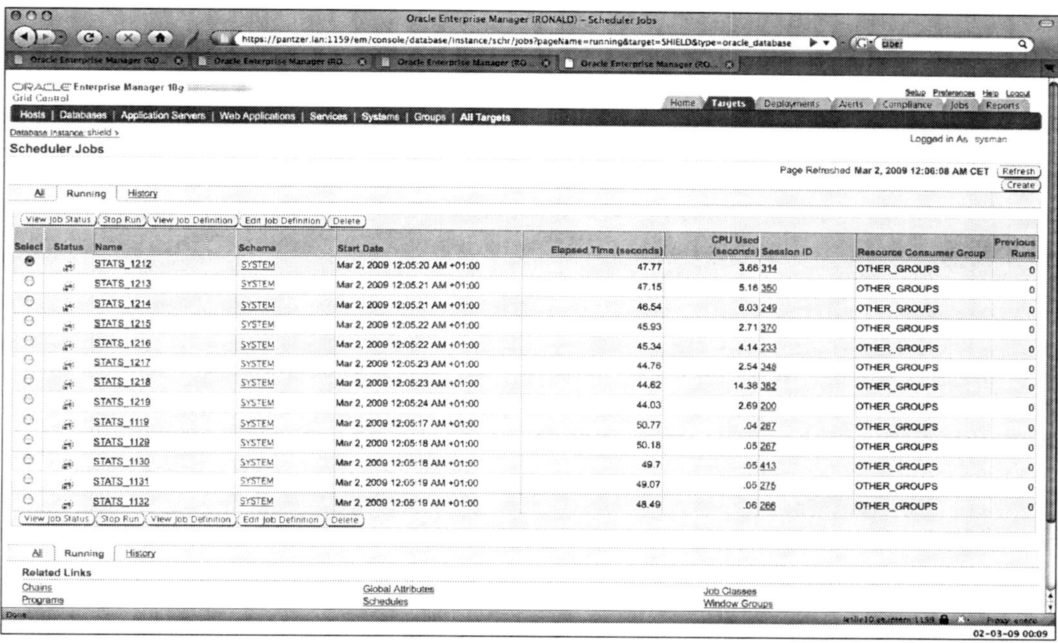

In this **Scheduler Jobs** screen, you can see the statistics collection in action. At this very moment, 13 STATS jobs are active. This will put some load on the system.

At first sight, this approach might seem a little overwhelming, but there is apparently no control on the load that is put on the system. This is where the real power of the Scheduler and Resource Manager combination kicks in. The jobs are defined and when their start time comes, they are queued. As soon as the Resource Manager tells the Scheduler that there is room for an extra job, the Scheduler selects the next job to start. It is completely controlled by the Resource Manager plan and consumer group definitions. This code is in use in data warehouses with a STALE_PCT of 5, and there the statistics are normally gathered within an hour. In the Resource Manager plan, the online users have the same amount of resources as the analyze process. They hardly notice the load that the analyze process puts on the system.

This was a simple example, but don't be fooled as it uses the full power of the product. A slightly more advanced use would be when we look more closely at the backups, as there are a few extra requirements that make this an interesting subject.

Backups

Before we begin, we will need to make sure the databases are running in the ARCHIVELOG mode. We are doing this just to be able to make an online backup, and do it at any arbitrary moment of the day. On many sites, there are databases that do not require full recovery, but they cannot be easily taken offline for a backup. Having the database run in ARCHIVELOG mode enables us to make a backup while users are still working in the database. When only a simple backup is enough and no full recovery is required, we might as well ditch the archived log files that are not needed to restore the database. When full recovery is required, we should also backup the archived log files. As said before, all the databases are running in the ARCHIVELOG mode and we need to save all of the archives for a few databases. For all the databases, we need to back up the archives that are generated during the back up. Failing to do so will make the backup completely useless. Because the customer is not paying to save all the archives, we are not going to back them up. Instead, we are going to trash them as soon as possible. If we don't do that, the ARCHIVELOG destinations will flood, causing the database to hang. This is where another part of the Service Level Agreement (SLA) comes in, which forces us to make the system available during the business hours. We need to make sure that the database is available at all times. This is because when the archiver can no longer write new archives, the database will come to a halt and users will no longer be able to do their work.

This is an interesting scenario that is not easily scheduled in cron, without making assumptions about the runtime of a backup. And before you know it, there is a time bomb in your hands!

Things that can scare you

On many sites, the actions handling the archives are scheduled in cron. The interesting decision to make here is whether to drop the archives or not, and is the backup system ready for use. The solution shown here takes lots of things into account. As is the case with many solutions, it's certainly not the only way and it also won't be the best possible way. However, it does show the power of the Scheduler. There are essentially three programs, and each program has an argument named `ORACLE_SID`.

One program calls the backup database script, another calls the backup archives script, and the last one calls the delete archives script. All of these programs are of the type `EXECUTABLE` and will be called as the remote external jobs.

To make things easier, there is a table that controls the way the databases listed must be backed up. These are a few things to enter for every database:

- `ORACLE_SID`
- Interval in minutes to run the backup or delete the archives script
- The host where the database resides
- The backup server to be used
- Last database backup duration
- The days on which the database backup has to run
- The time when the database backup preferably has to run

This is enough data to be able to generate the remote external jobs that we are going to deploy for this task. There are a few assumptions in place that are as follows:

- The database backup script is called `HOT_${ORACLE_SID}`.
- The archive backup script is called `BARC_${ORACLE_SID}`.
- The archive delete script is called `DARC_${ORACLE_SID}`.
- The archives are generated and backed up at a frequency that prevents flooding in the archives file location. When the archive delete script is running, it uses the same frequency as the delete script.
- If the `backup_type` is `SEMIHOT`, all the archives that are not needed to restore the database are trashed.
- If the `backup_type` is `HOT`, the simplest form, no task-specific control is needed.
- For a `SEMIHOT` backup, we stop the `DARC` script as soon as the `HOT` script is found to be starting.
- When the `SEMIHOT` backup is started, we schedule a `BARC` script to back up the archives that are generated during the backup with the same frequency that the `DARC` script used.
- When the `SEMIHOT` backup finishes, we run the final `BARC` script as soon as possible, before re-submitting the archives killer script `DARC` again.

The following flowchart gives a visual image of what should be done in case of a `SEMIHOT` backup:

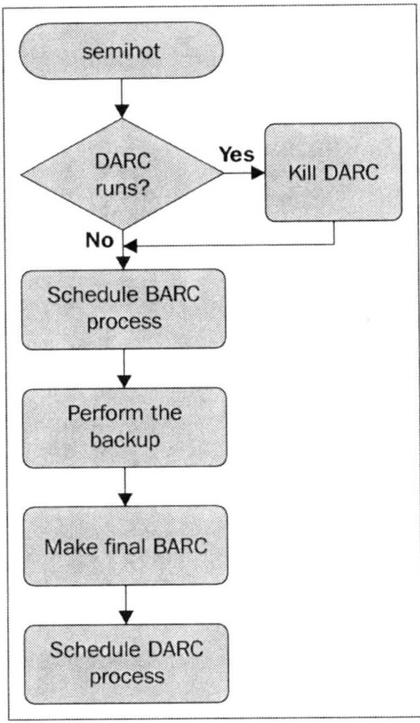

The last line, "Schedule `DARC` process" is the most important one here. We can, of course, schedule the `DARC` script as soon as the `HOT` script ends and give the `BARC` script a start time that tells the Scheduler, "Hey, start me now!" How long should we keep the `DARC` script waiting before it can go and do its job? There is only one answer for this—it has to wait until the `BARC` script has completed. Of course, we can use the `priority` attribute to make sure that the (short-running) `BARC` script gets priority over a (long-running) `HOT` script. However, there is no guarantee that it does get executed before the `DARC` job if both are scheduled at the same time. As mentioned before, this idea will be conveyed further when we consider the following figure, which represents the full cycle of a `SEMIHOT` backup:

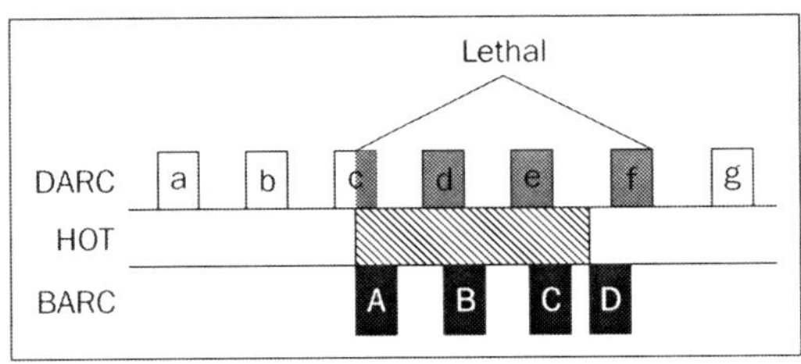

The white and grey boxes on the upper level represent the executions of the DARC process—shown as white where it is OK to run this and grey where it will cause havoc to the recoverability of the backup. The execution of the backup is represented by the striked box on the middle level, and the black boxes at the bottom represent the execution of the BARC processes intended to make the backup consistent. What we don't want is the DARC processes running while the HOT process is running. This also means that the execution of the DARC process "c" will have to be stopped when the HOT process starts. We also don't want the DARC process to run before the first BARC process after the HOT backup has ended. To make the period in which we are vulnerable to the loss of archives needed to make the backup consistent, we fire a BARC process as soon as the HOT process ends. After the BARC processes are ready, it is OK for the DARC processes to start running again. So, when BARC process "D" has succeeded, we can start killing archives again by scheduling the DARC processes.

The Scheduler gives us lots of handles to accomplish this. The most important thing is the HOT backup process and knowing when it is scheduled. If we know this and the frequency of the DARC processes, we can predefine the last execution of the DARC process. In the screenshot, we can clearly see that the third execution of the DARC process is marked "c", and will invalidate the backup. It should preferably not start running at all. For this, we define the DARC process with an `end_date` attribute set to the start time of the HOT backup minus the interval at which the DARC process runs. This will make sure that the DARC process execution marked "b" will be the last DARC process to start. To prevent accidents, we also set `auto_drop`, which makes sure that the process does not even exist during the vulnerable part of the backup process. In case it does run, we kill the job.

Because the DARC process has not been running for a while when the HOT backup starts, the first thing we need to do is schedule a BARC process and set it to start immediately when the HOT backup is seen starting. It gets the same run interval as the DARC process did. When the HOT backup finishes, we set the `max_runs` attribute of the BARC process in such a way that we have one BARC process starting after the HOT backup finishes and it starts within a minute after the completion of the HOT backup. When the final BARC process has finished, we reschedule the DARC processes again with the `end_date` attribute set to the next HOT backup start time. The BARC process also has `auto_drop` set to `true`. So when it is no longer needed, it does not exist.

Try this with any other Scheduler. It won't happen! Let's take a closer look at the interesting parts of the code.

Diving into the code

The most important part of this setup is the Scheduler event queue. The jobs will be generating events and we will use the Scheduler event queue to catch them and see the event that job generated. The events are very important and knowing which events are taking place is also important for us when debugging the system. For this reason, I normally make an `event_log` table that lists all the events that are seen along with the time at which the event is seen. In the payload for the event message is the timestamp at which the event has been generated.

Reading the event queue

We can read the Scheduler event queue as follows:

```
options_in dbms_aq.dequeue_options_t;
  props_out dbms_aq.message_properties_t;
  sid varchar2(30);
  host varchar2(30);
  destination varchar2(30);
  hot_state   varchar2(30);
  begin
    loop
      options_in.consumer_name := consumer;
     options_in.wait := dbms_aq.FOREVER;
      begin
        dbms_aq.dequeue ('sys.SCHEDULER$_EVENT_QUEUE'
                        , options_in,props_out
                        , msg
                        , msgid
                        );
      exception
        when dequeue_timeout
        then
          dbms_output.put_Line ('no event');
          props_out.state := DBMS_AQ.PROCESSED;
        when others
        then
          raise;
      end;
      if ( props_uit.state = dbms_aq.READY )
      then
        dbms_output.put_line ('msg.event_type:'||msg.event_type);
        dbms_output.put_line ('msg.object_owner:'||msg.object_owner);
```

```
dbms_output.put_line ('msg.object_name:'||msg.object_name);
dbms_output.put_line ('msg.event_timestamp:'
                     ||msg.event_timestamp);
dbms_output.put_line ('msg.error_code:'||msg.error_code);
dbms_output.put_line ('msg.error_msg:'||msg.error_msg);
dbms_output.put_line ('msg.event_status:'||msg.event_status);
dbms_output.put_line ('msg.log_id:'||msg.log_id);
dbms_output.put_line ('msg.run_count:'||msg.run_count);
dbms_output.put_line ('msg.failure_count:'||
                      msg.failure_count);
dbms_output.put_line ('msg.retry_count:'||msg.retry_count);
/* for debugging mostly */
insert into event_log
  (
    receive_date,
    event_type,
    object_owner,
    object_name,
    event_timestamp,
    error_code,
    error_msg,
    event_status,
    log_id,
    run_count,
    failure_count,
    retry_count
  )
values
 (
    current_timestamp
    msg.event_type,
    msg.object_owner,
    msg.object_name,
    msg.event_timestamp,
    msg.error_code,
    msg.error_msg,
    msg.event_status,
    msg.log_id,
    msg.run_count,
    msg.failure_count,
    msg.retry_count
 );

if msg.object_name != 'BACKUP_MONITOR_STOP' and
   msg.object_name != 'BACKUP_MONITOR_RUN'
```

This code is the heart of the system and waits for a Scheduler event to take place. The expected events are not only those of the BARC, DARC, and HOT processes, but also the BACKUP_MONITOR_STOP and BACKUP_MONITOR_RUN processes. The latter one is running the backup monitor code itself and the only task of the stop job is to pass its active existence to the backup monitor code, so that the monitor can stop in an orderly fashion. As you can see in the code above, the options_in.wait is given FOREVER. This keeps the system silent when nothing happens:

```
        if msg.error_code != 0
        then
          if (msg.error_code <> 27370 and msg.object_name not like
                                                          DARC_%')
            /* we kill DARC_ as soon as HOT_ begins so 27370 for
               DARC is ok */
          then
            send_nok
             (
               msg.object_owner,
               msg.object_name,
               msg.error_code,
               msg.error_msg
             );
          end if;
        end if;

        if (msg.object_name like 'HOT_%'  and
                    (msg.event_type = 'JOB_STARTED'
                  or msg.event_type = 'JOB_SUCCEEDED')
           )
            or  (msg.object_name like 'BARC_%' and
                    msg.event_type = 'JOB_COMPLETED')
        then
           /*
            * is HOT backup ended check for need of change BARC<>DARC
            */
            switch_BARC_DARC (msg.object_name, msg.event_type);
        end if; -- event received dbms_aq.ready

        commit;
        exit when msg.object_owner = consumer and
                  msg.object_name  = 'BACKUP_MONITOR_STOP';
      end if; /* msg received */
    end loop;
    dbms_output.put_line ('exiting watch_queue loop');
  END watch_queue;
```

As there is a chance that we need to kill the DARC job (we do this when it appears to run when HOT starts), ora-27370 is not an error when it is found for the DARC process. For other errors, we generate a mail for whoever should get notified. There are a few events that ask for our attention: JOB_STARTED and JOB_SUCCEEDED for the HOT backup job and also the JOB_COMPLETED event for the BARC job. There is a subtle difference between the JOB_SUCCEEDED and JOB_COMPLETED events. JOB_SUCCEEDED means that the job succeeded, whereas JOB_COMPLETED means that the JOB has completed its functional life and auto_drop has been executed. In our case, this means that the last BARC process (the one that has to start after the HOT backup competed) has done its job.

Scheduling for the HOT backups

The scheduling of the HOT backups is performed by the following snippet of code. The HOT backups are in control, as the start and the stop of the HOT backups control the behavior of the DARC and BARC processes.

```
dbms_scheduler.create_job
  (
    job_name          => i.hot_name,
    program_name      => 'backup_db_hot',
    repeat_interval   => 'freq=weekly'; byday='||i.backup_days||';
                         byhour='||to_char(i.backup_time,'hh24')||';'||
                         'byminute='||to_char(i.backup_time,'mi')||';',
    start_date        => current_timestamp,
    job_class         => i.server,
    auto_drop         => false,
    enabled           => false
  );
dbms_scheduler.set_attribute
  (
    name      => i.hot_name,
    attribute => 'raise_events',
    value     => dbms_scheduler.job_started +
                 dbms_scheduler.job_succeeded +
                 dbms_scheduler.job_failed +
                 dbms_scheduler.job_broken +
                 dbms_scheduler.job_completed +
                 dbms_scheduler.job_sch_lim_reached +
                 dbms_scheduler.job_disabled +
                 dbms_scheduler.job_chain_stalled
  );
```

```
dbms_scheduler.set_attribute
  (
    name          => i.hot_name,
    attribute     => 'logging_level',
    value         => DBMS_SCHEDULER.LOGGING_full
  );
dbms_scheduler.set_attribute
  (
    name          => i.hot_name,
    attribute     => 'job_priority',
    value         => 4
  );
dbms_scheduler.set_attribute
  (
    name        => i.hot_name,
    attribute   => 'MAX_RUN_DURATION',
    value       => numtodsinterval (i.backup_length * 1.2, 'hour')
  );
dbms_scheduler.set_attribute
  (
    name        => i.hot_name,
    attribute   => 'destination',
    value       => i.destination
  );
dbms_scheduler.set_attribute
  (
    name        => i.hot_name,
    attribute   => 'credential_name',
    value       => i.credential_owner||'.'||i.credential_name
  );
dbms_scheduler.set_job_argument_value
  (
    job_name          => i.hot_name,
    argument_name     => 'ORACLE_SID',
    argument_value    => i.oracle_sid
  );
dbms_scheduler.enable( i.hot_name );
```

This is a pretty straightforward piece of code! The priority for the `HOT` backup is `4`, meaning low priority. This is relative to the others in the same resource consumer group. The normal `BARC` and `DARC` processes get a little higher priority, that is `3`; whereas the final `BARC` process gets a priority `2`. We want to get a notification when the backup runs significantly longer than expected. So the `MAX_RUN_DURATION` value is used here, which will raise an event when this happens. However, it will not stop the job. The destination and the credential needed to run the job at the specified destination are specified as attributes of the job.

Scheduling the DARC process

When the SEMIHOT backup is done and the BARC process is completed, we can schedule the DARC process again. From this point in time, it can safely be scheduled until the next backup. We do this in such a way that the DARC job no longer exists when the backup starts.

```
procedure schedule_darc
  (
    job in varchar2, sid in varchar2,
    dest in varchar2, cred in varchar2,
    server in varchar2, interval in number,
    hot_job in varchar2
  )
as
  begin_hot timestamp;
begin
      dbms_scheduler.create_job
        (
          job_name        => job,
          program_name    => 'delete_arch',
          repeat_interval =>
          'FREQ=MINUTELY;INTERVAL='||interval,
          start_date      => current_timestamp,
          job_class       => 'default_job_class',
          auto_drop       => true,
          enabled         => false
        );
      dbms_scheduler.set_attribute
        (
          name      => job,
          attribute => 'raise_events',
          value     => dbms_scheduler.job_started +
                       dbms_scheduler.job_succeeded +
                       dbms_scheduler.job_failed +
                       dbms_scheduler.job_broken +
                       dbms_scheduler.job_completed +
                       dbms_scheduler.job_sch_lim_reached +
                       dbms_scheduler.job_disabled +
                       dbms_scheduler.job_chain_stalled
        );
      dbms_scheduler.set_attribute
        (
          name       => job,
          attribute  => 'logging_level',
          value      => DBMS_SCHEDULER.LOGGING_full
        );
```

```
dbms_scheduler.set_attribute
  (
    name        => job,
    attribute   => 'job_priority',
    value       => 4
  );
dbms_scheduler.set_attribute
  (
    name        => job,
    attribute   => 'destination',
    value       => dest
  );
dbms_scheduler.set_attribute
  (
    name        => job,
    attribute   => 'credential_name',
    value       => cred
  );
/* the backup is scheduled, as is the DARC job.
 * if this monitor code is not running, make sure that
 * the DARC job is NOT going to interfere with the HOT backup.
 * there will be problems because the archives are not backed up but
 * that will be noticed by other monitoring processes in grid control
 */
 select next_run_date - ((1/24/60)*interval) into begin_hot
/* last run is ultimately available to start until interval (minutes)
 * before the start of the hot backup
 */
        from user_scheduler_jobs
        where job_name = hot_job;
dbms_scheduler.set_attribute
  (
    name           => job,
    attribute      => 'end_date',
    value          => begin_hot -- HOT backups begins after
                                            interval minutes
   );
dbms_scheduler.set_job_argument_value
  (
    job_name        => job,
    argument_name   => 'ORACLE_SID',
    argument_value  => sid
  );
dbms_scheduler.set_job_argument_value
  (
    job_name        => job,
    argument_name   => 'KEEP_HOURS',
    argument_value  => '0'
  );
dbms_scheduler.enable( job );
```

The majority of the code used here is the same as for the BARC process. The most important difference is the setting of the end_date, which is based on the NEXT_RUN_DATE of the corresponding HOT job and the interval in which the DARC and BARC processes run. This is incorporated to make sure that no DARC process will be running when the corresponding HOT backup is going to start. This also ensures that when the backup monitoring process is not running, the first series of backups will have correct results. Normally, the backup monitoring software will be running, but you are not always aware.

Scheduling the final BARC process

When the end of the backup is detected, we will need to make sure that the final ARCHIVELOG backups are created and that too as soon as possible.

```
begin
  select state, run_count into barc_state, barc_runs
  from user_scheduler_jobs
  where job_name = i.job_name;
if barc_state <> 'RUNNING'
then
              /* start the last archives backup ASAP */
  dbms_scheduler.disable (i.job_name);
  dbms_scheduler.set_attribute
    (
      name        => i.job_name,
      attribute   => 'job_priority',
      value       => 1
    );
  dbms_scheduler.set_attribute
    (
      name       => i.job_name,
      attribute  => 'start_date',
      value      => current_timestamp
    );
  dbms_scheduler.enable (i.job_name);
else /* already running, ad 1 extra run ASAP for BARC */
  dbms_scheduler.set_attribute
    (
      name      => i.job_name,
      attribute => 'max_runs',
      value     => barc_runs + 2
    );
```

```
    dbms_scheduler.set_attribute
      (
        name      => i.job_name,
        attribute => 'repeat_interval',
        value     => 'FREQ=MINUTELY; INTERVAL=1'
      );
    dbms_scheduler.set_attribute
      (
        name      => i.job_name,
        attribute => 'job_priority',
        value     => 1
      );
    dbms_scheduler.set_attribute
      (
         name      => i.job_name,
         attribute => 'start_date',
         value     => current_timestamp
      );
  end if;
```

If the `BARC` job is already running, we set `max_runs` to the current `run_count` plus `2`, while at the same time we set the repeat interval to `1` minute. This makes sure that when the currently running `BARC` is ready, the next one is started within a minute thereafter. After that final run, the `max_runs` count setting makes sure that the `BARC` job is dropped and we receive the `JOB_COMPLETED` event for the `BARC` process. The job priority is set to `1`, the topmost priority, just to ensure that our most wanted job does not have to wait any longer and is served as soon as possible. On the web site (`http://www.packtpub.com/files/code/5982_Code.zip`), the full code will be available for download.

How to use the calendar

In the forums, some questions are repeated over and over again. One of them is how to use or create a schedule. The Oracle documentation makes some attempt to explain the use of the calendar, but fails to use real examples. Here, we will see some examples that explain some of the real-life questions:

- How to schedule on the first day of a month?
- How to schedule only on Monday?
- How to schedule on the first Monday of a month?
- How to schedule on the first working day of a month?
- How to schedule on the first working Monday of a month?
- How to schedule on the nth Monday of a month?

- How to schedule on the last working day of a month?
- How to schedule in the first quarter of a year?
- How to schedule on the first Monday of the first quarter of a year?

Tools

Before diving into the calendars, it would be good to know that there is a very useful tool in the database that can help debugging a calendar. This tool is the `evaluate_calendar`, which is found in the `dbms_scheduler` package. This procedure can show the next run date for a given start date. To make it easier to use, we can add the following code to the database:

```
create or replace type calendar_row_type as object (next_run_date
                                        timestamp with time zone);
create or replace type calendar_table_type as table of
                                       calendar_row_type;
CREATE OR REPLACE FUNCTION ANA_SCHED (start_time in timestamp,
                        calendar in varchar2, steps in number)
RETURN calendar_table_type pipelined AS start_date TIMESTAMP;
 return_date_after TIMESTAMP;
 next_run_date TIMESTAMP;
BEGIN
  start_date := start_time;
  return_date_after := start_date;
  FOR i IN 1.steps
  LOOP
    dbms_scheduler.evaluate_calendar_string(calendar,
        start_date, return_date_after, next_run_date);
  -- next_run_date has to popup somewhere as a column
    pipe row (calendar_row_type(next_run_date));
    return_date_after := next_run_date;
  END LOOP;
  return;
END ana_sched;
/
```

The code is a simple pipelined function that generates a row for the requested number of next executions, starting from the specified start date. We can use the `ana_sched` function as follows:

```
select next_run_date, to_char(next_run_date,'dy') day from table
                 (ana_sched(sysdate, 'freq=weekly;byday=mon;',5));
```

This shows the next `5` Mondays since today. This function is also available in DbVisualizer and DB Console.

How to schedule on the first day of a month

The `create_schedule` procedure is all we need for creating a simple calendar. The following code shows a calendar that simply lists the first day of every month:

```
BEGIN
dbms_scheduler.create_schedule(
                              schedule_name     => 'firstday',
                              start_date        => NULL,
                              repeat_interval   => 'freq=monthly;'||
                                                   'bymonthday=1',
                              end_date          => NULL, comments=>NULL
                                );
END;
```

This gives a run date for the first day of every month. The start time of the runs is equal to the time on which we created the schedule.

How to schedule only on Monday

This is also a simple example that enlists all the Mondays. Again, the start time is the same as the time on which we created the schedule.

```
BEGIN
dbms_scheduler.create_schedule(
                              schedule_name     => 'mondays',
                              start_date        => NULL,
                              repeat_interval   => 'freq=weekly;'||
                                                   'byday=mon',
                              end_date          => NULL,
                              comments          => NULL
                              );
END;
```

This code defines a schedule called `mondays` that lists all the Mondays—nothing more, nothing less. As we have a Monday in every week, the frequency is weekly.

```
select next_run_date, to_char(next_run_date,'dy') day from table
                              (ana_sched(sysdate, 'mondays',5));
```

How to schedule on the first Monday of a month

Now, list only the first Monday of every month:

```
BEGIN
dbms_scheduler.create_schedule(
                              schedule_name     => 'first_mondays',
                              start_date        => NULL,
                              repeat_interval   => 'freq=monthly;'||
                                                   'byday=mon;
                                                    bysetpos=1;',
```

```
                                end_date            => NULL,
                                comments            => NULL
                               );
  END;
```

As we have a monthly interval now, we have to define accordingly. In the monthly interval, we choose the day by `byday=mon`. As there are multiple Mondays in a month, we specify which Monday we want to use by `bysetpos=1`. This gives us the first Monday of the month.

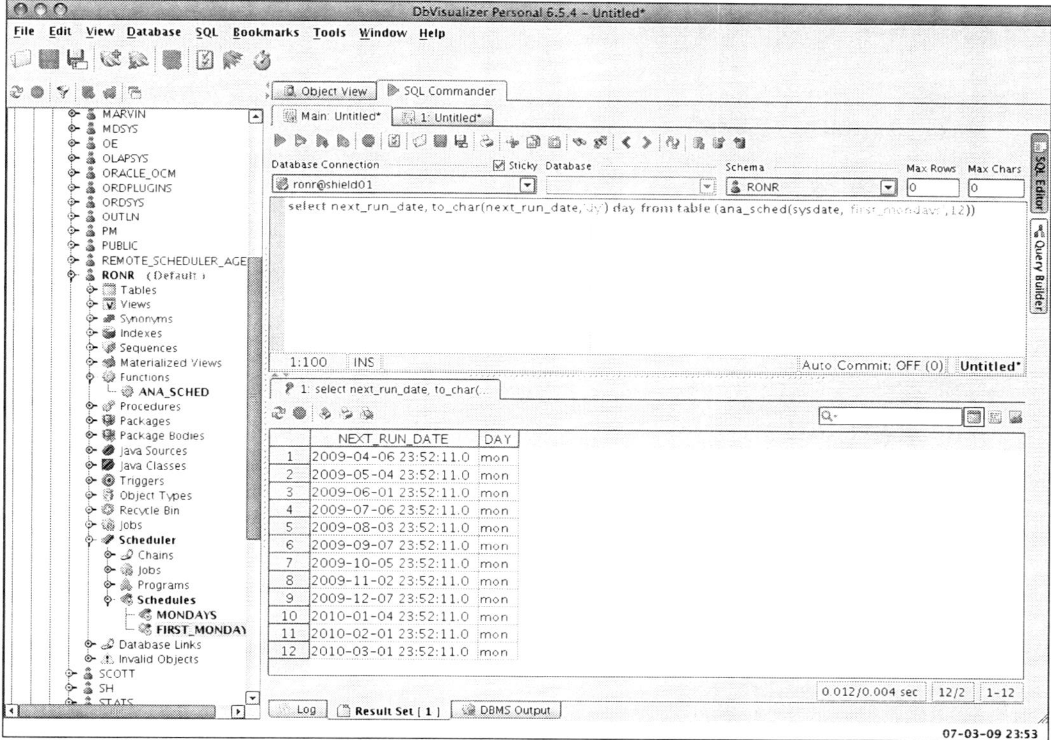

How to schedule on the first working day of a month

What should be listed depends a lot on what the definition of a working day is. In this case, we define a working day as the days that do not fall into the weekend or the free day category. Here comes more power of the calendaring possibilities of `dbms_scheduler`. We can combine the schedules. Let's first define the weekends and then the free days. The weekend schedule can be defined as follows:

```
--/
begin
dbms_scheduler.create_schedule
```

```
    (
      schedule_name         => 'weekend',
      start_date            => NULL,
      repeat_interval       => 'freq=weekly; byday=Sat,Sun',
      end_date              => NULL,
      comments              => 'weekends'
    );
  end;
  /
```

We have a weekend every week, so the frequency is weekly. Now let's make a schedule that defines the special days:

```
--/
BEGIN
  dbms_scheduler.create_schedule
    (
      schedule_name     => 'july_6',
      start_date        => NULL,
      repeat_interval   => 'freq=yearly; bydate=0706',
      end_date          => NULL,
      comments          => NULL
    );
  dbms_scheduler.create_schedule
    (
      schedule_name     => 'june_14',
      start_date        => NULL,
      repeat_interval   => 'freq=yearly; bydate=0614',
      end_date          => NULL,
      comments          => NULL
    );
END;
/
```

The code above lists some very important days that are not working days. We will combine them in schedule `special_days`:

```
--/
BEGIN
  dbms_scheduler.create_schedule
    (
      schedule_name     => 'special_days',
      start_date        => NULL,
      repeat_interval   => 'june_14,july_6',
      end_date          => NULL,
      comments          => NULL
    );
END;
/
```

Now we have a list of special days that we don't work on and when they are combined with the weekends, it returns the free days. So why not make a schedule for this? Let's prepare it using the following:

```
--/
BEGIN
  dbms_scheduler.create_schedule
    (
      schedule_name      => 'free_days',
      start_date         => NULL,
      repeat_interval    => 'weekend,free_days',
      end_date           => NULL,
      comments           => NULL
    );
END;
/
```

The `free_days` schedule lists all the days that are not working days. The original question was about the first working day of a month. Here, again we can make a combination of existing schedules, in this case by using `exclude`. We essentially use all the days, minus the `free_days`. We can do this as follows:

```
--/
BEGIN
  dbms_scheduler.create_schedule
    (
      schedule_name      => 'firstworkingday',
      start_date         => NULL,
      repeat_interval    => 'freq=monthly; byday=Mon,Tue,Wed,Thu,Fri;'||
                            'exclude=free_days;bysetpos=1',
      end_date           => NULL,
      comments           => NULL
    );
END;
/
```

The `firstworkingday` schedule lists the first working day of a month, assuming a working day is on a week day.

How to schedule on the first working Monday of a month

From the previous example, it is easy to refine to the first working Monday of a month:

```
--/
BEGIN
  dbms_scheduler.create_schedule
    (
      schedule_name      => 'firstworkingmonday',
      start_date         => NULL,
      repeat_interval    => 'freq=monthly; byday=Mon;'||
                            'exclude=free_days; bysetpos=1',
      end_date           => NULL,
      comments           => NULL
    );
END;
/
```

The `firstworkingmonday` schedule lists the first working Monday of a month.

How to schedule on the nth Monday of a month

We can use an approach that is very similar to the above using `setbypos`. We pick the second Monday of every month as follows:

```
--/
BEGIN
  dbms_scheduler.create_schedule
    (
      schedule_name        => 'secondworkingmonday',
      start_date           => NULL,
      repeat_interval      => 'freq=monthly; byday=Mon;'||
                              'exclude=free_days; bysetpos=2',
      end_date            => NULL,
      comments            => NULL
    );
END;
/
```

The `secondworkingmonday` schedule lists the second working Monday of a month based on the `free_days` definition as mentioned before.

How to schedule on the last working day of a month

The step to the last Monday of a month is also defined by `bysetpos`, counting back from the end specified by a negative number.

```
--/
BEGIN
  dbms_scheduler.create_schedule
    (
      schedule_name      => 'lastworkingday',
      start_date         => NULL,
      repeat_interval    => 'freq=monthly;'||
                            'byday=Mon,Tue,Wed,Thu,Fri;'||
                            'exclude=free_days;bysetpos=-1',
      end_date           => NULL, comments=>NULL
    );
END;
/
```

Here, we used the fact that a negative value for `bysetpos` leads to backward counting.

How to schedule in the first quarter of a year

It is simple to define the first quarter:

```
--/
BEGIN
  dbms_scheduler.create_schedule
    (
      schedule_name      => 'q1',
      start_date         => NULL,
      repeat_interval    => 'freq=daily; bymonth=1,2,3',
      end_date           => NULL,
      comments           => NULL
    );
END;
/
```

The `q1` schedule selects all the days of the first quarter of a year.

How to schedule on the first Monday of the first quarter

How can we use the previously defined schedule `firstworkingmonday` to show only the first working Mondays in the first quarter? This can be done with the intersect operator as follows:

```
select next_run_date, to_char(next_run_date,'dy') day
from table (ana_sched(sysdate, 'q1;intersect=firstworkmonday;
                                          bymonth=1',40));
```

This shows the schedule that lists the dates in the `q1` schedule, which are also present in the `firstworkingmondays` schedule, delimited to month `1`. Needless to say, this is incredibly powerful, impossible to describe in cron or `dbms_jobs`. This should give enough grip to be able to create almost any schedule that one can imagine.

Summary

In this chapter, we examined the various uses of Oracle Scheduler and, ultimately, the power of the Oracle Scheduler when used in real-world scenarios.

We covered:

- How to dequeue the Scheduler event queue
- How to save the events for debugging
- How to specify `job_weight` for a job with parallelism
- How to specify `job_priority`
- How to specify `max_job_duration`
- How to specify which events should be generated by a job
- How to interpret `job_completed`
- How to make use the `max_runs` job attribute
- How to make use the `end_date` job attribute
- How to make use of the `auto_drop` job attribute
- How to generate the job names using a prefix
- How to use the Scheduler for advanced backup setups
- How to use the Scheduler to generate object statistics without impacting the other users
- How to create a schedule
- How to combine schedules to make advanced schedules

There seems to be only one limitation of the Oracle Scheduler—our lack of imagination to make it work to its full advantage. I hope now it's overcome. The only known limitation is the poor imagination of human beings who have to make the Scheduler work. In the next chapter, we will explore other configurations that Oracle Scheduler can run in, and various other things that can be arranged.

9 Other Configurations

I hope that the previous chapters gave enough handles to start working with the Scheduler. I am aware that there is a lot more to tell about the Scheduler, and this chapter will shed light on some other configurations where the Scheduler can be used. This time it is about **RAC** (**Real Application Clusters**) and the standby databases.

RAC

When the jobs you are running depend on things other than just the database, it might be interesting to know what these other things are, and where they can be found. There are several ways to control which instance a job is going to run, some of which are:

- Define `instance_id` in the job definition
- Use `instance_stickiness` in the job definition
- Define `service_name` in the job class definition for the job

To be able to show what exactly happens, we need an RAC installation. The RAC installation used here runs on two nodes—`oralin01` and `oralin02`—using the shared storage that is exported as `iSCSI` disks from the *of01* server running openfiler. The database called "shields" is using the `iSCSI` disks through the ASM. The instances of this database are `shields1` and `shields2`. In the default setup, every instance of the cluster supports the service whose name is the same as the database name. For demonstration purposes, the services departures and arrivals have been defined. The preferred instance for the arrivals service is `shields2` and the preferred instance for the departures service is `shields1`. The shields service runs on both the instances.

To find out where a service is currently running, we can use the `gv$active_services` view. This view lists things such as the `instance_id` and the services running on that instance. Combine it with `instance_name` from `v$instance` to find out on which instance the query runs:

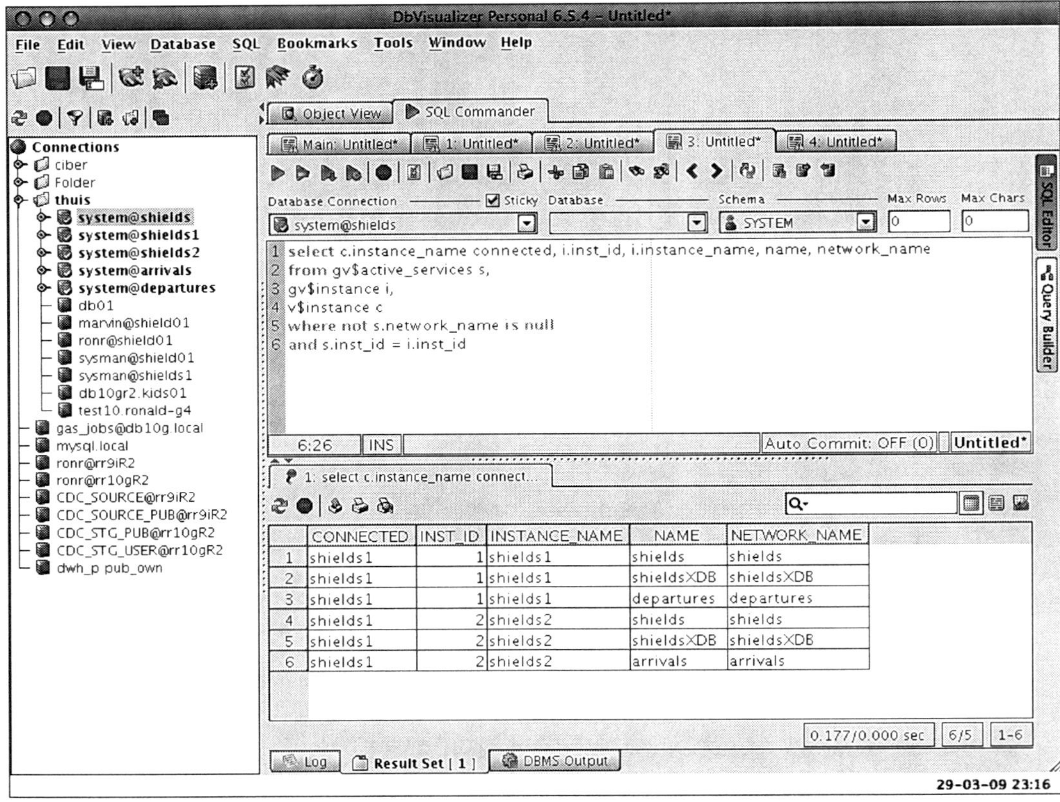

In this output, we can see that we are connected on the **shields1** instance. Currently, the **departures** service is running on **shields1**, which is the preferred instance of this service. The **arrivals** service is running on the **shields2** instance. The other services are either the default shields services and the **shieldsXDB** service.

Another view that is interesting in this regard is the `v$session` view. It lists through which service name what connection was made:

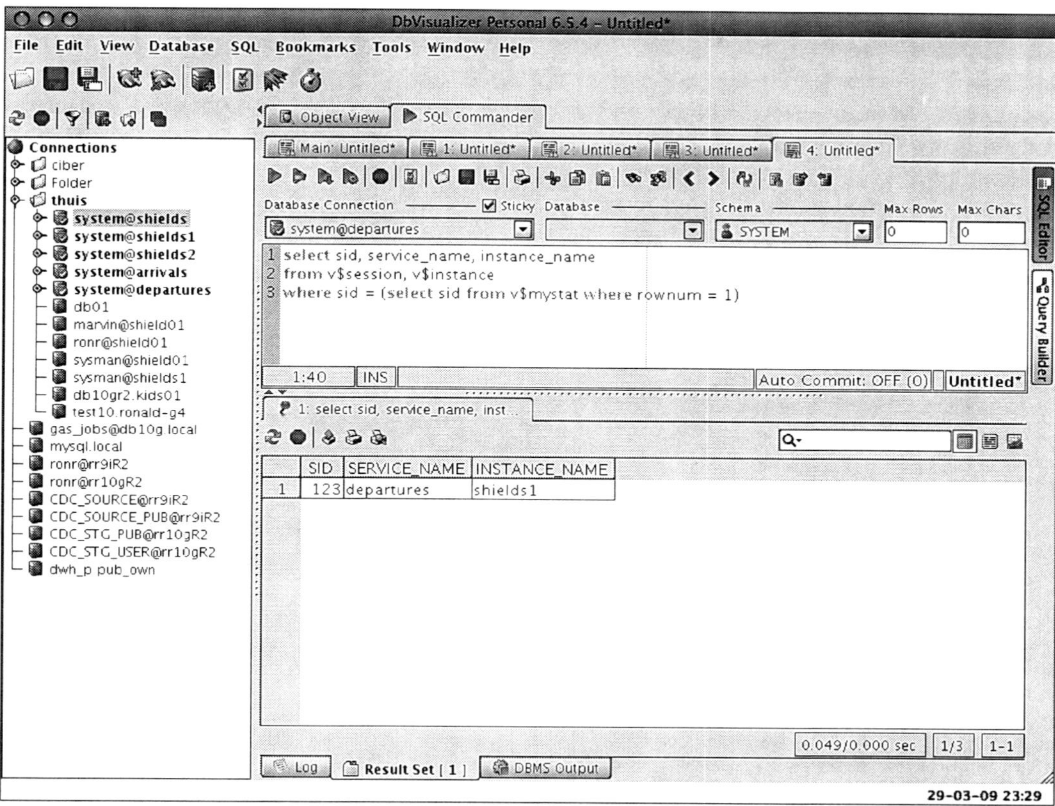

In this output, we can see that the Session ID is **123**, the session is connected on the **departures** service, and the instance is **shields1**.

In this case, the configuration is made such that the departures and the arrivals service each run on their preferred instance. It could very well be that these services run on more instances. Using service management, we can define on which instances a service is allowed to run and which one is the preferred instance. Enough has been said about RAC. For now, let's go back to the Scheduler jobs.

Job creation/modification

On the most detailed level of the job, the instance can be selected by assigning an instance ID to the `instance_id` attribute. This might be a little surprising as we are all educated to use `service_name`. There is a reason for this. Sometimes, a job should not run if the selected instance is not available. In that case, a hardcoded link to the `instance_idinstance_id` could be very valid. The definition indicates the instance on which the job is to be run. If the instance is not running, the job cannot run. The following job can only run when `instance_id 1` is open:

```
--/
begin
  dbms_scheduler.create_job
    (
      job_name        => 'RAC01',
      job_class       => 'DEFAULT_JOB_CLASS',
      job_type        => 'plsql_block',
      job_action      => 'begin insert into test_rac
                         (sid,instance_name,service_name,time)
                          select sid, instance_name, service_name,
                          systimestamp from v$session, v$instance
                          where sid = (select sid from v$mystat
                                                where rownum = 1);
                               end;',
      repeat_interval => 'freq=minutely;interval=2'
    );
  dbms_scheduler.set_attribute
    (
      name            => 'RAC01',
      attribute       => 'instance_id',
      value           => 1
    );
  dbms_scheduler.enable('RAC01');
end;
/
```

The output of this job is in the `test_rac` table, which is defined as:

```
CREATE
  TABLE test_rac
   (
     sid NUMBER,
     service_name VARCHAR2(30),
     instance_name VARCHAR2(30),
     TIME TIMESTAMP WITH TIME zone
    );
```

The job runs every 2 minutes and inserts a line into the `test_rac` table. Note that this job has the `instance_id` hardcoded into it. This means that the job will not run if this instance is not running. It also means that the `service_name` found in the `v$session` view for this job is the `SYS$USERS`, a default service name.

What should we do when we want a job to switch to an available instance automatically after the original instance has terminated for whatever reason? We should tie the job to a service name. The way to do this is by creating a job class that connects to the desired service. In this case, the job class connects to the departures service:

```
--/
begin
  dbms_scheduler.create_job_class
    (
      job_class_name    => 'departures_class',
      service           => 'departures',
      logging_level     => DBMS_SCHEDULER.LOGGING_RUNS,
      comments          => 'run on the departures service'
    );
end;
/
```

Now, we will change the previously defined job `RAC01` so that it falls in the `departures_class` by running this piece of code:

```
--/
begin
  dbms_scheduler.set_attribute
    (
      name            => 'RAC01',
      attribute       => 'job_class',
      value           => 'departures_class'
    );
end;
/
```

From this moment on, the job output will look a little different as we can see in the following `test_rac` table:

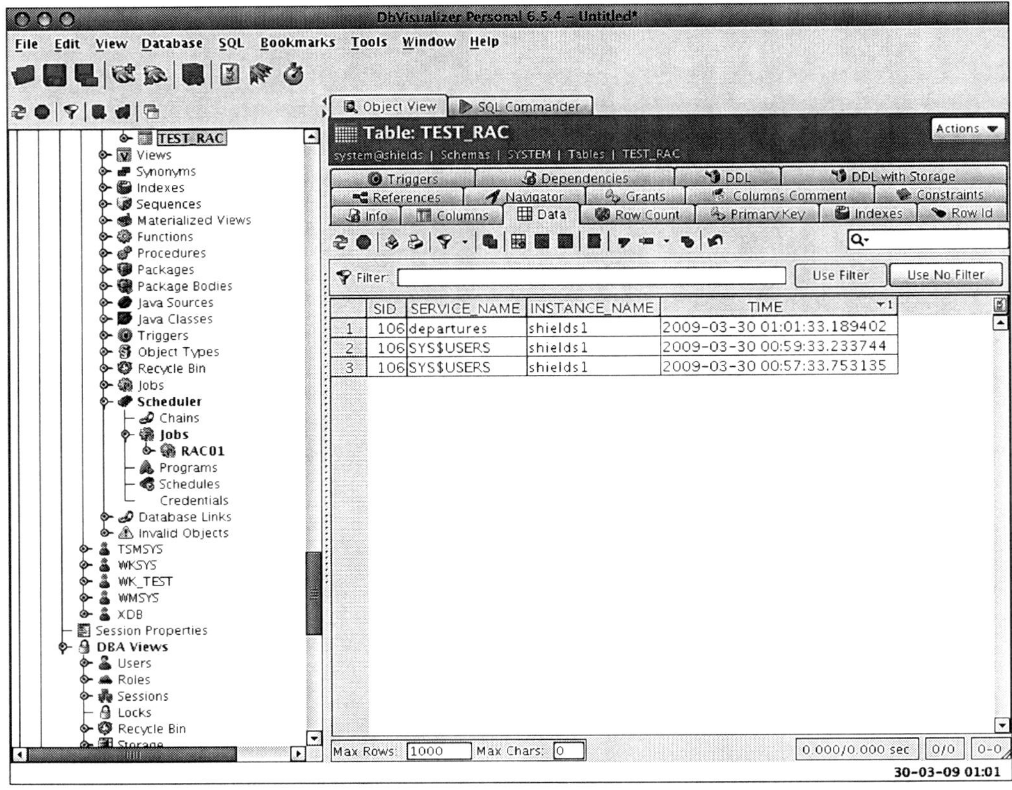

See how the default service name is changed to the desired service name **departures**. The departures service currently runs in the **shields1** instance.

Let's consider a hypothetical situation where a disaster strikes all of a sudden and the host that serves the **shields1** instance is shut down. After a while, we can see that the departures service has moved to the **shields2** instance.

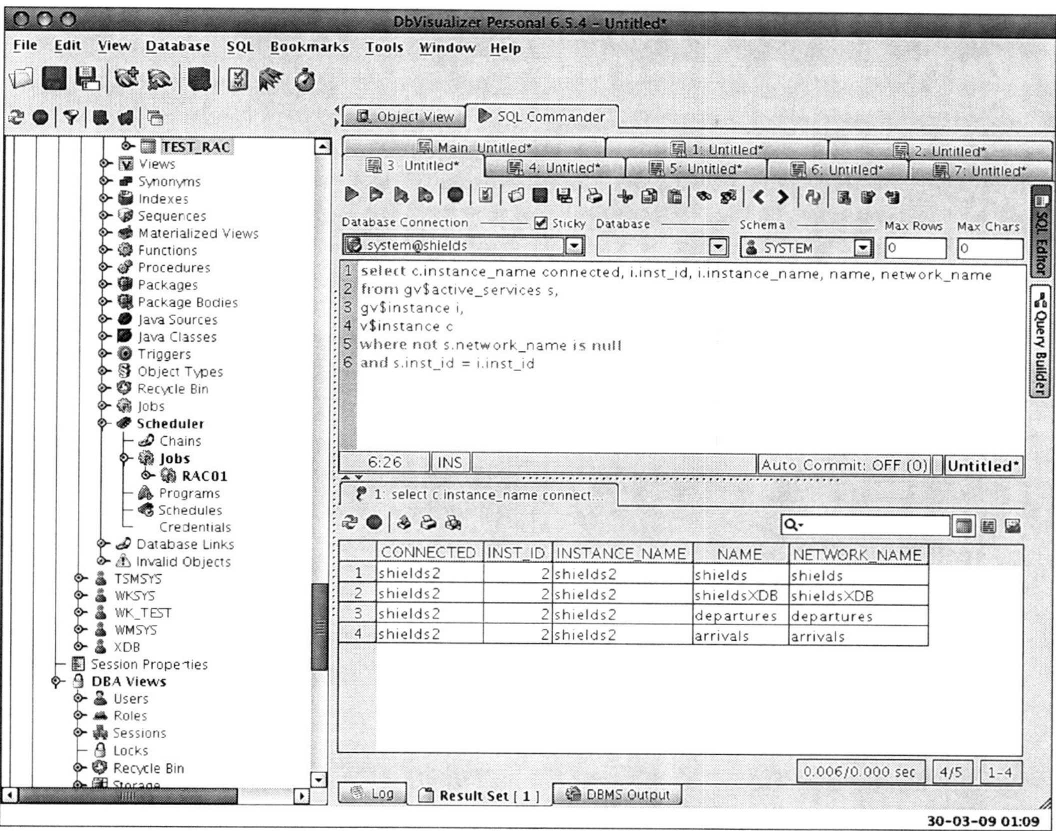

Now that the service is running on a different instance, we expect that the job is also going to run. Minutes later, we find that the job is still not running. How can this be? Here we find a nice default value for the `instance_stickiness` attribute of the job. This tells the Scheduler to try to run the job on the same instance where it started for the first time.

The first time, if no explicit instance selection is made, the job will run on the instance (that runs that service) with the lightest load that is available at that moment. The tricky bit here is in the definition, which tells us that if the interval between the runs is large, `instance_stickiness` will be ignored and if the instance where the job should run is unable to run the job for a significant period of time, another instance will run the job. Pay attention to this parameter as it might help you. But if it's used in a wrong way, it may have a few surprises up its sleeve. In our hypothetical scenario, we had hoped that the job would fluently switch over to the other instance when the service was relocated to the surviving instance.

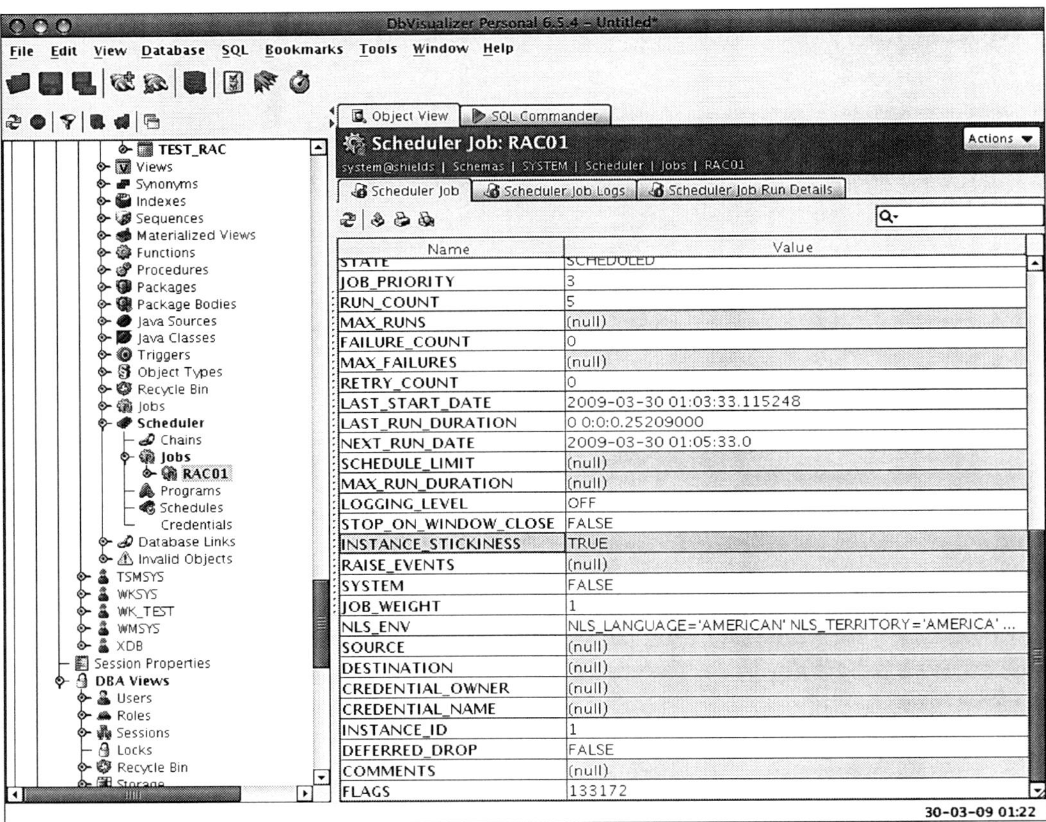

As we are not willing to delay the departing passengers any longer, we reset the `instance_stickiness` parameter to `false` and the `instance_id` to `NULL`.

```
--/
begin
  dbms_scheduler.set_attribute
```

```
    (
      name      => 'RAC01',
      attribute => 'instance_stickiness',
      value     => false
    );
end;
/
```

It would be better to create the job with `instance_stickiness` set to `false` from the beginning and `instance_id` to `null` if we want to be flexible.

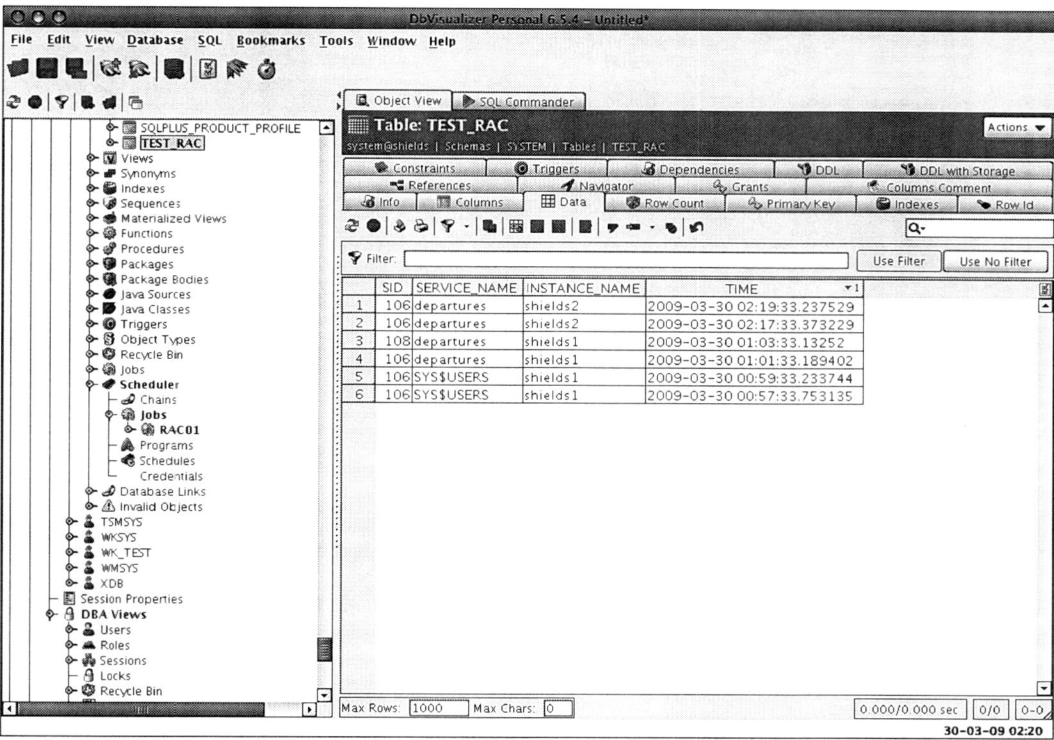

Here, we clearly see the switch to the other instance. This took a bit of extra time, caused by the default behavior of `dbms_scheduler.create_job`. The default behavior is to create a job that runs on the instance where the job was created and to keep it running there. So now we change the following attributes:

- `instance_id` = `NULL`
- `instance_stickiness` = `false`

We should be able to get the job quickly running on the other instance again. In the meantime, the **shields1** instance has been restarted, so now let's shut down the host of **shields2** instance and see what happens.

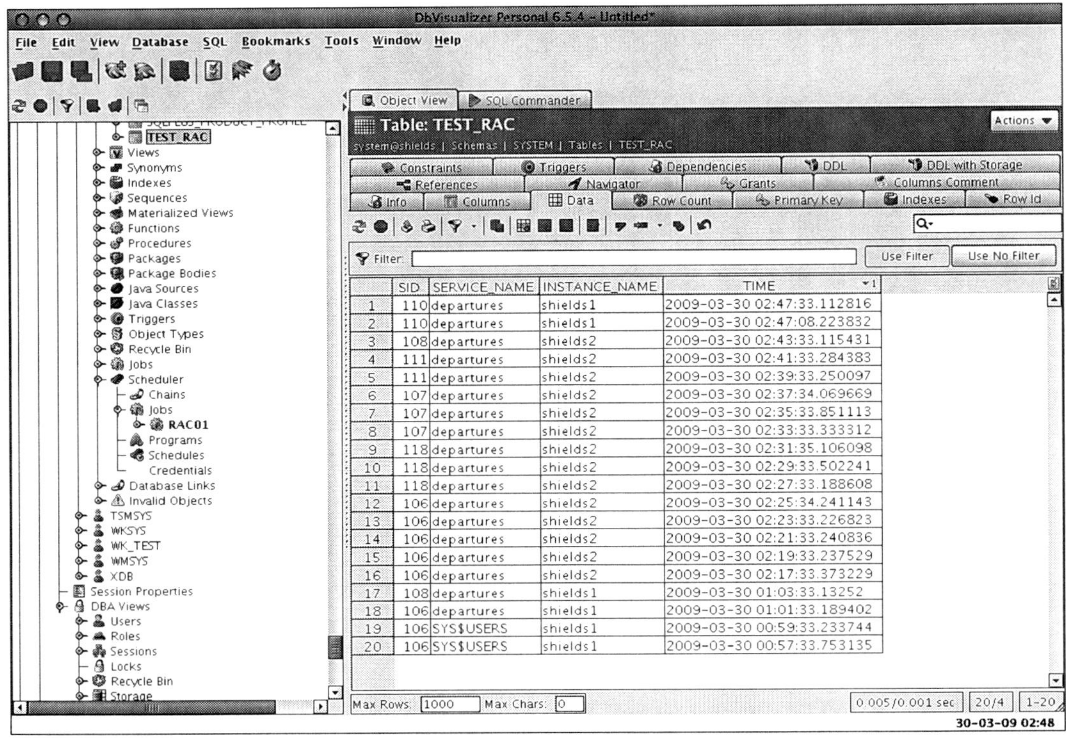

Almost immediately, the job starts running on the `shields1` instance where the departures service was relocated by the cluster software when we crashed the node of the `shields2` instance.

The job_class definition

The selection of the instance where a job should run can also be handed over to the job class. In the `job_class`, we can define a `service_name` on which the jobs of that class should run. This gives the Scheduler more freedom to select an available instance that supports the defined service. If the specified service is dropped, the jobs automatically fall back to the default service.

Service selection can also be controlled by `resource_consumer_group`. The `resource_consumer_group` definition will take precedence if a job class has a service defined, this service is also mapped to a resource consumer group, and at the same time the job class also has a `resource_consumer_group` defined.

Standby databases

Jobs are mostly defined in a normal primary database. There are reasons for desiring jobs to run in a standby database. Oracle 11g introduces the database roles for this purpose. In the `database_role` attribute of a job, we can specify when a job should run. Should it run when the database is run in the PRIMARY role, or should it run when the database runs in the LOGICAL STANDBY role? There is no option for the PHYSICAL STANDBY role. It is understandable that the PHYSICAL STANDBY role is not implemented. But at the same time there could be some valid reasons to still want jobs to run with the database in the PHYSICAL STANDBY role. That would, of course, be without the fancy logging, but what about the maintenance of the applied archives? This still has to be scheduled outside the database that needs this maintenance.

Creating jobs in a logical standby database

The job creation in DDL is not propagated to the logical standby database. However, you can create Scheduler jobs in the logical standby database. After the job creation, the role of the Scheduler job is inherited from the `database_role` where the job was created. This just means that if you create a job in the primary database, the job will run in the primary database. If you create a job in the logical standby database, it will inherit the LOGICAL STANDBY role from the database. It is possible to change the `database_role` for an existing job by running this:

```
--/
begin
  DBMS_SCHEDULER.SET_ATTRIBUTE('your_job_name','database_role',
                                               'LOGICAL STANDBY');
end;
/
```

The job role is listed in the `DBA_SCHEDULER_JOB_ROLES` view, and not in the `*_SCHEDULER_JOBS` views.

Role transition means the primary database can exchange its role with the standby database and you have jobs that should run not only when the database is in the PRIMARY role, but also when the database is in the LOGICAL STANDBY role. If a role transition is to be expected, you need to create two copies of that job in the same database—one copy that has the PRIMARY role and the other has the LOGICAL STANDBY role.

For this sample job, we need to create a table to hold the job logging in the primary database as follows:

```
CREATE
  TABLE PZ
    (
      T TIMESTAMP(6) WITH TIME ZONE,
      INSTANCE_NAME VARCHAR2(30),
      ROLE VARCHAR2(30),
      M VARCHAR2(30)
    )
/
```

Do this in the primary database. It is automatically propagated to the logical standby database when the Redo Apply process is running.

In order to be able to create a job, the Redo Apply process must first be stopped and Data Guard must be disabled. If you try to create a job without this preparation, you will get the **ORA-01031: insufficient privileges** error. The following code stops the Redo Apply process and disables the Data Guard. This enables us to create the job like this:

```
ALTER DATABASE STOP LOGICAL STANDBY APPLY;
ALTER session DISABLE GUARD;
--/
BEGIN
  dbms_scheduler.create_job
    (
      job_name            => 'teststby_stby',
      job_class           => 'DEFAULT_JOB_CLASS',
      comments            => 'test in logical standby database',
      auto_drop           => TRUE,
      job_type            => 'plsql_block',
      job_action          => 'begin insert into pz (t,instance_name,
                                                          role, m)
                              select systimestamp, i.instance_name,
                              d.database_role, ''teststby from stby''
                              from v$instance i, v$database d;
                              end;',
      number_of_arguments => 0,
      start_date          => NULL,
      repeat_interval     => 'freq=minutely;interval=2;',
      end_date            => NULL);
END;
/
ALTER session ENABLE GUARD;
ALTER DATABASE START LOGICAL STANDBY APPLY;
```

This code creates the job. This does not mean that the job is going to run now. The job will run when the guard status is `STANDBY`.

Running jobs in a logical standby database

Once the job is created in the logical standby database, we can run it. However, first we must switch the logical standby database into the correct mode as shown here:

```
alter database guard standby;
```

However, how successful that job will be depends on what it should do. If the job updates a table that is guarded, there will be other errors such as:

```
PL/SQL: ORA-16224: Database Guard is enabled
```

It is possible to successfully run such a job by running:

```
alter database guard none;
```

Now, tables whose changes are propagated from the primary database are editable for the job. So the job that tries this has more chance for success.

To stop this, we can set it back using:

```
alter database guard all;
```

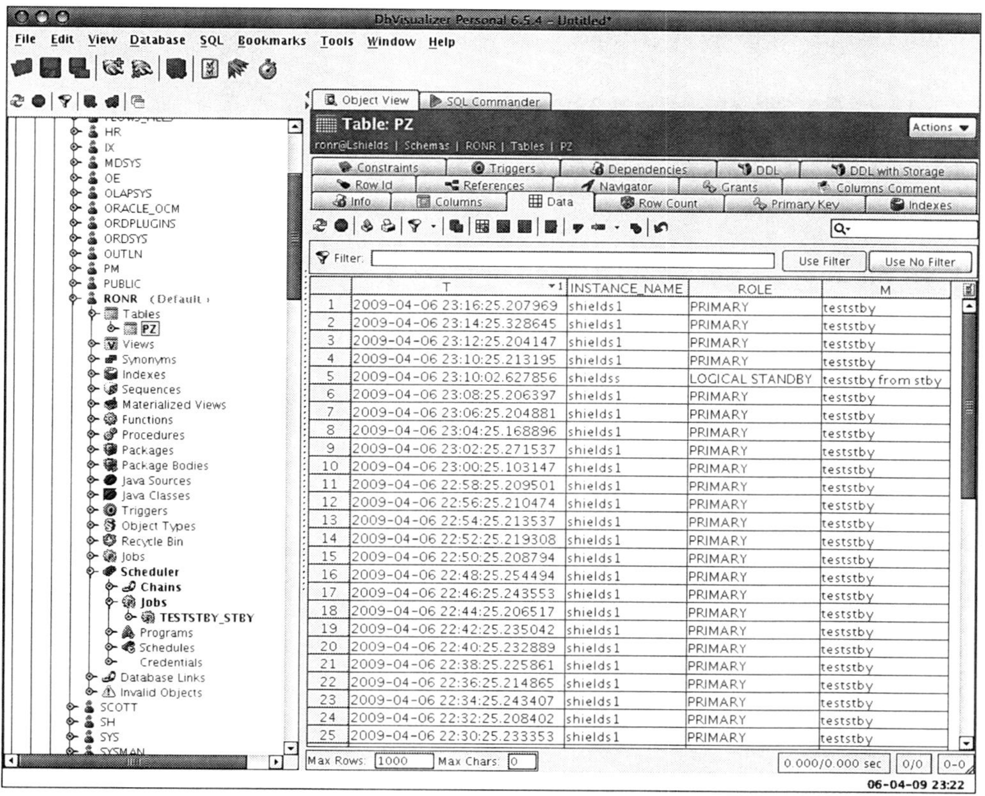

In this screenshot, you can see that a job was running in the primary database all the time. The logical standby database was altered to allow a job to run for a short while, after which the Redo Apply process was restarted.

Summary

In this chapter we have seen:

- How to tie a job to a specific RAC instance
- How to tie a job to a specific service
- How `instance_stickiness` and `instance_id` can prevent jobs from running
- How we can achieve a job to keep running when a service gets relocated
- How we can create and run jobs in a logical standby database

In the next chapter, we will take a look at the tools that are available for us to increase our productivity when working with the Scheduler.

10
Scheduler GUI Tools

We have already seen a lot of the power of the Scheduler. We worked with the Scheduler mostly using SQL*Plus and DB Console. Although everything can be done using SQL*Plus, it can hardly be called the "user interface" that the Scheduler deserves. The DB Console supports lots of features of the Scheduler, but it is not exactly a friendly tool. Also, it does not show the flexibility of the Scheduler and is not always available. The Grid control is more or less the same, but is comparatively hard to set up. Searching the Web for more tools is a bit disappointing. Since a few years, there is a nice little multiplatform, multidatabase tool called DbVisualizer. This tool offers tremendous flexibility by virtue of its design. In this chapter, we will walk through the tools, DB Console, and DbVisualizer and see how they work.

DB Console

DB Console is a free tool that has been included in the database installation since Oracle 10g. It is a web application, and it works reasonably well in most browsers. It needs a separate configuration for every database that you want to work with, which makes it a burden for your system. When working with many databases, this hardly makes sense. In that case, Grid Control is a better choice; but, it lacks the features that are present in DB Console.

After the installation, the URL for DB Console is shown. When launching the browser to the specified URL, we get to see the logon screen as follows:

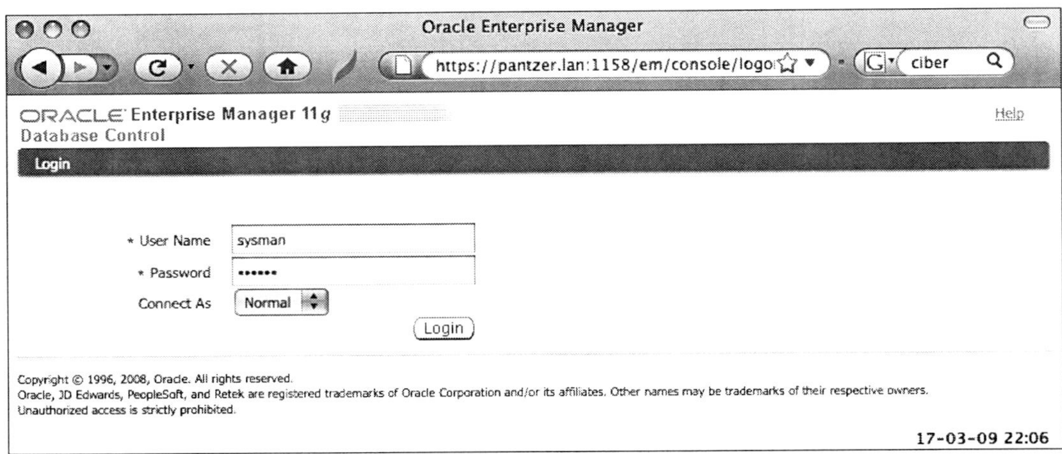

We can use this tool from a remote location as long as it is somehow reachable from your current location. This is great and can be very useful. After entering **User Name** and **Password**, we get to the DB Console home page. Here, you can see a quick overview of the database that the DB Console is working on:

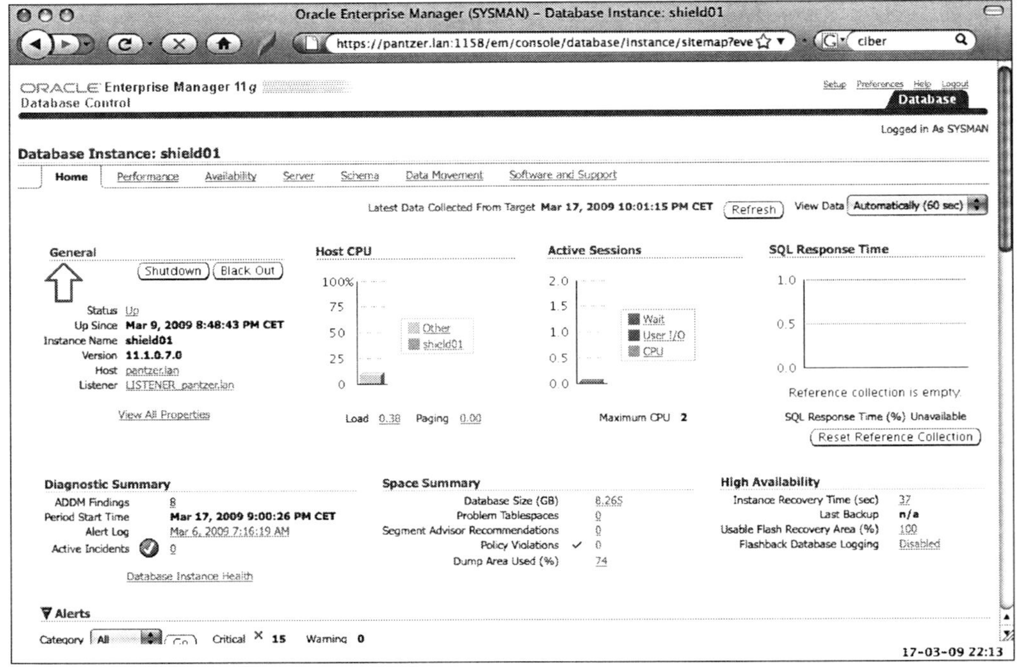

In this case, the database's name is **shield01** and it's located on the pantzer server. The Scheduler can be found in the **Server** tab, as shown in the following screenshot:

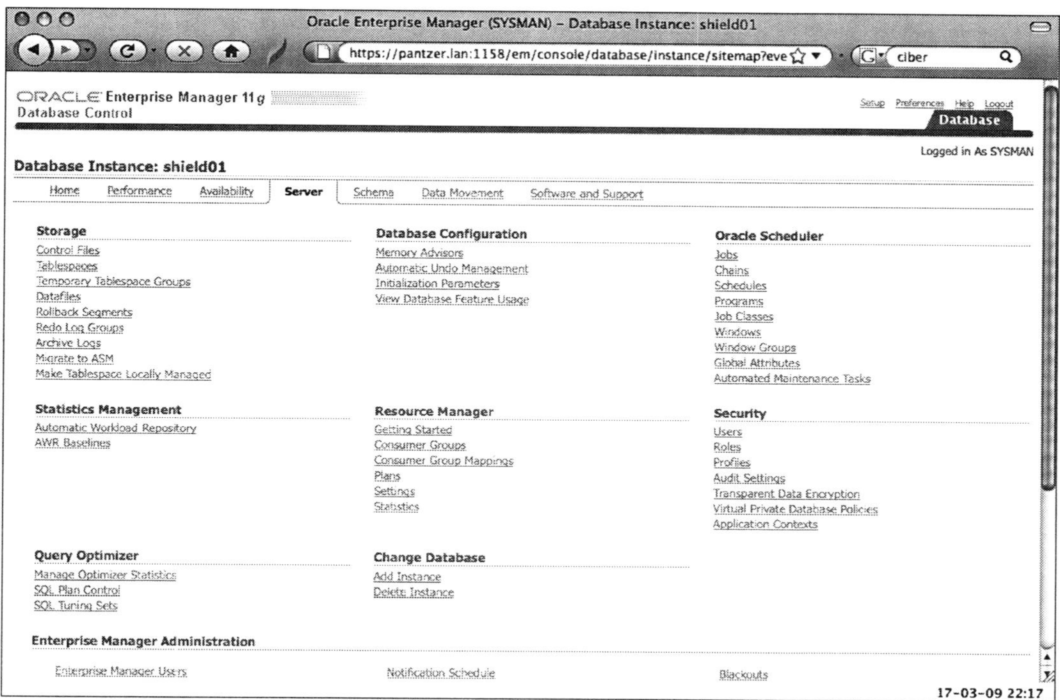

In this screenshot, we can see the **Resource Manager** and **Oracle Scheduler** columns. For now, we just dive into the **Oracle Scheduler** column. The entries to manage **Jobs**, **Chains**, **Schedules**, **Programs**, **Job Classes**, **Windows**, **Windows Groups**, **Global Attributes**, and **Automated Maintenance Tasks** are all here. Missing from this list is an entry for the credentials. The **Automated Maintenance Tasks** screen is very nice to see. This view was missing in 10g which made the important tasks invisible.

Now, you can see them listed in the following screenshot:

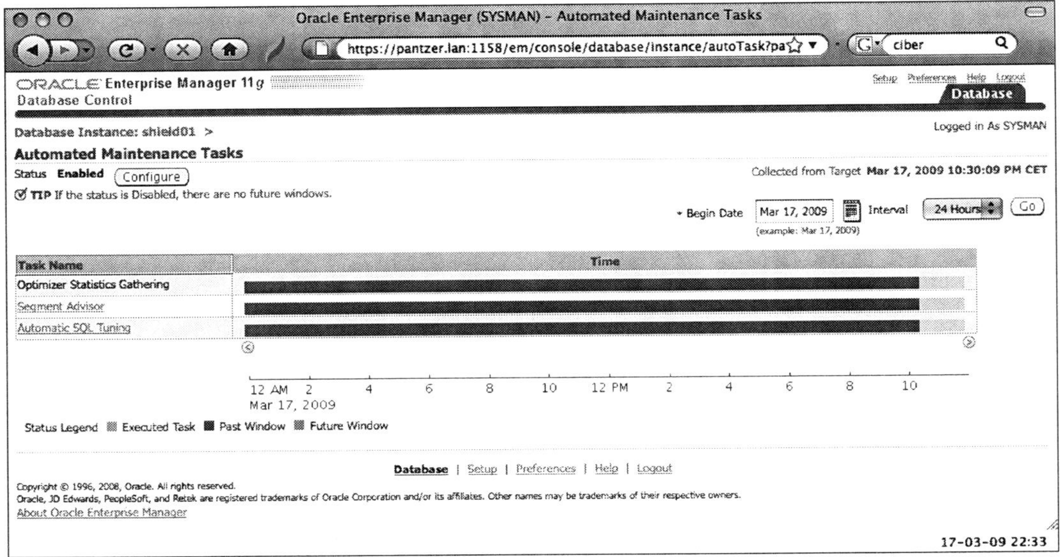

On this screen, we can clearly see the **Optimizer Statistics Gathering**, **Segment Advisor**, and **Automatic SQL Tuning** jobs. Normally, we don't need to bother with them and can let them be. When needed, you now know where to find them. Clicking on **Database Instance: shield01** brings us back to the previous screen. From there, we select the **Jobs** view that pops up on the screen:

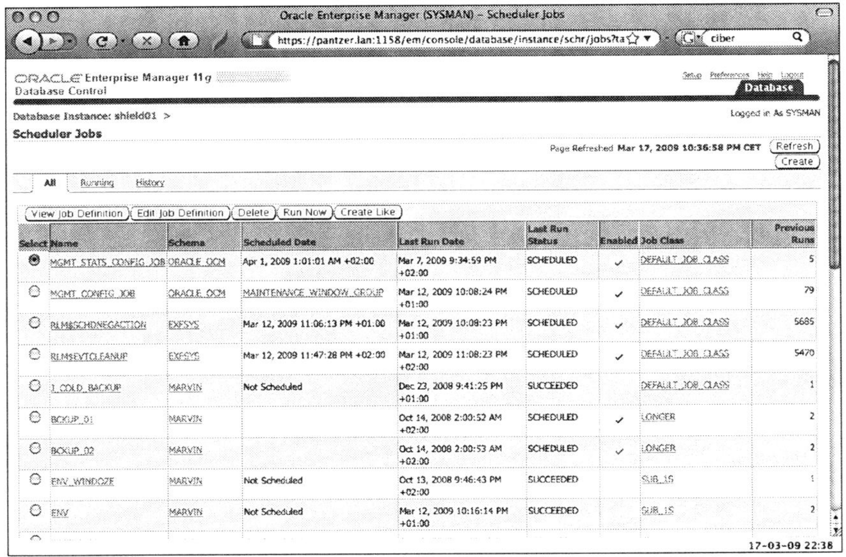

This screen is mostly used to review jobs. It lists all the defined jobs that the connected user can see. It shows which jobs exist, their status information, and the job class that the job belongs to. This can be a long list when you use jobs that generate lots of other jobs. When a job is running, you can see in the following screenshot that the **Scheduled Date** column shows **now running**, and the **Last Run Status** column shows **RUNNING**:

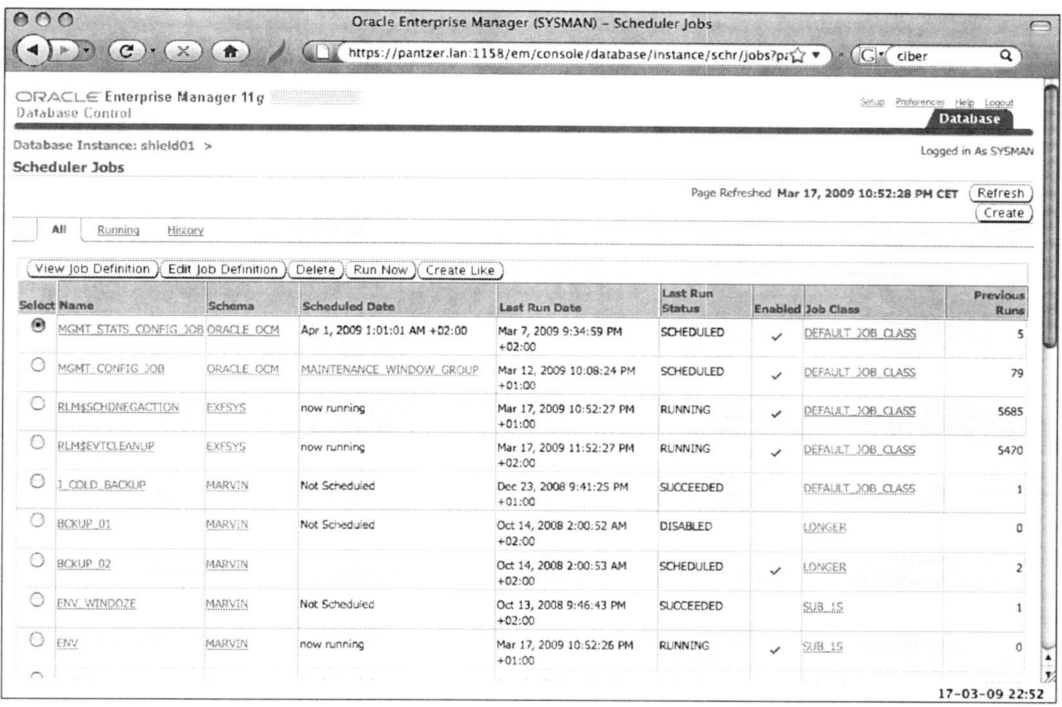

The running jobs also have their own dedicated space in the **Running** tab. In the **Running** tab, it is not surprising that we can see which jobs are running. This is shown in the following screenshot:

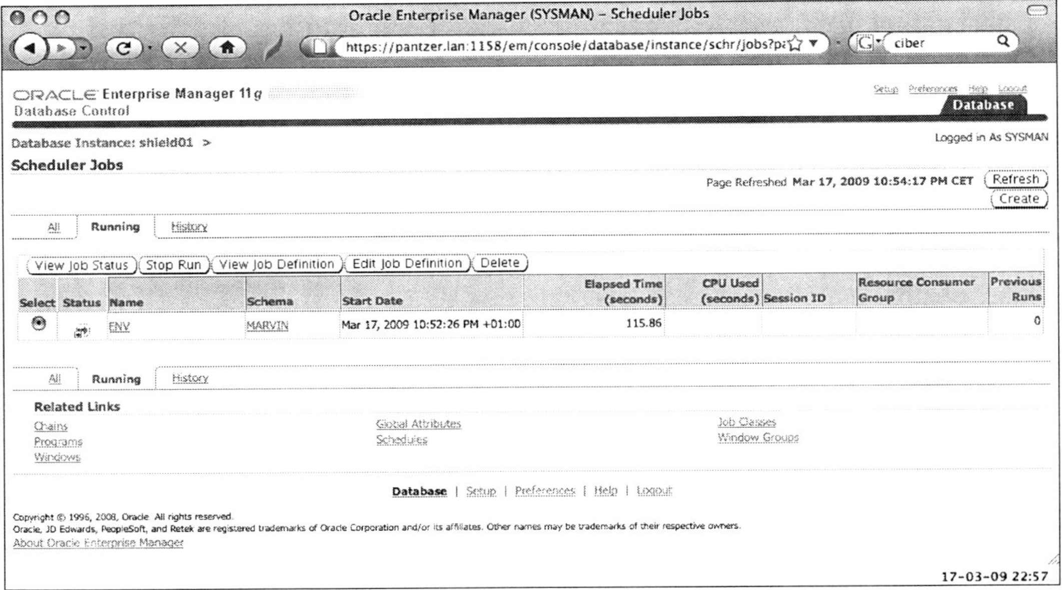

Looking at the running jobs, we can see more details such as when the job started and how long it has been running. In this case, it is an external job and so there is no information for **CPU Used**, **Session ID**, and **Resource Consumer Group**.

Using the **Stop Run** button, we can stop the job. The other buttons are not unique for running jobs. After a while, all the jobs end up in the **History** section. So, in the **History** tab, we get to see which jobs ran recently.

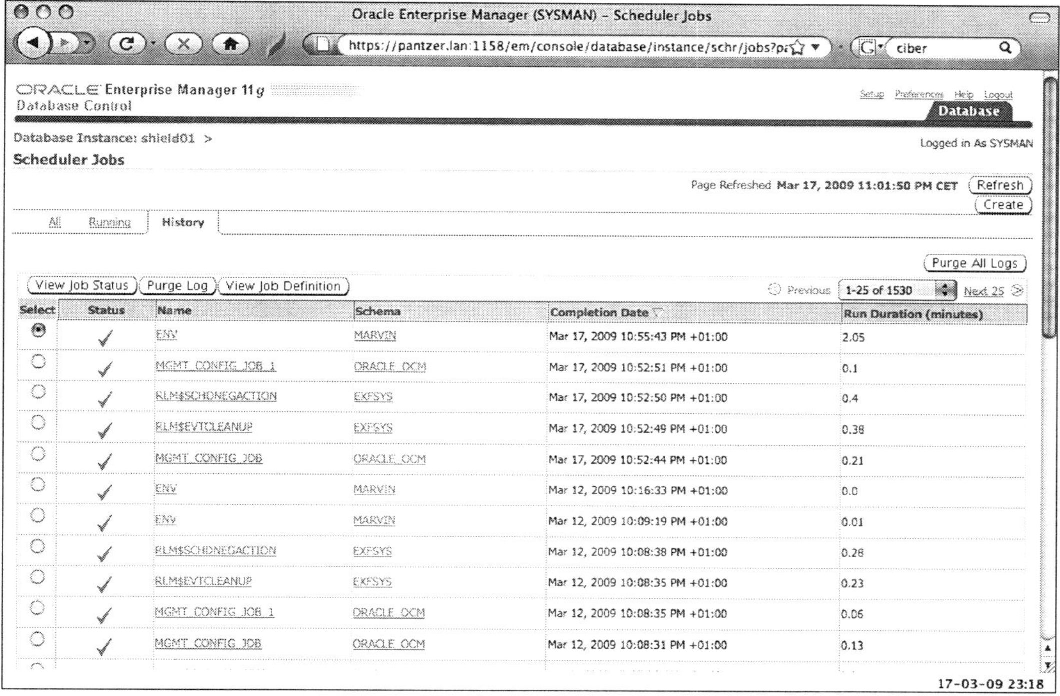

When looking for a specific job execution, it could be easier to start from a job definition in the **All** tab. Click on the job name to see the job definition, which is **ENV** in this case.

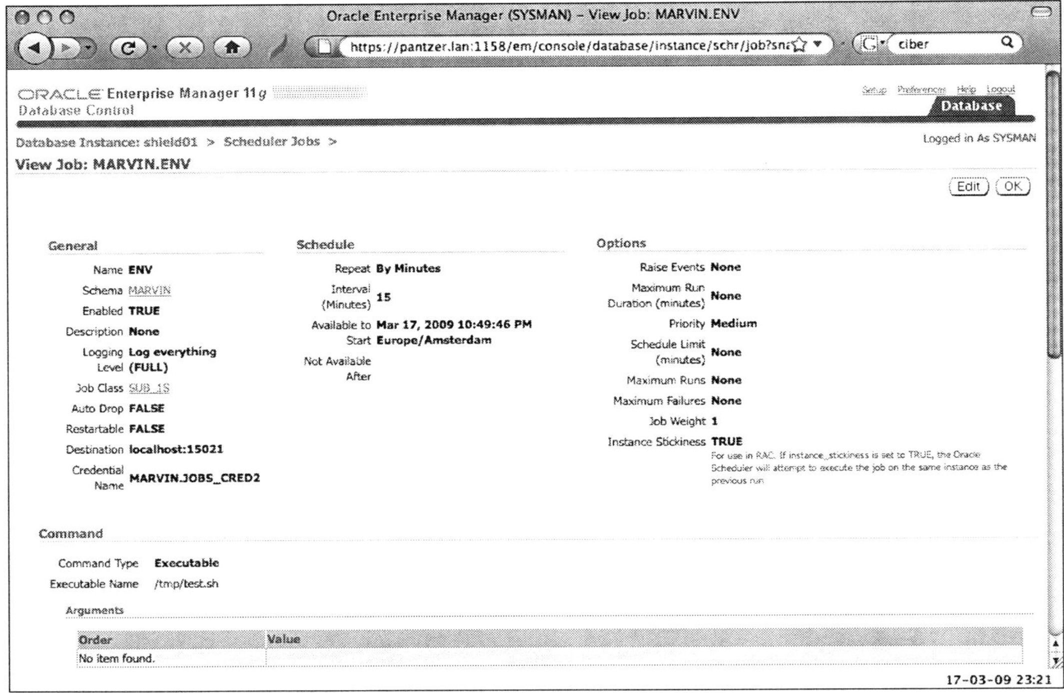

On scrolling down, we come to the **Operation Detail**:

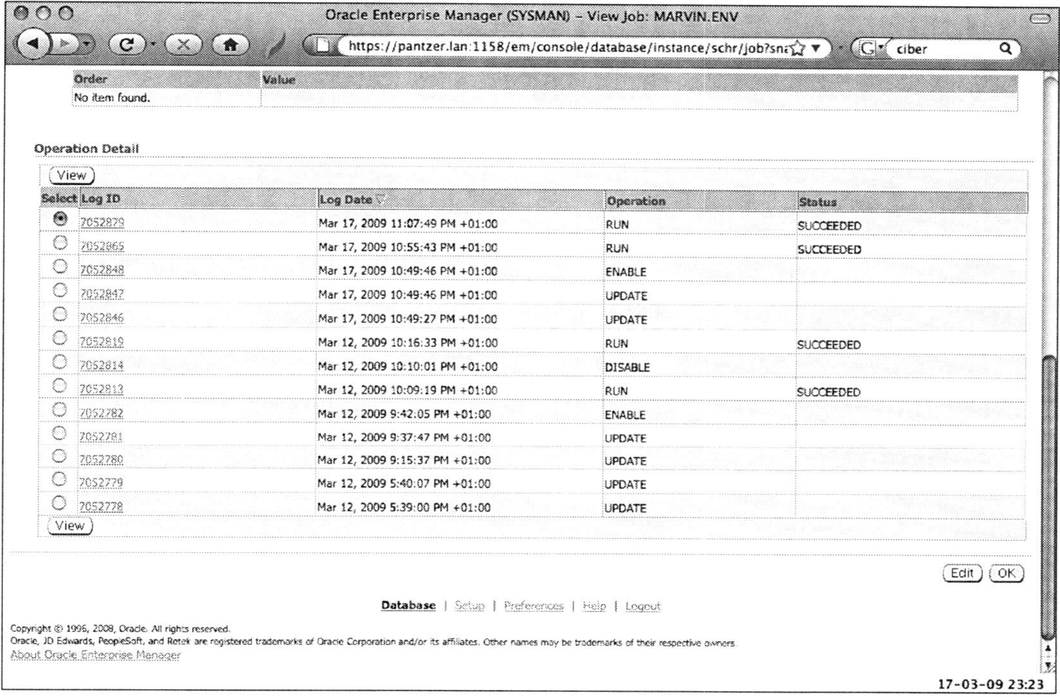

We can see the execution details of the operations in this screen. We get to see the same details here as we would when browsing using the **History** tab.

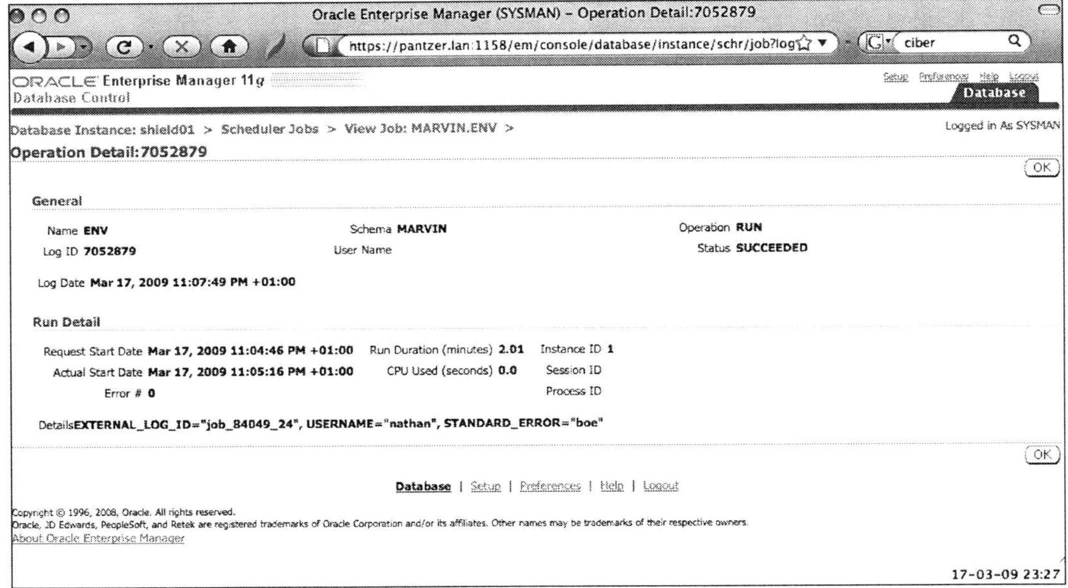

We can see that the job ran externally using the operating system user **Nathan**. Also, the job has a log file called **job_84049_24** and it received a message on the standard error. The job operation is **RUN**, which means that it is a job execution. The status is **SUCCEEDED**, which means that the return code of the job was `0`. There is no way to see the contents of the external log file using DB Console. If we want to see the external log file, we need to go to the server where the agent runs. There, we can find the log file in the agent's execution data directory in the logs directory.

The **Chains** entry in the **Oracle Scheduler** column in the **Server** tab is very useful. It shows the defined chains with buttons to create a job that runs the selected chain, and also edit, view, create, or delete a chain.

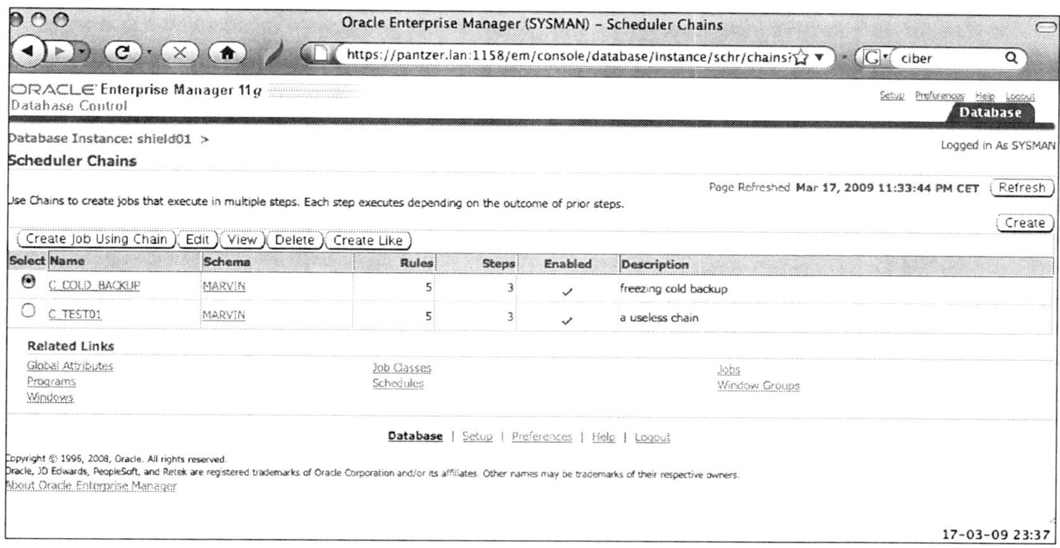

The **Create Job Using Chain** button makes using chains a little easier. It essentially lists a pre-filled screen that is very similar to the **Create Job** screen that is shown here:

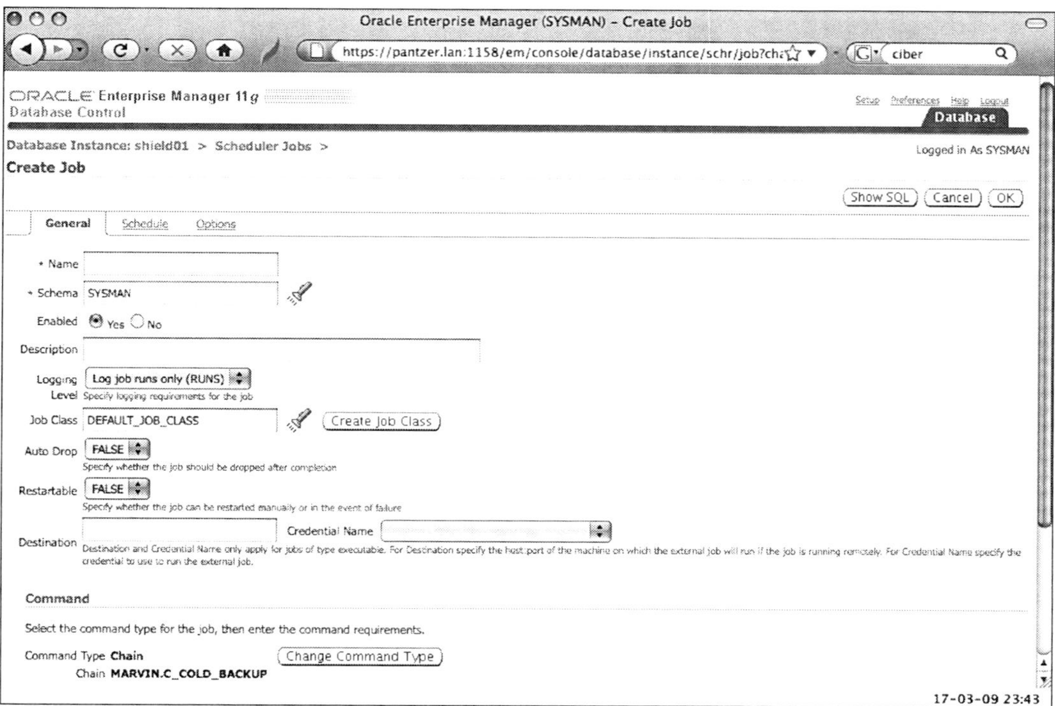

In the **Create Job** screen, we can enter the general properties of a job in the **General** tab. Scheduling can be set up in the **Schedule** tab. Here, the DB Console is a bit limited as we can only specify one **Time** and **Repeat** interval, and we cannot use the normal "frequency = definition" that `dbms_scheduler` allows. We can see this in the following screenshot:

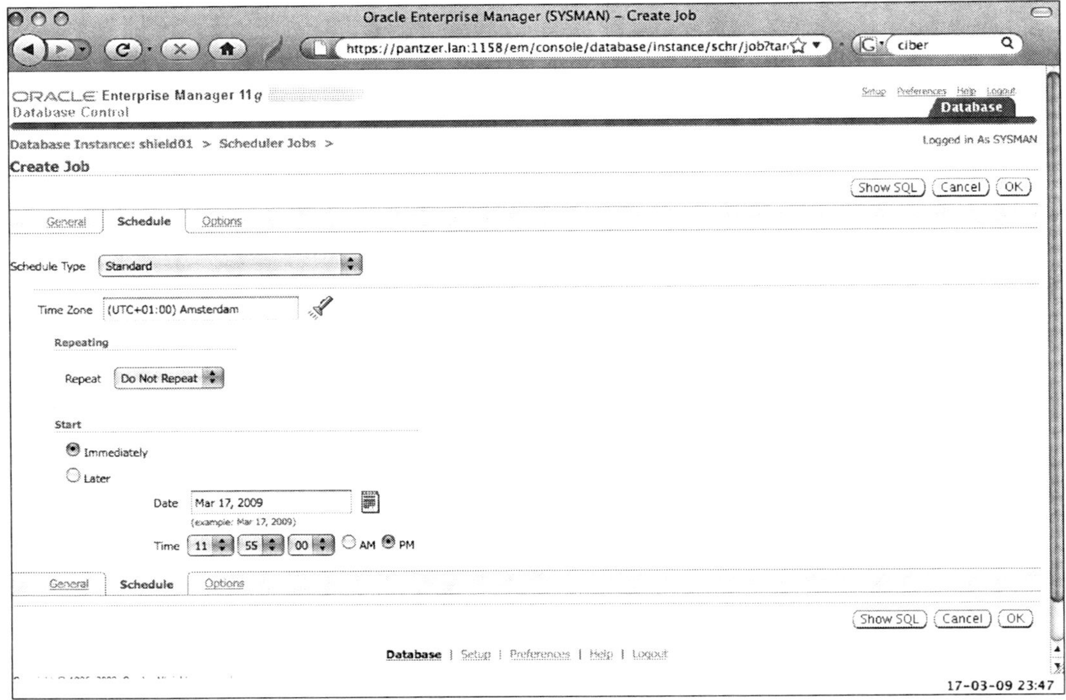

We can set a job to repeat, but when we want a job to run daily at `05:00` and `17:00`, we cannot do that using this screen unless we have predefined a schedule that does this. In the **Options** tab, we can specify which events a job has to generate:

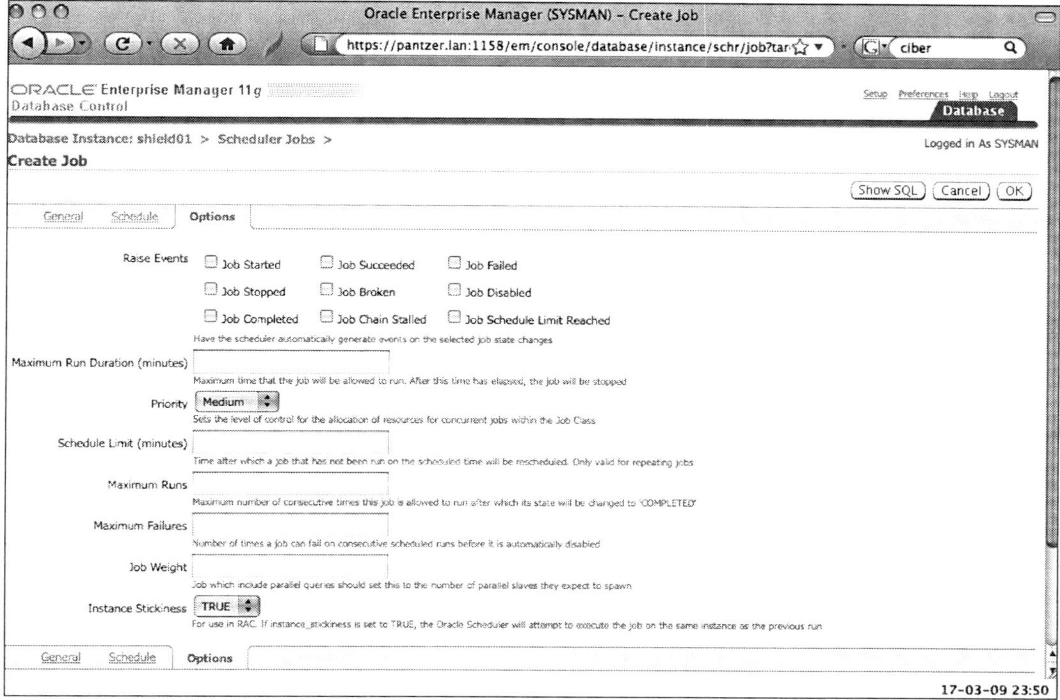

Go back to the Server page and select the **Schedules** entry in the **Oracle Scheduler** column. We come to the following screen where schedules are created and maintained:

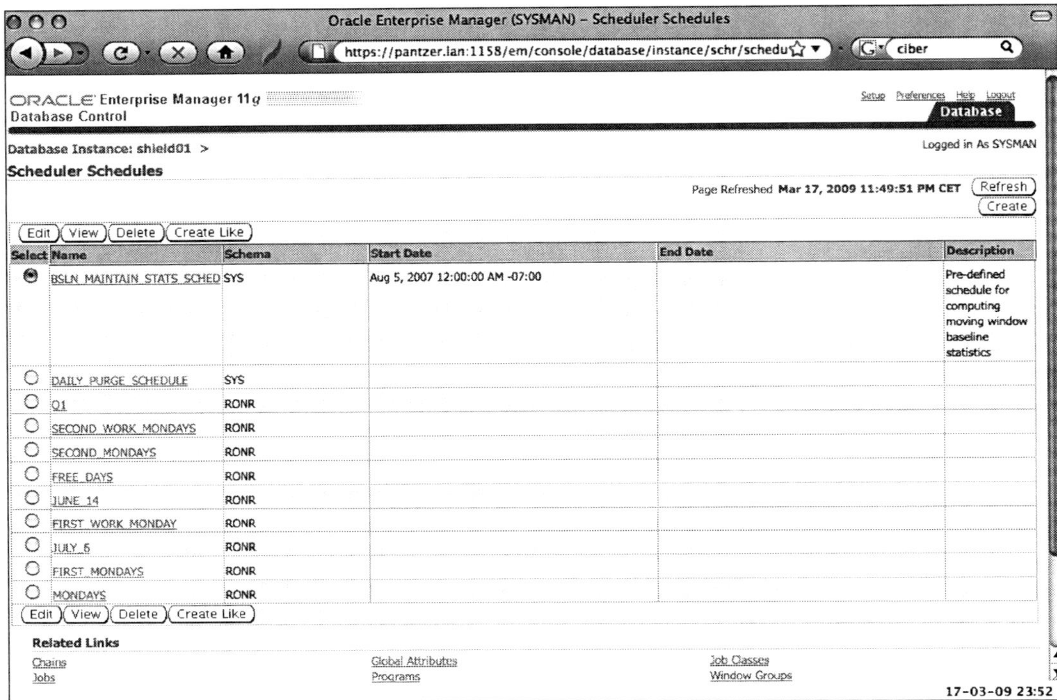

The **Edit**, **Create**, and **Create Like** buttons have a very interesting thing in common—they all show the first few scheduled dates that are generated using the definition that is being entered.

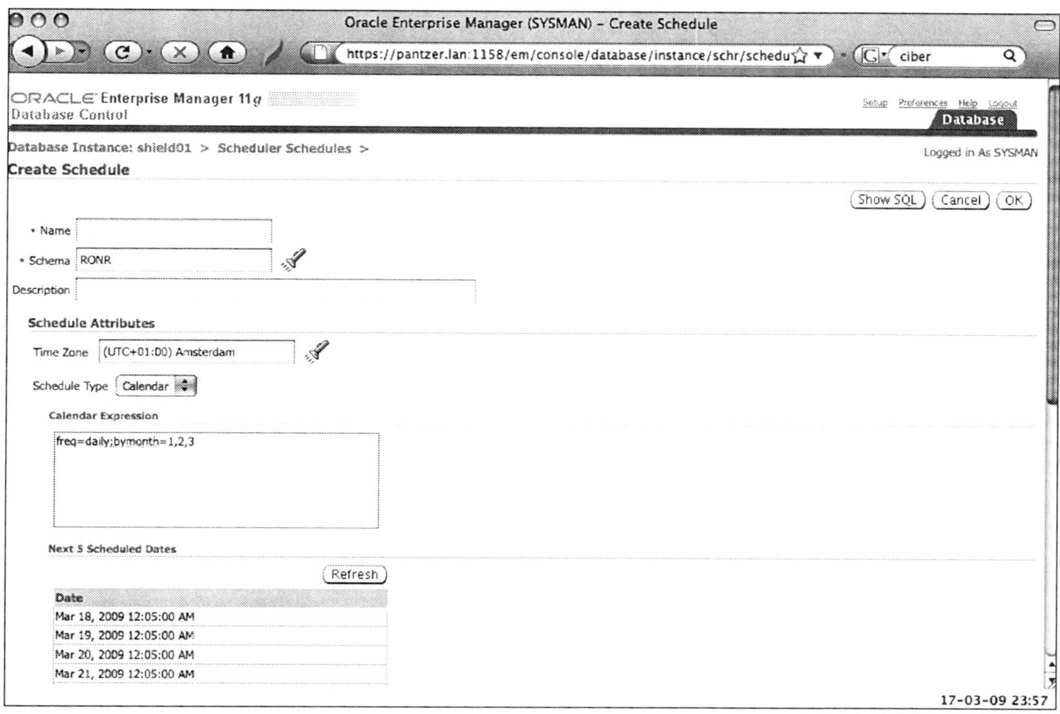

See the lower part of the screen. It is very helpful and can prevent unpleasant surprises. This screen is very convenient because it immediately shows the results of your Scheduler definition.

Back in the main Scheduler column, we now pick the **Programs** entry to see where can we create, delete, copy, and edit program definitions. Even in an empty database, there are quite a lot of programs defined as you can see in the following screenshot:

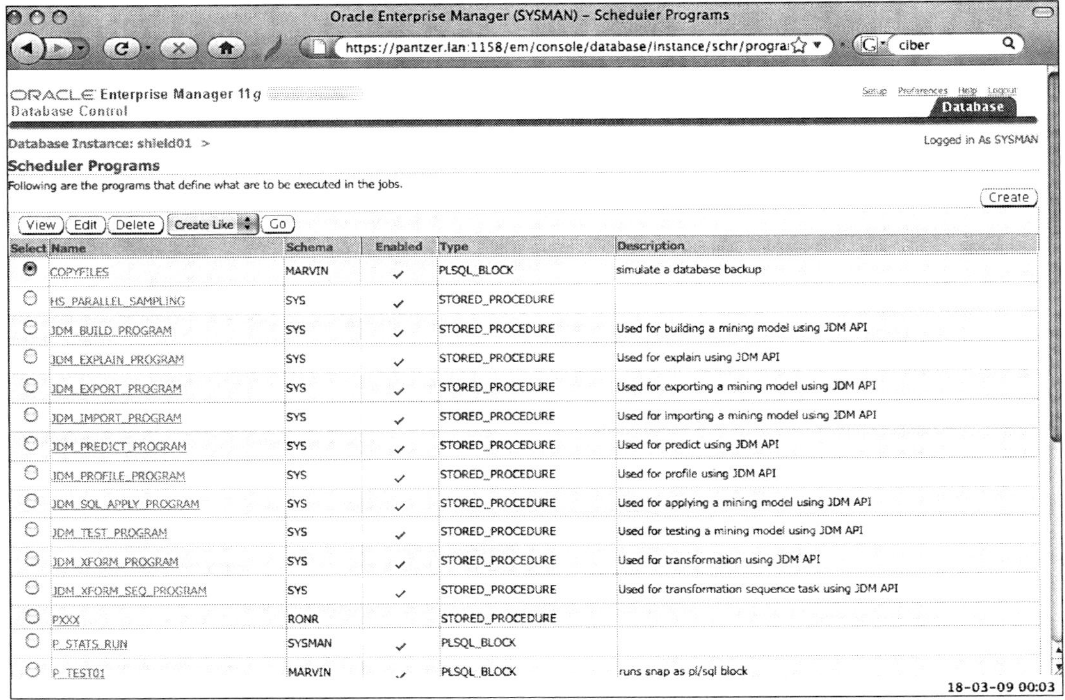

Now, we click on the **Edit** button to see some more details. In this case, the program is of the PL/SQL type, so we don't have the option to add program arguments.

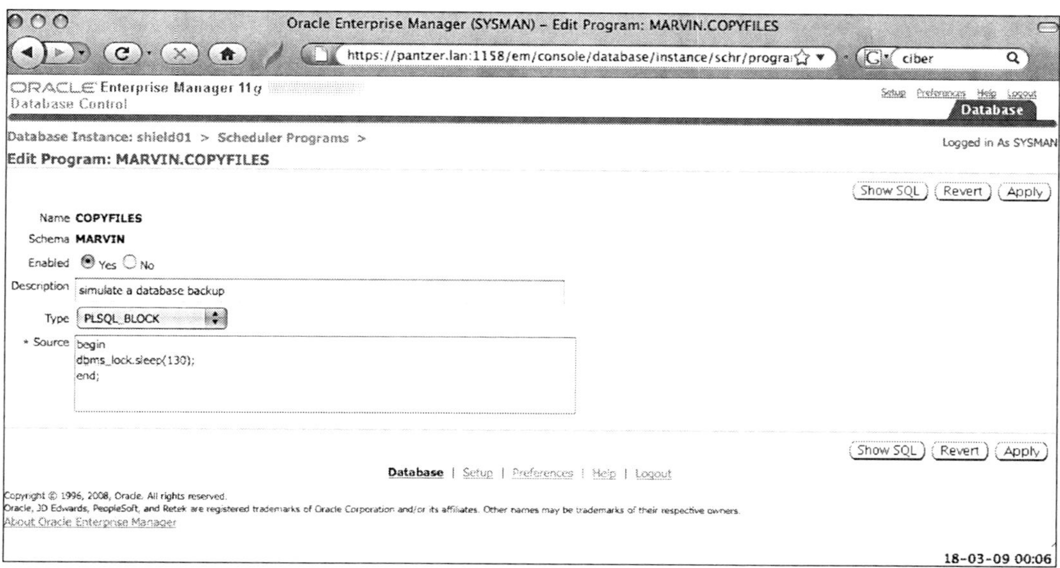

For the other types—**STORED_PROCEDURE** and **EXECUTABLE**—we have the facility to add arguments when appropriate. This is to say, when you select a procedure that has arguments, they are listed as named arguments with the option to give them a default value.

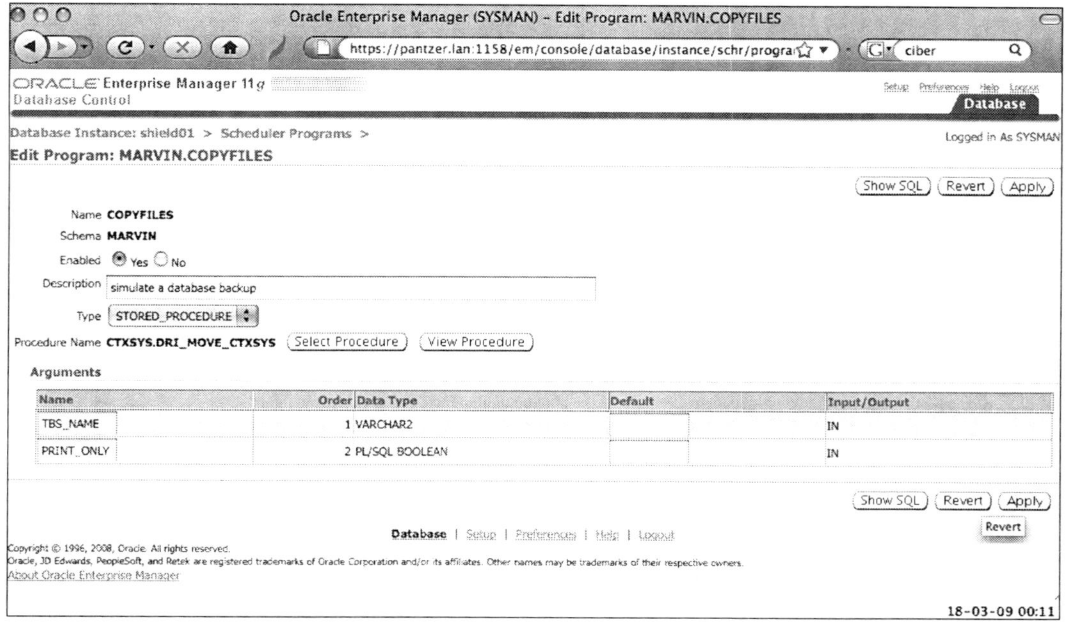

When the type is **EXECUTABLE**, Oracle has no way of knowing what the executable program expects, so there we can manually add arguments.

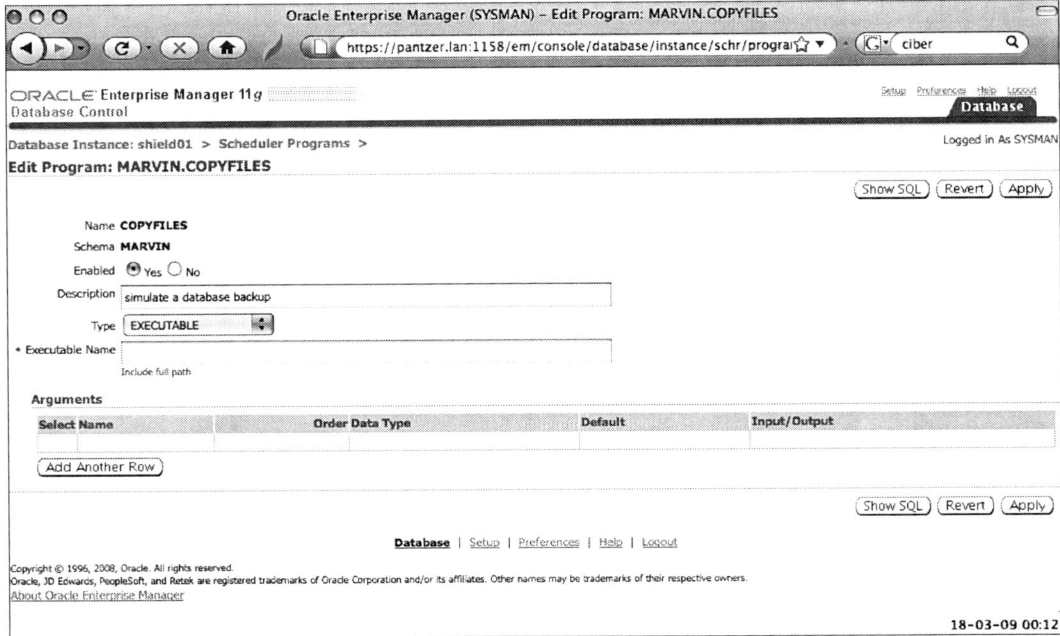

In the **Scheduler Job Classes** screen, we can manage job classes. Go and take a look at this page in a new database and check **Log Retention Period**. You might want to make some changes there. In this database, the job classes have already been modified to keep just 120-days' worth of logging as shown in the following screenshot:

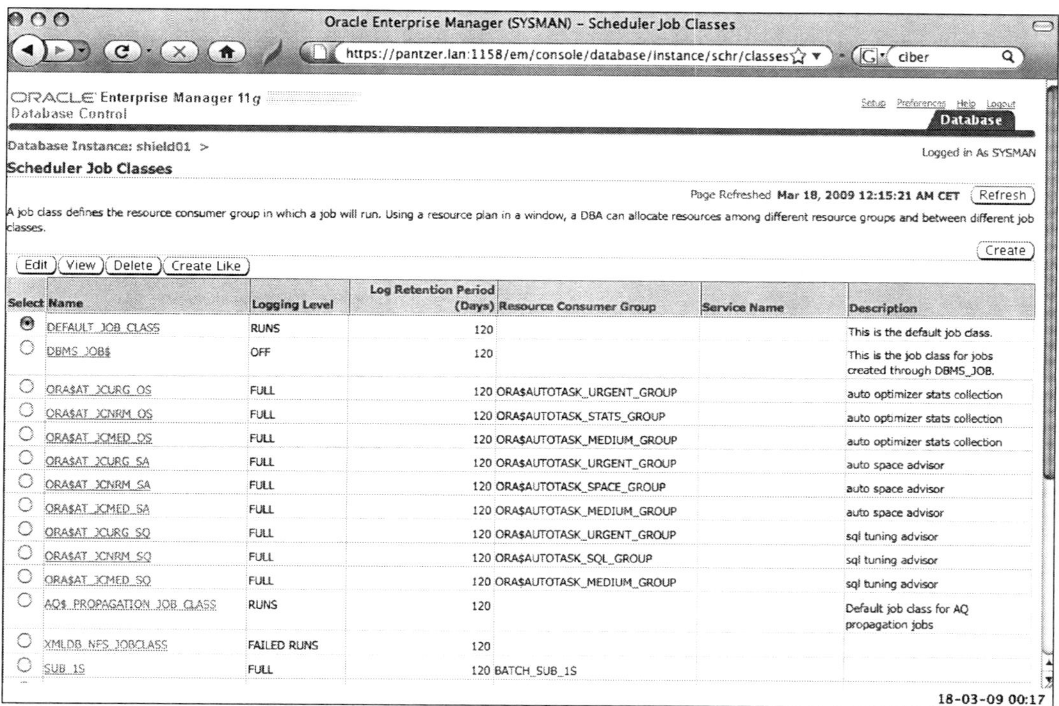

In the **Scheduler Windows** page, we can define a window. Here, we can define which **Resource Plan** is active during which period. A window can be attached to a predefined schedule. However, it can also have its own repeat interval like jobs.

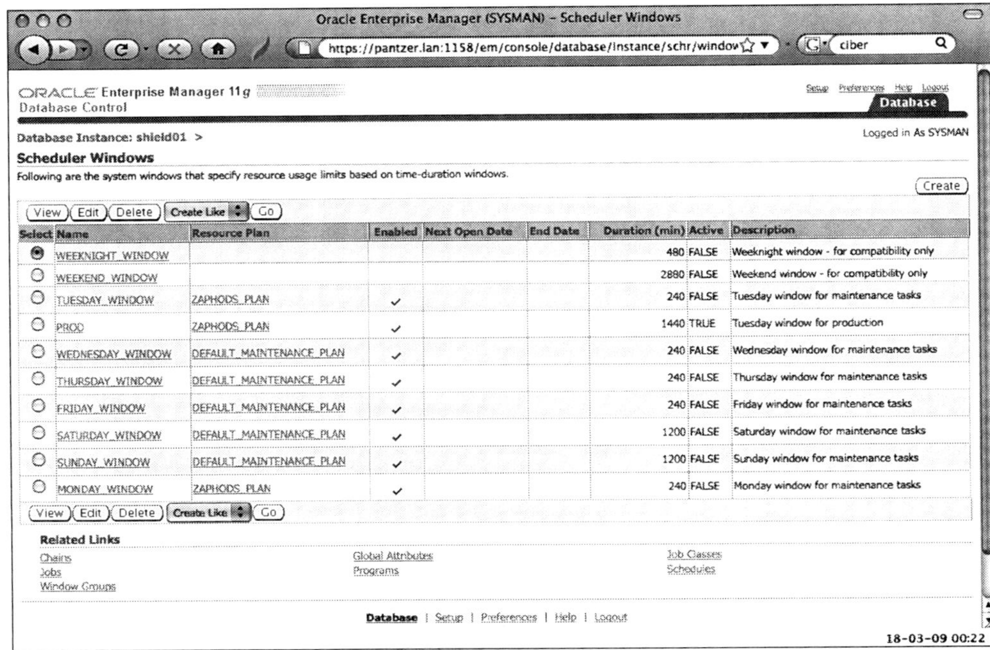

In the **Scheduler Window Groups** screen, we can combine windows in the Window Groups. The groups shown in this screenshot are all predefined:

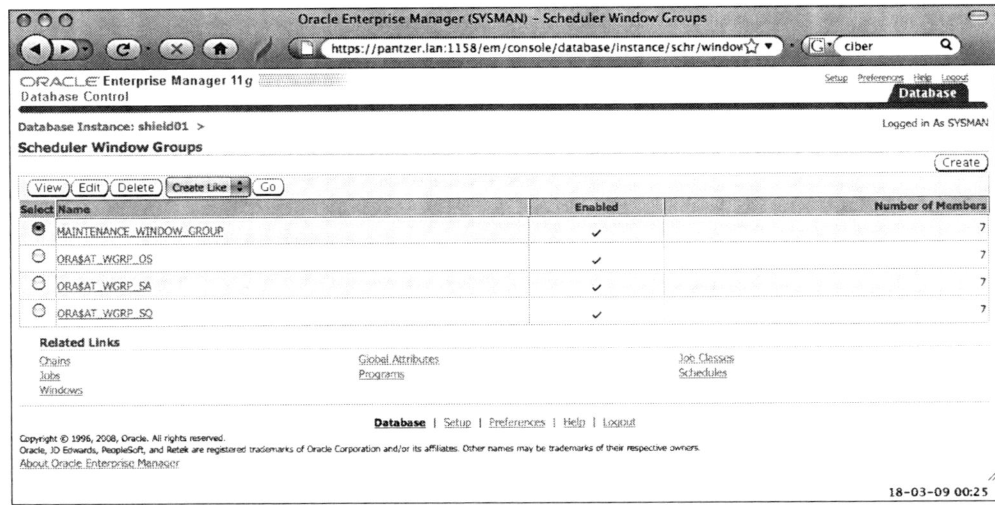

The last window is the one that holds the Global Scheduler Attributes.

It is important to have the correct time zone listed in the Global Scheduler Attributes. If the time zone is missing here, and if it is also missing in the job and the schedule definitions, switching to daylight saving time will be a problem.

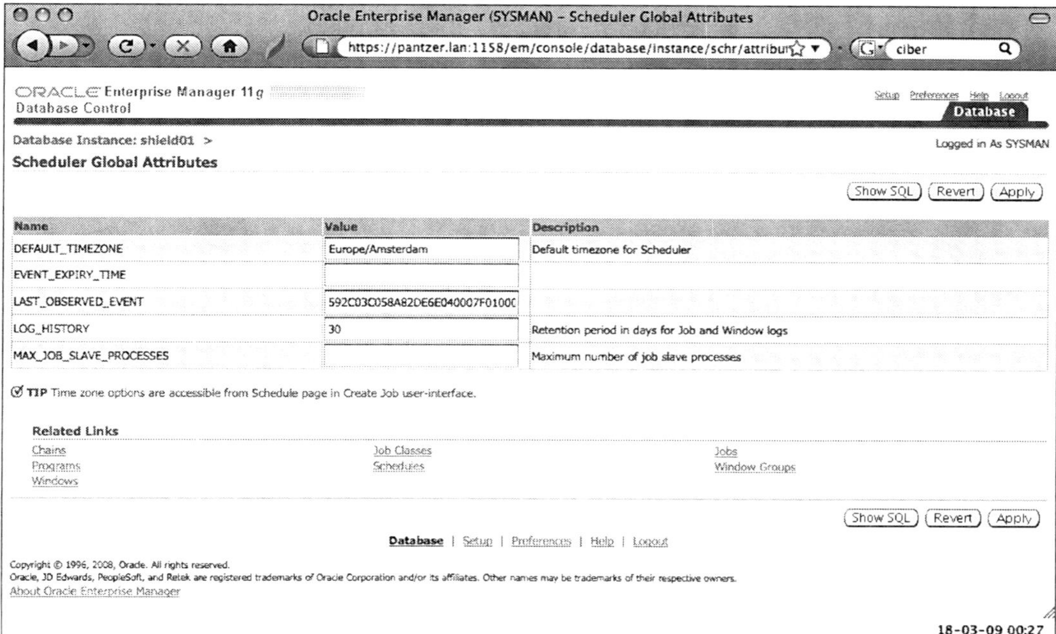

The **MAX_JOB_SLAVE_PROCESSES** attribute can be used to put a little control over the number of the jobs that can maximally run together. This is the only option to limit jobs where Resource Manager is not an option for some reason.

Grid Control

In Grid Control, we are also able to manage jobs, much like in DB Console. The Scheduler objects can be found in the **Administration** tab of a database.

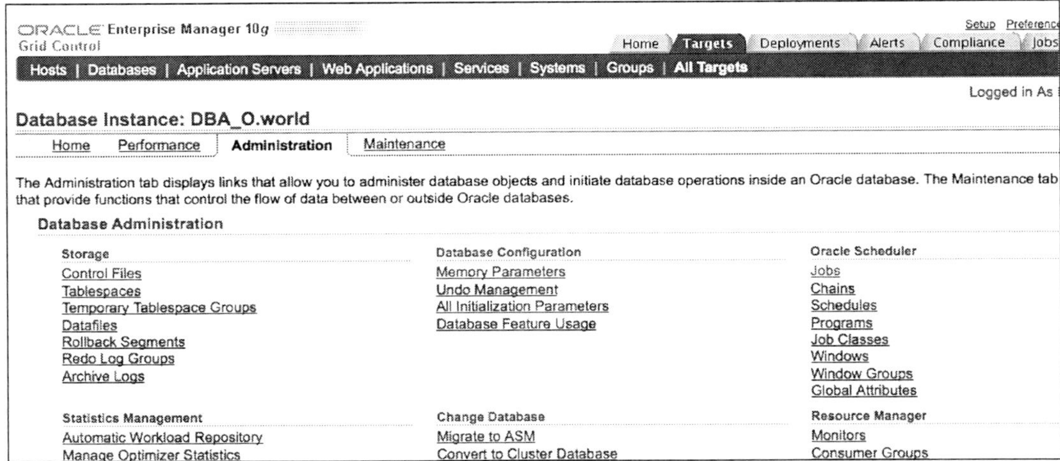

There is no support for the remote job agent in Grid Control 10g. This is not strange considering the fact that this type of agent popped up in 11g for the first time. The GUI works the same as for DB Console.

DbVisualizer

At this moment, the only other tool available that has a decent Scheduler support is DbVisualizer. There may be more tools, but this one runs on multiple platforms and is very easily configurable.

This tool has some surprises. Initially, it was only a browsing tool, but that has changed over time. If you have the chance to play with it, *Ctrl* + click on everything you see in the object tree. When you do so, you will see a pop-up menu that lists actions that can be performed on the selected object. This is very context-sensitive and gives a clean user interface.

The Scheduler support built into DbVisualizer is the users' contributions, from Nathan Aaron and someone who is writing about Oracle Scheduler and was missing a simple Scheduler interface (that's me), to the tool. Take a look at `http://dbvis.com/` and ask for a demo license. It works on almost anything that has a CPU in it. DbVisualizer uses the JDBC interface to connect to the database. When connected, you get to see a list of connections that can be grouped in folders.

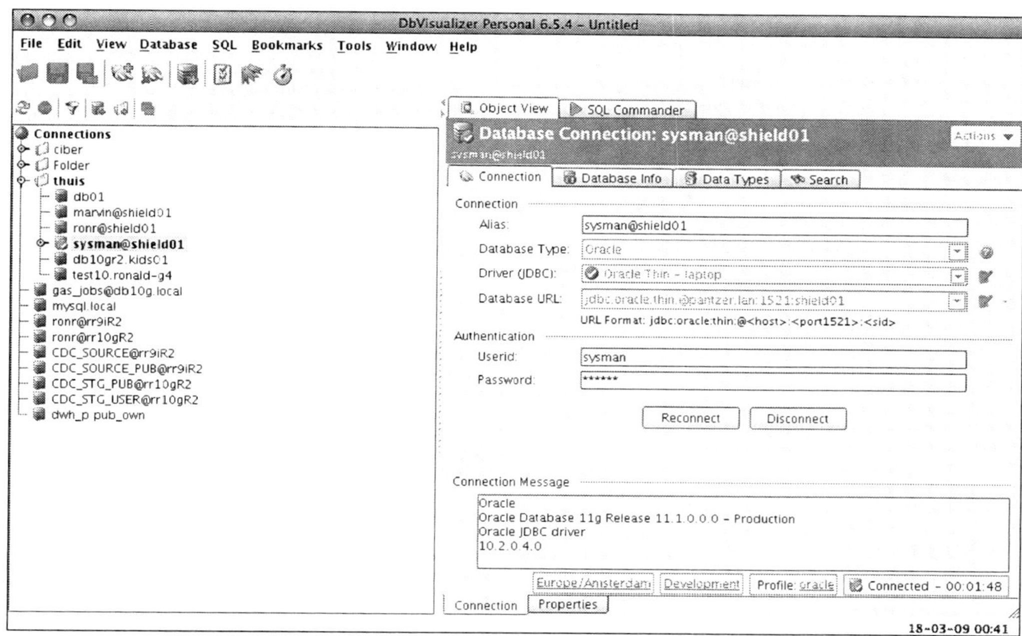

Open the connection where you want to work and see the top-level object tree: **Schemas, Session Properties**, and **DBA Views**.

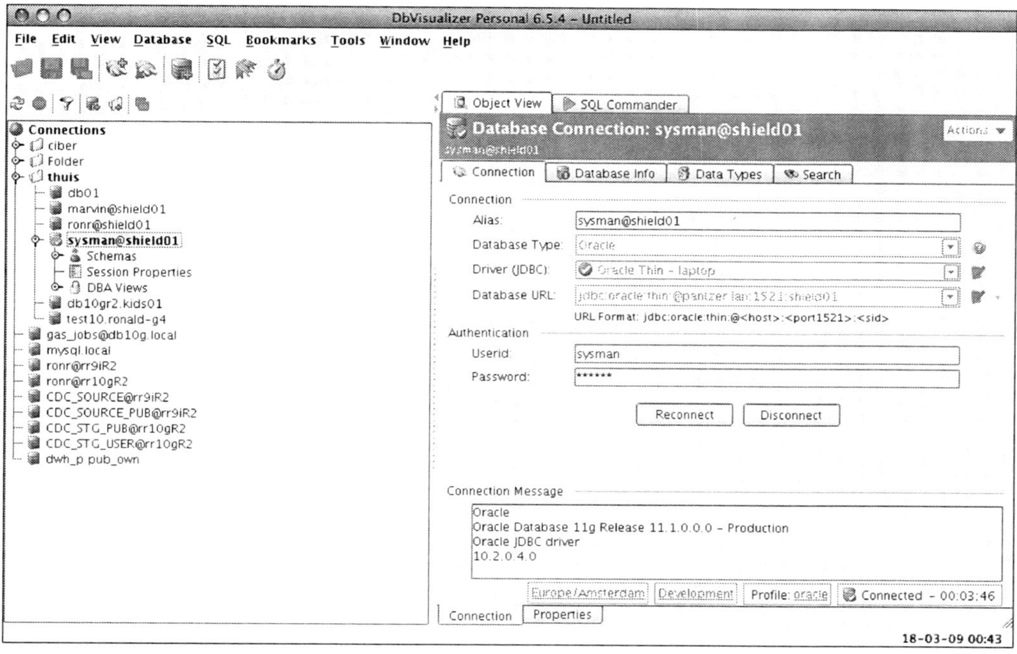

The Scheduler support is located in **Schemas** and **DBA Views**.

The **DBA Views** contain the items that should be managed centrally, most likely by a DBA. Here, you can find **Global Attributes**, **Windows**, and **Job Classes**.

In the **Schemas** tree, there are the objects that are a part of an application such as the jobs, programs, chains, schedules, and credentials.

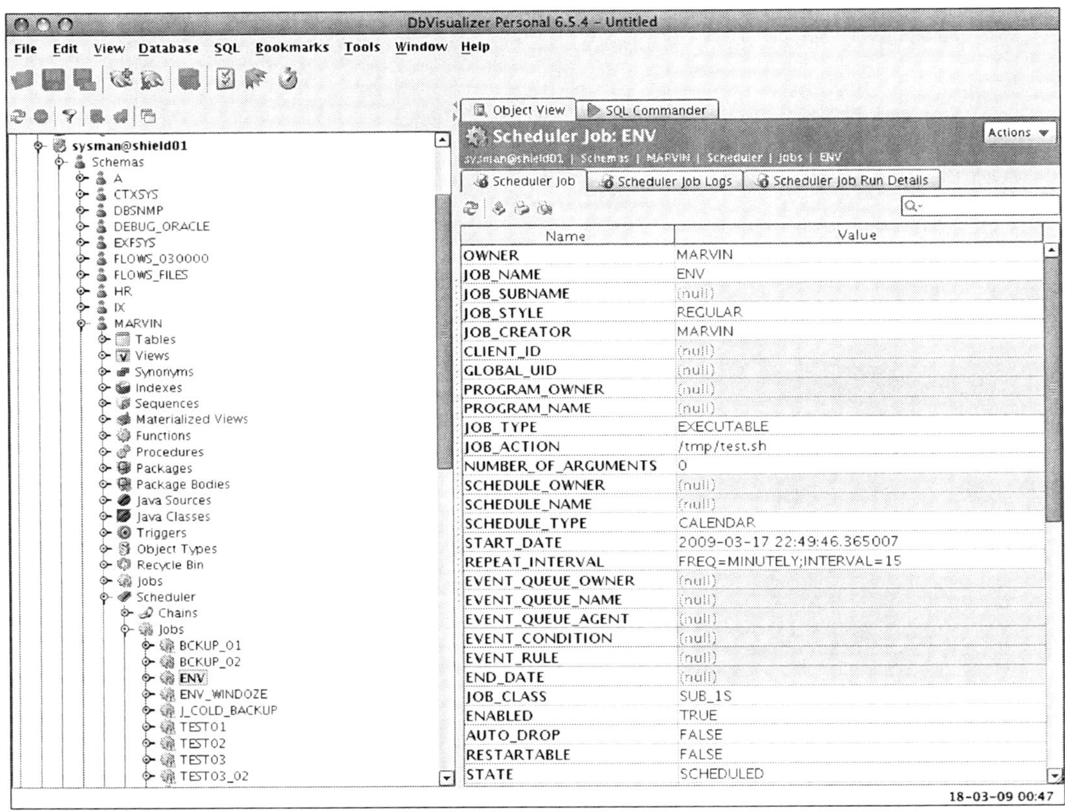

The Oracle Scheduler support is grouped in the **Scheduler** subtree of **Schemas**. In this screenshot, you can see the jobs of **MARVIN**, the same as the ones shown earlier in DB Console. In the lefthand pane is the object tree, and in the righthand pane are the details of the selected object—in this case, the **ENV** job. The righthand pane also has a few tabs where the Scheduler job logs and the Scheduler job run details are shown for the selected job.

Take a little time to explore the tool and don't forget to right-click on everything you see in the object tree. You will like it. For example, see what happens when you right-click on **Jobs**:

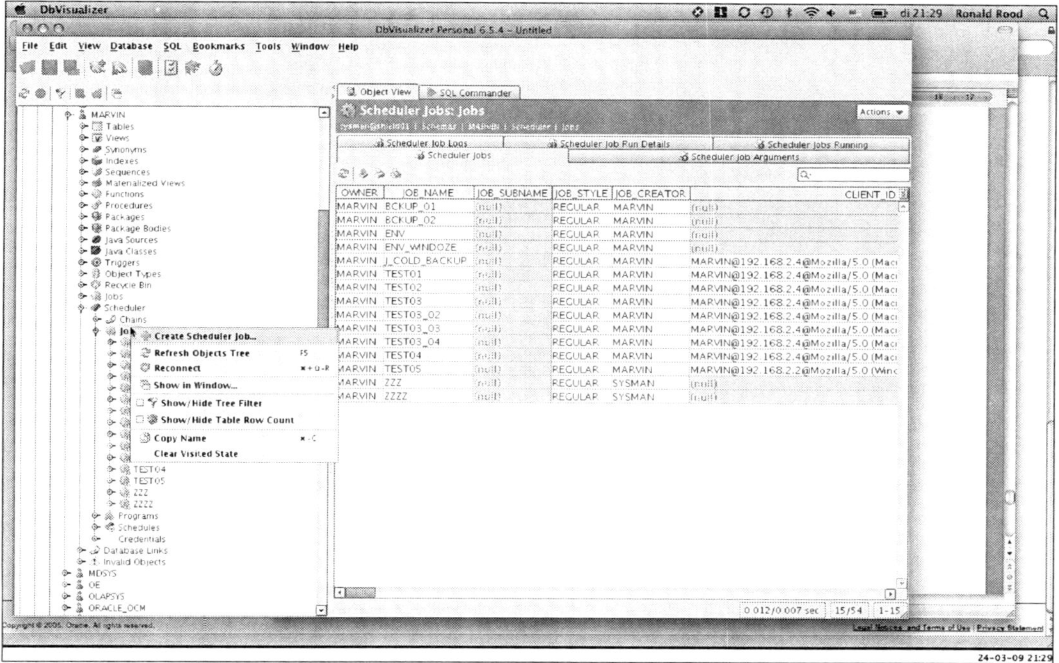

Select the **Create Scheduler Job** option from the menu. You will have something similar to the following screenshot on your screen:

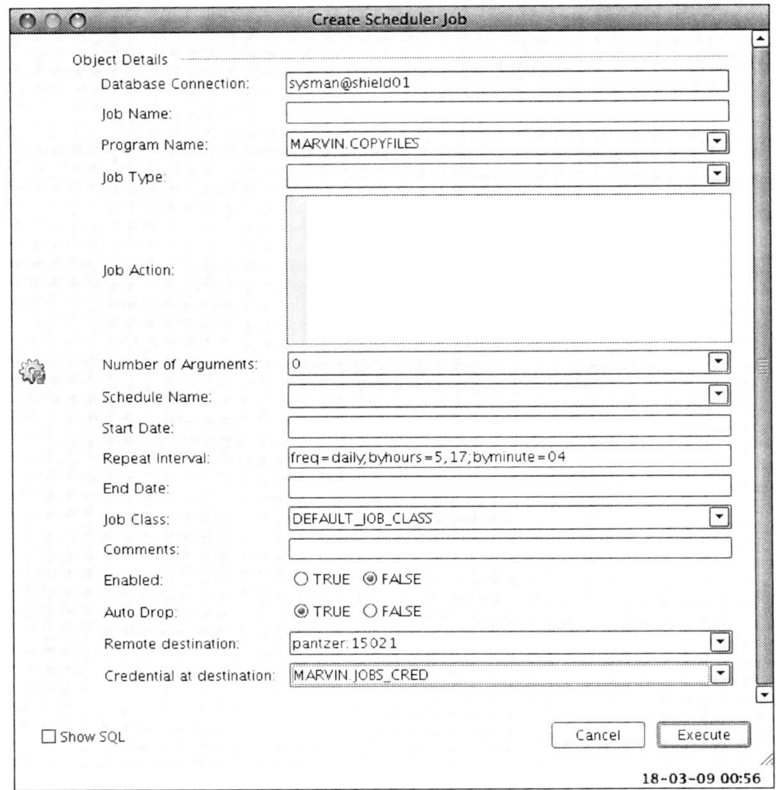

This **Create Scheduler Job** window pops up and allows you to define anything you want to put into a job. Don't forget that this is all contributed by users without even having to code a single line in the tool itself. It is all done in a text file called `oracle.xml`. When enabling the **Show SQL** checkbox, you get to see the PL/SQL that is generated for you. This can easily be copied to the SQL editor in case it does not completely fit your needs. The only limitation around here is imagination and time. It does take a little time to implement these things. This tool has a very context-sensitive setup and only shows the actions that are appropriate for an active context. It doesn't exactly have a large bunch of buttons like some other applications, where every new option has a new button that is always present on the main toolbar.

Summary

This was again a quick tour through the Scheduler, purely using the currently available graphical tools. We saw DB Console—a web application that comes for free with the database and DbVisualizer—a client-server application. Both have their strong points. The customization of DbVisualizer is so strong that you really should take a look at it.

Finally, we have reached the end of this book. We have seen a lot of the Scheduler and hopefully more than what the PL/SQL packages and Types manual show. The goal was to explain how the Scheduler could be used and how to get most out of it in a step-by-step approach. We began with a simple job, waded through chains, and found out how to control the resource consumption. The newest thing we saw was the remote external job agent that is a great enhancement compared to the classical external job.

We have also seen some advanced items such as event handling, job generation, debugging Scheduler jobs, some real-life scripts, and jobs in RAC databases and logical standby databases. Finally, this chapter showed some tooling for the Scheduler and also showed that what has not been already made can be made by us.

Index

A

AQ_TM_PROCESSES parameter 134
arguments
- defining 22
- metadata arguments 22
- normal application arguments 25

attributes, job
- job_priority 61
- max_run_duration 63
- restartable 63
- schedule_limit 62

B

backups
- BARC process, scheduling 171, 172
- DARC process, scheduling 169-171
- HOT backups, scheduling 167, 168
- scheduler event queue, reading 164-167

bugs 145

C

chain definition, DB Console 41
chains
- about 29-31
- creating 35
- programs 35
- rules 31

class, resource manager 80, 81
create external job privilege 57
create job privilege 57
credentials 120, 121

D

database
- backing up 160-163
- checking 149-151
- security 104

database_role attribute 191
DB Console
- about 38, 195
- automated maintenance tasks screen 197
- chain, analyzing 52-54
- chain, running 48
- chain definition 41-47
- create button 209
- create iob screen 206
- create job screen 205
- create job using chain button 205
- create like button 209
- database overview 196
- edit button 209
- executable 19
- features 7, 195, 196
- general tab 206
- Global Scheduler attributes 215
- history tab 200, 204
- jobs, running 8
- options tab 207
- oracle scheduler column 197
- PL/SQL block 9
- program 20
- programs, building 38-40
- resource manager column 197
- running chains, manipulating 51
- running tab 200

scheduler column 210
scheduler job classes screen 213
Scheduler Window Groups screen 214
Scheduler Windows page 214
server tab 204
shield01 database 197
stop run button 200
stored procedure 15
tricks, with chain 49, 51
user, creating 8
DBMS_SCHEDULER package 59
DbVisualizer
about 216
create scheduler job window 220
database connections 217
DBA views 218
features 216, 217
Schemas tree 218
drop any job privilege 59

E

evaluate_calendar tool
about 173
create_schedule procedure 174
first day of month, scheduling for 174
first monday of first quarter, scheduling for 179
first monday of month, scheduling for 174
first quarter of year, scheduling for 179
first working day of month, scheduling for 175, 177
first working monday of month, scheduling for 178
last working day of month, scheduling for 179
nth monday of month, scheduling for 178
only mondays, scheduling for 174
evaluation interval 32, 33
event-based scheduling
about 129-140
event handler
creating 130
example 130
events
about 129
generating 133
raising 132
events, in chains 130
executable, job type
about 19
external jobs, creating 19
execute privilege 59

G

Grid Control
about 216
features 216

I

instance_id = NULL attribute 189
instance_stickiness = false attribute 190
instance consolidation 99
issues, resource manager 97, 99

J

job
attributes 61
creating 57
job class 80
job environment 148
job events
monitoring 129
job execution privileges 63, 66
jobs 30

L

log detail level
about 68
defining 68, 70
logging
about 68
log detail level 68
log purging 70
log purging 70-72

M

metadata arguments
about 22
assigning, to program 22, 23

monitoring, resource manager 92, 93
multiple agents
configuring, on single host 118, 119

N

Non Uniform Memory Architecture. *See* **NUMA**
normal application arguments
assigning, to program 25, 26
NUMA 98

O

Oracle 11g 103
Oracle Scheduler
10.2.0.1 142
10.2.0.2 142, 143
11g release 144
about 57
backups 160
bugs 145-148
calendar 172
database, checking 149
evaluate_calendar tool 173
job environment 148
releases 141
resources, managing 75
statistic collection 153
Windows usage 144
oralin01 node 181
oralin02 node 181

P

pending area 77
PL/SQL block
about 9
job, creating 9-15
plan, resource manager
about 82
creating 83-90
making 82
scenario 83
privileges 34
privileges, for creating job
about 57
create any jobs 58
create external jobs 58
create jobs 58
dbms_rule_adm.grant_system_privilege 58
execute any class 58
execute any program 58
manage scheduler 58
system privilege 57
program, DB Console 20
programs, chains
about 36
COPYFILES 36
program state 37
SHUTDOWN 36
STARTUP 37

Q

queue_spec parameter 138

R

RAC
about 181
installation, need for 181
installation, running on nodes 181
instance_id, defining 182
instance_stickiness, using 181, 188
job, creating 184-190
job, modifying 184-190
job_class definition 190
jobs, running ways 181
oralin01, nodes 181
oralin02, nodes 181
service_name, defining 181
Real Application Clusters. *See* **RAC**
Real Application Clusters database 151
remote job agent
about 103
configuring 116
database, preparing 113
features 118
installing, on Linux 110, 111
installing, on Windows 105-109
silent install option 112
upgrading 111
remote job agent, configuring
about 116
troubleshooting 117, 118

remote job agent, preparing
about 113
HTTP port, setting 114, 115
registration password, setting 115
remote Scheduler objects, creating 115
XDB installing, verifying 114
remote Scheduler
runtime observations 126
resource consumer group
about 75-77
class 80
creating 77-79
resource manager
about 75, 127
issues 97
monitoring 92-97
plan 82
troubleshooting 99
window 91
window groups 92
rules 30, 31
rule set 34

S

Scheduler GUI tools
about 195
DB Console 195
DbVisualizer 216
Grid Control 216
scheduler management 66, 67
security 103, 104
shields 181
silent install, remote job agent
base release 112
latest available level, patching 112
simple jobs 72
standby databases
about 191
jobs, creating 191, 192
jobs, running 193, 194
statistic collection
about 153
analysis, performing 158
drop_jobs procedure 155
jobs, generating 155-157
procedures 153
run procedure 154
schedule_run procedure 154
scheduled run, generating 158, 159
statob procedure 155
status 30
statuses 30
stored procedure
about 15
command type, changing 16, 17
snap procedure 17

T

troubleshooting, remote job agent 117, 118
troubleshooting, resource manager 99, 100

U

ulimits 148
UNIX
targeting, as remote platform 121-124
Unix system
file privileges, for external job 141

W

window, resource manager 91
window groups, resource manager 92
Windows
file privileges, for external job 144
targeting, as remote platform 125

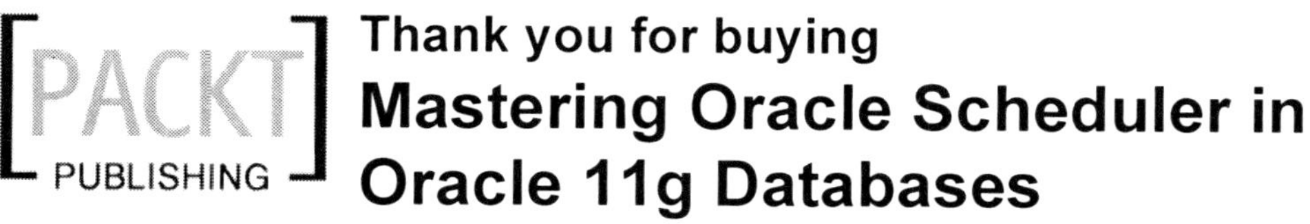

About Packt Publishing

Packt, pronounced 'packed', published its first book "*Mastering phpMyAdmin for Effective MySQL Management*" in April 2004 and subsequently continued to specialize in publishing highly focused books on specific technologies and solutions.

Our books and publications share the experiences of your fellow IT professionals in adapting and customizing today's systems, applications, and frameworks. Our solution based books give you the knowledge and power to customize the software and technologies you're using to get the job done. Packt books are more specific and less general than the IT books you have seen in the past. Our unique business model allows us to bring you more focused information, giving you more of what you need to know, and less of what you don't.

Packt is a modern, yet unique publishing company, which focuses on producing quality, cutting-edge books for communities of developers, administrators, and newbies alike. For more information, please visit our website: `www.packtpub.com`.

Writing for Packt

We welcome all inquiries from people who are interested in authoring. Book proposals should be sent to `author@packtpub.com`. If your book idea is still at an early stage and you would like to discuss it first before writing a formal book proposal, contact us; one of our commissioning editors will get in touch with you.

We're not just looking for published authors; if you have strong technical skills but no writing experience, our experienced editors can help you develop a writing career, or simply get some additional reward for your expertise.

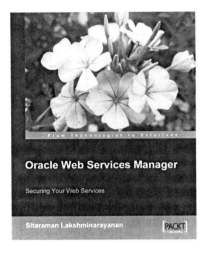

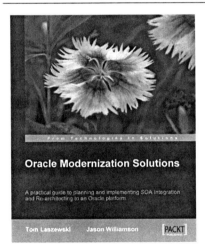

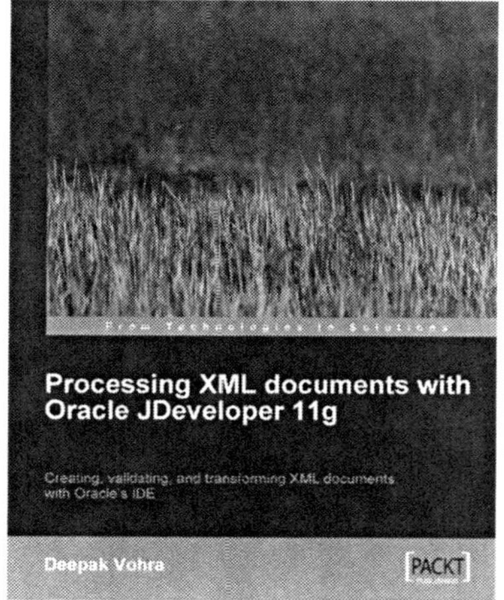

Processing XML documents with Oracle JDeveloper 11g

ISBN: 978-1-847196-66-8 Paperback: 384 pages

Creating, validating, and transforming XML documents with Oracle's IDE

1. Will get the reader developing applications for processing XML in JDeveloper 11g quickly and easily
2. Self-contained chapters provide thorough, comprehensive instructions on how to use JDeveloper to create, validate, parse, transform, and compare XML documents
3. The only title to cover XML processing in Oracle JDeveloper 11g, this book includes information on the Oracle XDK 11g APIs

---

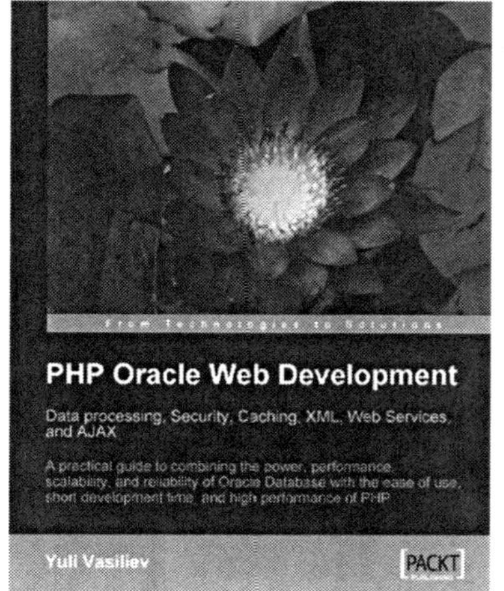

PHP Oracle Web Development

ISBN: 978-1-847193-63-6 Paperback: 396 pages

A practical guide to combining the power, performance, scalability, and reliability of the Oracle Database with the ease of use, short development time, and high performance of PHP

1. Program your own PHP/Oracle application
2. Move data processing inside the database
3. Distribute data processing between the web/PHP and Oracle database servers
4. Create reusable building blocks for PHP/Oracle solutions
5. Use up-to-date technologies, such as Ajax and web services, in PHP Oracle development

Please check **www.PacktPub.com** for information on our titles

Printed in the United Kingdom by
Lightning Source UK Ltd., Milton Keynes
140789UK00001B/26/P